Studying Children
and Schools

Studying Children and Schools

Qualitative Research Traditions

David F. Lancy
Utah State University

WAVELAND

PRESS, INC.

Prospect Heights, Illinois

For information about this book, contact:
Waveland Press, Inc.
P.O. Box 400
Prospect Heights, Illinois 60070
(847) 634-0081
www.waveland.com

Cover photo: © David Samuel Robbins/CORBIS

For all the students who became my teachers

Contents

Preface

When I began my own research career, the sine qua non of research methodology in the study of children was the *experiment*; for teachers, it was the *survey*. These highly quantitative and distanced means of acquiring data have gradually been augmented by more intimate qualitative approaches. It is the aim of this book to introduce the reader to many of these approaches—especially those taken by anthropologists. Unlike typical introductory research texts, this work presents the *substance* or content of qualitative research as well as its methods. I have chosen this approach for several reasons. Qualitative research is commonly distinguished from quantitative research on the basis that the former is inductive while the latter is deductive, meaning that in qualitative research one observes reality—the particular—and extrapolates to the general. Hence, we will *induce* the general principles from an examination of particular examples of qualitative research. Another reason for focusing on substantive issues is that qualitative research is much more than a collection of techniques. It is often addressed to different issues and incorporates different assumptions about reality than quantitative research.

Another unusual aspect of this text is that I organize the material according to several distinct "traditions." I would argue that to understand qualitative research, one must know something about the disciplinary training of the researchers, their preferences in terms of topics of study, and the customs and rituals that have grown up around the methods they use. In other words, qualitative research has been conducted by individuals who share and work from a set of tools and ideas that coalesce into what I'm calling a "tradition." Further, many qualitative research texts actually focus rather exclusively on ethnography; most *exclude* such robust traditions of qualitative research as case study, ethnomethodology and biography.

This work is meant for those who would do qualitative research as well as those whose goal is only to be able to read these studies with a critical and discerning eye. I will lead the reader through a representative sample of work in the field and, along the way, point out critical features that make a work qualitative and also note features that we might consider strengths or benefits of this approach as well as weaknesses or liabilities.

Another reason for offering the reader a chance to sample a rather extensive catalog of discrete studies flows from my desire to forego paradigmatic purity for pragmatic utility. Many research texts focus exclusively on what should be—and this may be defined very narrowly—rather than on what is. Among my early mentors were Mike Cole and Millard Madsen, two experimental psychologists who introduced the study of culture into their work, and Jack (John W.) Roberts, a cultural anthropologist who used experiments, questionnaires, and other quantitative data collection techniques. Hence, I willingly err on the side of being over-inclusive and include work that might be considered only marginally qualitative. This eclecticism permits me to stress "crossing points" between qualitative and quantitative methods. Ultimately, my aim is to promote the development of resourceful investigators who use whatever means at their disposal to pursue interesting questions and pressing problems.

Much of the material in this text was originally published in *Qualitative Research in Education: An Introduction to the Major Traditions* (Lancy 1993). This work is shorter and, I hope, more coherent. Two traditions—cognitive studies and history—have been dropped from this edition. Several studies have been added, as there has been a huge flood of publications featuring qualitative research in the last decade. However, I have to agree with Dick Wisniewski (2000), founding editor of the *International Journal for Qualitative Studies in Education*, who finds that most of this literature is *about* qualitative research rather than the reporting of truly original findings. He laments: "I wonder if, as researchers become as precise as possible about the conduct of their work, there may be the unanticipated consequence of doing less of the actual work— the conduct of studies?" (p. 7). One reason for this dilemma is that, about 1990, the postmodernism wave began, and in the process virtually all research *traditions* have been questioned and/or cast aside, which has had a rather chilling effect on research, it seems to me. The reader can be reassured that we will keep our feet dry, skirting around the postmodern flood as much as possible.

The book is divided into three parts. Chapter one consists of a lengthy introduction to the field of qualitative research. It is designed to make the reader aware of critical issues that will be raised again and again throughout the text, such as what role the qualitative researcher should assume. The chapter also delineates areas of widespread agreement in the field regarding the identifying features of qualitative research. These features will then be instantiated with numerous examples throughout the text, for example, *deriving theory from data*.

The second part of the book consists of five chapters, each dealing with a distinct "tradition" of child/school study. Many would argue that qualitative (as opposed to quantitative) research cannot be viewed as a unitary, monolithic body of shared assumptions and tools. Rather, it has evolved in the context of the more narrowly focused and discipline-based traditions such as anthropology, sociology, and psychology. Uneven chapter lengths reflect the varying popularity of these traditions. There are literally hundreds of published scholars in the field of educational anthropology, for example, while one finds only a dozen or so active ecological psychologists. Each chapter reviews several studies on particular topics in considerable depth. This permits an examination of the kinds of issues that unite scholars in this particular tradition as well as the development of a more discerning and critical approach to the research literature. An underlying premise here is that one must first read and digest a fairly large body of qualitative research before attempting to do it oneself.

In the last chapter of the book, we take up the practical problems involved in getting started on a qualitative research project.

What is Qualitative Research?

You know my method. It is founded upon the observation of trifles.
—Sherlock Holmes, in *The Boscombe Valley Mystery* by A. Conan Doyle

Anthropologists who study children and schools face somewhat of a dilemma. For many, the methods and assumptions of cultural anthropology—tenets like participant observation, holism and key informants—work just fine. We can conduct and report our work to fellow anthropologists, who will judge it on its merits, and our names will be inscribed in the annals of the discipline . . . or not. But the study of children and schools has, historically, been the provenance of psychologists and others whose notions of science are quite different. Our "qualitative" research is trumped by their more experimental, rigorous "quantitative" research. So how can anthropologists join the larger conversation? By becoming qualitative researchers. What exactly *is* qualitative research? Eisner and Peshkin (1990) seem to despair of an answer: "There is . . . no general agreement about the conduct of . . . qualitative inquiry; perhaps there never will or can be consensus of the sort that is embodied in the standardized procedures of quantitative research . . ." (p. 1).

I'm not nearly so pessimistic. I've found that the best way to proceed with prospective qualitative researchers is to conduct a kind of fashion show—to march a cross-section of past studies that have yielded important results down the runway for their inspection. You should be able to "try on" these various approaches to see what fits best with your own goals, skills and temperament. A major goal of this book, then, is to introduce you to the empirical research literature, conducted qualitatively, especially as it reflects attempts to account for differences in children's developmental trajectories and/or academic achievement. But before we begin to look at specific studies, let's first examine some broader, more general issues.

THE RELATIONSHIP BETWEEN
QUALITATIVE AND QUANTITATIVE RESEARCH

Early on during any class with a research focus,[1] students begin to formulate their problem. Inevitably it is stated in quantitative, often experimental, terms. The medical research model—fundamentally quantitative—is so pervasive in our society that it is hard to imagine any other way of proceeding. Hence, we might start our consideration of qualitative research by contrasting it with quantitative research. The following table of comparisons is representative of that way of thinking.

Table 1.1
Characteristics of Qualitative Contrasted with Quantitative Studies

Qualitative	Quantitative
The investigator has chosen a topic or issue to study. Task is to *discover*, hypotheses emerge.	Investigator goes much further, delimiting the study, selecting variables, making predictions, etc. His/her task is to *verify or refute*. Hypotheses are stated in advance.
The site/individuals chosen for the study governed by topic . . . sites/individuals/cases relatively few in number.	Sample size is governed ideally by considerations of statistical "power." "N" is preferably large.
The investigator is the principal "instrument" for data collection.	The investigator should remain anonymous and neutral vis-à-vis the research/site/subjects. He/she gathers data via intermediary instruments like questionnaires, tests, structured observation schemes, etc.
The research process is designed to intrude as little as possible in the *natural, ongoing* lives of those under study.	Intrusion may be extreme in that *subjects* may be *paid* to participate in a *laboratory simulation*. At a minimum those being studied will be aware that they are part of an "experiment."
Investigator aware of his/her own *biases* and strives to capture the *subjective reality* of participants.	Investigator assumes an *unbiased* stance; safeguards are employed to maintain *objectivity*.
Investigator uses "wide-angle lens" to record *context* surrounding phenomena under study. Focus may shift as analytical categories and theory "emerge" from the data.	Context is seen as potentially contaminating the integrity of study. Procedures employed to reduce *extraneous factors*.
Typical study lasts some months, perhaps years.	Typical study lasts some hours, perhaps some days.
Report utilizes *narrative* format; there is a story with episodes.	Report is *expository* in nature, consisting of a series of interlocking *arguments*.

Given that qualitative and quantitative research clearly have different means and, perhaps, different raisons d'être, what should be the relationship between the two?[2] Lincoln and Guba (1985), who have done a thorough job of building a rationale for the naturalistic paradigm by attacking positivism, see qualitative research as utterly *antithetical* to quantitative research. "The design specifications of the [quantitative] paradigm form a procrustean bed of such a nature as to make it impossible for the [qualitative researcher] to lie in it—not only uncomfortably, but at all" (p. 225). Meanwhile, "Critics of qualitative inquiry have charged that the approach is too subjective, in large part because the researcher is the instrument of both data collection and data interpretation, and because a qualitative strategy includes having personal contact with and getting close to the people and the situation under study" (Patton 1990:54).

Rury's (1991) study of nineteenth-century women's participation in high school is but one example of many studies where qualitative data are used to *complement* quantitative data. Qualitative and quantitative methods may be combined in a single study, or a qualitative researcher may rely heavily on previous quantitative research on the topic in constructing his/her literature review and rationale.

Patton (1990) describes using qualitative research as, essentially, the "natural history" stage of a quantitative study. He and his colleagues were to carry out a summative evaluation of a "leadership program." Before designing the study they became participant observers in the program, which was essential as ". . . the program . . . bore little resemblance to our expectations, what people had told us, or the official program description" (p. 202). We must be very cautious in promoting this *antecedent* use of qualitative research; as Glaser and Strauss (1967) indignantly point out, it suggests that "real" research must be quantitative.

Another possible relationship occurs when investigators *imbed* qualitative case studies in an essentially quantitative study. Sylvia Hart-Landsberg (1982), for example, conducted a case study of one classroom's use of *Think-About*, an instructional television program that was also evaluated by more conventional means. The "real world" material she gathered from the single classroom was used to flesh out the bare skeleton of achievement test and opinionnaire data from the larger study.

As the mirror image of the quantitative researcher, engaging in an initial natural history phase to identify variables, formulate hypotheses, and so on, it has become extremely common for qualitative researchers to utilize various quantitative techniques, especially experiments and attitude surveys *at the end* or near the end of their study. They do so for several reasons, but one of the most common is to determine whether the views they have obtained from a small sample of informants who they have interviewed at length are consistent, in the main, with those held by the larger group to which their informants belong. Another possibility occurred in my ethnographic study of Kpelle children's play; I had formulated some ideas about the way in which children learn folktales, which I proceeded to "test" using standard experimental procedures (Lancy 1977).

Finally, we should consider the possibility of qualitative and quantitative researchers working *in parallel*. Educational anthropologists see themselves as focusing on different issues than the educational psychologist, for example. That is, the ethnographer seeks to capture "the big picture," "culture," "surrounding context," and so on, or the ethnographer looks at what lurks in the interstices of the setting, finding "hidden curricula" (Gearing & Epstein 1982). At the time I undertook an ethnographic study of Longbranch Elementary School,* many aspects of the innovative instructional program used in the school had been extensively evaluated (Glaser 1976). However, by taking a phenomenological perspective on the views and experience of pupils in the school I addressed issues, questions, and problems that no one had looked at before (Lancy 1976 a, b, c). The study was not, however, designed to complement in any direct sense the previous quantitative research.

Ultimately, of course, to understand the nature of education we will need much additional research of all stripes. Consider trying to characterize someone's "quality of life" *without* reference to quantitative data of any kind, e.g., age, income, and family size, or *only* with reference to these various quantifiable criteria. Clearly either extreme is unsound.

QUALITATIVE RESEARCH TRADITIONS

The comparison with quantitative research has its limitations, however, and when I first began teaching qualitative research I found it useful to focus on what has come to be called "traditions." Essentially, we proceed inductively, arguing in effect that qualitative research is what those who consider themselves qualitative researchers do. In quantitative inquiry there is, in theory if not always in practice, a clear separation between the issue studied and the methodology used to conduct the study. The sensorimotor development of infants, the effect of gender on math achievement and the side effects produced by a new drug can all be studied via *experiments*. Thus quantitative methodology, along with its handmaiden mathematics (including, but not limited to, statistics), has developed as a loosely united and relatively independent field of endeavor. There is a large cadre of "research methodologists" whose intellectual investment is made not in answering questions or solving real-world problems but in trying to improve the tools employed to do these things. Thus quantitative research methodology grows and expands much like new limbs on a tree. It is possible to connect every little twig, eventually, to a single trunk. Some limbs cease to receive nutrients or are storm-damaged, die and fall off. Newer limbs, their leaves reaching for the sun, grow vigorously.

By contrast, topic, theory and methodology are usually closely interrelated in qualitative research. Following Kuhn (1970), Jacob (1987) has chosen to discuss qualitative research as manifested in the differing guises of several scholarly traditions. For her, a tradition is established when ". . . a group of scholars . . . share . . . assumptions . . . about the nature of the human universe, theory, legitimate questions or problems, and appropriate

*The names of all schools discussed in the text have been changed to protect anonymity.

methodologies" (p. 250). I would add that many, if not most, practicing qualitative researchers learned their "craft" not from a text but primarily by studying under a recognized "master," again reinforcing the notion of tradition. For example, I studied the tradition of *educational anthropology* under John Singleton, the first editor of what was to become the principal journal in the field (*Anthropology and Education Quarterly*, see Singleton 1984). Singleton, in turn, studied (see Singleton 1967) under George Spindler, one of the acknowledged founders of this particular tradition (Spindler 1955).

Examined within the "traditions" framework, qualitative research more closely resembles a "mixed forest" than the "mighty oak" of quantitative research. While there is some cross-pollination, by and large these traditions are like distinct trees representing different species, or at least subspecies. In many cases their growth has not been spectacular, and some trees appear to be almost moribund. That is, whole traditions seem to spring up ("critical ethnography," Anderson 1989) while others slowly die out ("ecological psychology," Barker & Gump 1964).

The chapters that follow correspond, to a great extent, to these different traditions. We begin with anthropology (chapter 2), then move on to other, related traditions. Anthropology is, perhaps, the oldest and certainly one of the most prolific, in terms of number of distinct studies—traditions of qualitative research on children and schools. I will trace this history showing that the earliest educational anthropologists sought to fill holes in the ethnographic documentation of non-Western peoples by describing indigenous patterns of education (= *enculturation*) as well as the initial impact of introduced, European-style schools. Underlying concerns will be identified, such as a preoccupation with culture—the rules that underlie the patterned behavior of people who've lived together and interacted long enough to have reached consensus about what those rules should be. I will discuss two of the three different traditions that Jacob (1987) isolates which grew from anthropology, namely, *holistic ethnography* and *cognitive anthropology*. The former is more concerned with a full description of culturally patterned behaviors, while the latter is more concerned with the rules as "natives" see them.

The kinds of assumptions educational anthropologists hold, the methods they use, and the controversies that divide them will be examined in the course of describing several noteworthy research studies. These studies contribute to our understanding of prominent topics that have preoccupied many educational anthropologists, namely, school-community relations and the nature of the student culture.

Where the anthropologist employs the *ethnographic* method to study *culture*, the sociologist (third chapter) conducts a *field study* to document a *community*. These community studies had their origins in the Department of Sociology at The University of Chicago in the 1920s and, as early anthropologists brought back the first sympathetic, non-ethnocentric portraits of the culture of peoples in Africa, Asia, Oceania, and other places (as contrasted with the reports of missionaries, soldiers, capitalists and bureaucrats), so, too,

University of Chicago-trained sociologists provided relatively sympathetic portrayals of ghetto dwellers, bar patrons, gang members and so on. Those researchers have a common view that communities are created and held together by the interaction of their members.

The most visible group of scholars practicing in this tradition in education is in the United Kingdom. Another tradition which one can identify as fundamentally sociological is *ethnomethodology*. The ethnomethodologist is especially concerned with the relatively unnoticed, routine, informal interactions that take place in human communities.

The researchers whose work I will review in the fourth chapter share a concern for documenting *universal* aspects of human behavior and human institutions. With intellectual roots in natural history, these scholars have a close affinity with modern field biologists who meticulously record the behaviors of a particular species over prolonged periods of time. *Human ethologists* constitute one biological tradition that has produced work of importance in the study of children. Their "field" is the nursery school, the playground, the summer camp; and their species human beings, especially younger members of the species. *Ecological psychologists* use biological constructs and assumptions in an analogous rather than literal manner. They treat culturally patterned behavior as if it were species-specific in order to get at some of the ways that the environment might influence behavior, such as Barker and Gump's (1964) study of the influence of school size on student behavior. This chapter has three themes: dominance hierarchies, rough-and-tumble play, and the effects of density on behavior.

Case Studies, our focus in the fifth chapter, deviates from the pattern established so far, in that people who do them probably *do not* have a sense that they are carrying on a "tradition." I would argue that despite this, case studies do have two vital features in common: they all address very directly the improvement of practice, and all are designed to influence educational policy (Stenhouse 1985).

The traditions discussed to this point all promote "basic" research, the accumulation of findings that gradually give us a better understanding of some educational or psychological phenomenon. However, any given finding from a single study may not lead directly to a recommendation or conclusion. In the case study, however, either a problem is identified in advance or the investigator proceeds on the assumption that problems will be uncovered in the course of the research, obligating him/her to look for possible solutions. The case-study literature reviewed in chapter 5 ranges on a continuum from small-scale projects involving a single case to large-scale evaluation efforts with multiple cases. The theme we will address in this chapter is instructional innovation.

The "traditions" framework will again have to be stretched a bit to accommodate the material gathered together in the personal accounts chapter (chapter 6). It is argued that many disparate stands of scholarship are just now coalescing or being woven into what I believe is an emerging tradition. Anthropologists have used biography to illuminate enculturation processes, and Wolcott conducted an "ethnographic-type account" (1974:176) of the daily life and work of an elementary school principal that has become a classic; teachers' diaries have been used to illuminate the history of schooling (e.g., Kinkead 1997), and teachers are now being trained to observe and record life in their own classrooms. It has only been recently, however, that contemporary and archival personal accounts as well as concurrent in-depth studies of individual actors on the education scene have been viewed as having unique properties that set them apart from other traditions (Bruner 1986). Among the topics we will treat is the process of becoming a teacher.

In the last chapter, "Decisions, Decisions," I walk with the aspirant qualitative researcher through the decisions that will be made in the course of planning and executing a qualitative study.

THE NATURE OF QUALITATIVE RESEARCH

Distinct traditions aside, trying to determine the essence of qualitative research has been complicated by the fact that the term and its putative synonyms (ethnography, naturalistic inquiry, case study, field study) have at least three distinct referents.

Qualitative research is most commonly thought of as a *method*, a program or set of procedures for designing, conducting and reporting research (e.g., Bogdan & Biklen 1982). However, Lincoln and Guba (1985), among others, see it ". . . defined not at the level of *method* but at the level of *paradigm*" (p. 250). This distinction is captured in anthropologist Ray Rist's lament over the increasing popularity of ethnography: "The term ethnographer is now being used to describe researchers who neither studied nor were trained in the method . . . the traditional "rite of passage"—a prolonged field study—has now been bypassed . . . the idea of going into the field and allowing the issues and problems to emerge . . . has . . . given way to the preformulation of research problems, to the specifying of precise activities that are to be observed, and to the analytic framework within which the study is to be conducted. And all of this prior to the first site visit" (1978, p. 9). At the level of paradigm, qualitative research is distinguished from quantitative research in terms of their respective underlying *epistemologies*. That is, they differ in basic assumptions made about how one derives truth, the purpose of inquiry, the role of the scientist/investigator, what constitutes evidence, how one evaluates the quality of a given study, and so on.

As if two levels were not enough, I must warn you that many omnibus research methods texts consider qualitative research to be no more than a set of otherwise unrelated *techniques* such as "content analysis," "open-ended interviews," and "behavior observation," where the subject's possible responses are relatively unconstrained compared to more formally structured data-gathering methods such as multiple choice tests, rating scales, and the like. Hence, before one discusses what is or is not qualitative research, one must first establish whether the discussion is occurring at the level of paradigm, method, or technique. To sum up: When one follows the qualitative *paradigm*, one buys into an entire philosophy of inquiry (see the next section) that stands in sharp contrast to the tenets underlying quantitative research; one may follow a particular qualitative research *method* (e.g., case study) that deviates somewhat from the purest form of the paradigm; and one can work entirely within the quantitative paradigm and yet, occasionally, use a qualitative *technique* such as conducting open-ended interviews as a preliminary step in the design of a standardized survey instrument.

PHENOMENOLOGY AND THE QUALITATIVE PARADIGM

Those who subscribe to the qualitative paradigm conduct their work within a *phenomenological* framework. Its wellsprings are found in the earliest writings of Edmund Husserl (1859–1938) (see especially Husserl 1962). As a method, phenomenology has been most fully elaborated by the ethnomethodology school of sociology; as a philosophy by the French existentialist school; and as a theory by the Gestalt and symbolic interactionist schools of social psychology. Certain cherished tools of the scientist are abandoned or at least handled with caution. Thus, a researcher taking a phenomenological approach avoids, as much as possible, the use of *assumptions* about the phenomenon under study; avoids reducing complex reality to a few *variables*; and minimizes the use of instruments that are reactive and that greatly influence the reality she or he is trying to study. Such a researcher tries to go into the field with an open mind, to carry out investigations in which the conclusions are post hoc rather than a priori. Operating like the natural historian, the researcher observes, records, classifies and concludes, seeking, wherever possible, to capture the reality of the *subjects* and not only her or his own reality.

Reality, however, is constantly changing. This change process may be described as progress, as evolution, as entropy, or in any number of ways, but the researcher who employs the phenomenological perspective will be aware of it. Subjective realities are therefore often studied comparatively and historically to determine the kind and rate of change that affects them.

Obviously, there is a need for openness to afford the investigator the opportunity ". . . to be impressed by recurrent themes . . ." (Diesing 1971:145). The phenomenological researcher is open to alternative constructions of reality, open to many possible explanations for observed phenomena (few of which, in the absence of hypotheses or assumptions, can be ruled out in advance of the study), and open to a variety of data from many sources because no specified set of research techniques follows from the paradigm. Finally, the openness is demonstrated in the open-ended time frame in which change becomes part of the study rather than invalidating it.

Hence, the qualitative paradigm is ideal for phenomena that are patently complex and about which little is known with certainty. For less complex topics, phenomenology captures too much; it is wasteful (e.g., a phenomenological study of hiccuping). For phenomena about which a great deal is known, it would again be wasteful to throw away the known, to start from scratch as a phenomenological study would do (e.g., a phenomenological study of maze learning in the Norway rat in which nothing is assumed about the effects of handling, reward, or punishment). The phenomenological researcher is, above all, opportunistic. By being on the scene, the researcher observes and collects incidents, artifacts, and quotations that illuminate the phenomena. For this reason, phenomenology is best employed in situations that have relatively confined temporal and physical boundaries.

Another fundamental element in the qualitative paradigm is the use of "grounded theory." The concept was developed and elaborated in a book by Barney Glaser and Anselm Strauss entitled *The Discovery of Grounded Theory* (1967), undoubtedly the most influential work published to date on qualitative research. Glaser and Strauss were seeking a compromise between the relatively atheoretical community studies of the Chicago School of Sociology and the hypertheoretical, reified formulations of scientific sociologists like Merton and Parsons. They argue that theory should be grounded in the *data*. It is wrested from the data in the course of research rather than being imposed in a pre-ordained fashion: "Theory should emerge . . . it should never just be put together" (1967:41). They describe the "constant comparative" method where potential categories are identified, tried, and discarded until a "fit" between theory and data is achieved. In a study of parental influence on children's reading of storybooks, Kelly Draper and I videotaped 32 parent-child pairs as they read to each other. We had few if any preconceptions about what we would find, only that we hoped that distinct patterns would emerge and that these would be associated with the children's evident ease/difficulty in learning to read. I spent literally dozens of hours viewing these videotapes, developing, using, and casting aside various categories until I found two clusters of characteristics which I called "reductionist" and "expansionist" that accounted for a large portion of the variation among parents' reading/listening styles. I was, of course, guided in my search for appropriate categories by my ". . . experience with the setting . . ." (Patton 1990:14) and by the transcripts of our interview with each parent (Lancy, Draper & Boyce 1989).

Bronislaw Malinowski (1922) discovered anthropology's version of grounded theory nearly 50 years earlier when, stranded by the outbreak of World War I, he was forced to spend much longer doing fieldwork in the small Pacific community of the Trobriand Islands (just off the eastern tip of New Guinea) than he had intended. His prolonged stay had several consequences. He got to know the islands much better than he might have and was able to ". . . grasp the native's point of view, his vision of his world" (1922:25).[3] His prolonged stay permitted him to develop and test a variety of explanations for the elaborate *Kula* ceremony that was practiced in the area before arriving at an account consistent with his observations and the natives' beliefs. Malinowski's method is still held up today as the ideal, for anthropologists in general and educational anthropologists in particular (Goetz & LeCompte 1984).

DOING QUALITATIVE RESEARCH

A primary distinction between qualitative and quantitative research relates to data-gathering instruments. As shown in table 1.1, the quantitative researcher deliberately distances him/herself from his/her subjects. I make no claim that the information the qualitative researcher obtains is any more true, valid, or generalizable than the quantitative researcher's data, but the conclusions the two will draw from their research may be quite different. Further, the qualitative researcher who is herself the *principal research instrument* will certainly feel much more confident about her conclusions, having gotten it all straight from the horse's mouth, so to speak. The point here is that qualitative researchers, regardless of the tradition to which they adhere, regardless of the degree to which they adhere to the paradigm, *must experience the phenomenon firsthand* in order to, at the least, develop what Hemingway called a "crap detector" (Baker 1969). Like Malinowski in the Trobriands, the ideal participant observer becomes intimately involved in the life of the "tribe" under study.[4]

Of course, defining precisely how this human instrument is supposed to function is far from straightforward. (See Bogdan & Biklen 1982:119–127 on procedures for doing fieldwork.) The ideal occurs when the investigator can play a legitimate role within the setting. Note taking and interviewing occur during natural breaks from one's "duties," or after school is out. Annette Lareau functioned as an instructional aide in her comparative study of two elementary schools.[5] I was the computer lab supervisor in several studies of children's adaptation to this new medium (Lancy, Forsyth, & Meeks 1987).

One can become a participant by just *being there*, until gradually one is accepted (Cusick 1973). However, *non-participant* observation is also extremely common, and as Goetz and LeCompte (1984) point out: "Nonparticipant observation requires a detached, neutral and unobtrusive observer. The researcher's objective shifts from a central concern for participant meaning to focus on participant behavior" (p. 145). Further, they advise that "nonparticipant observation rarely is used as the initial, exploratory technique . . . it is more appropriate for refinement and verification stages of the research process" (p. 145). In my study of students at Longbranch Elementary School, I derived behavior categories (e.g., goofing off, making contraptions, passing out folders) and their definitions from several months' participant observation and student interviews. I then used them to construct a Behavior Observation Checklist, which I used, with the aid of an assistant, as a nonparticipant observer in several classes to code the stream of behavior and thereby obtain a sense of the frequency of these various student-identified activities (Lancy 1976a). Clearly there are a variety of roles open to the qualitative researcher, and Table 1.2 illustrates several.

To be a participant observer means working *in the field*, and . . . "Field work involves getting one's hand's dirty" (Patton 1990:47). Pursuing one's quarry through the corridors, on the swings, or in the boardroom is unpredictable and complex; there are numerous blind alleys and wasted initiatives;

Table 1.2
Role of the Investigator (I) Vis-à-Vis the Informant

Role	Examples	Comments
Interviewer	Case study: Chapters 5, 6	Importance of rapport between researcher and subjects . . . .
Nonparticpant observer	Human ethology, ecological psychology: Chapter 4	Generally more distant and structured than participant observation, but I. may have conducted prior P.O. . . . use of predefined categories for behavior . . . video-audio tape recording likely . . . use of one-way mirror . . . remote T.V. camera.
Participant observer	Case study: Chapter 5	Degree of participation generally low. I. maintains a degree of detachment.
	Anthropological . . . Sociological perspectives: Chapters 2 and 3	Degree of participation varies a great deal as does the degree of detachment . . . I. may identify with one set of participants (students) to the exclusion of another (teachers). High degree of participation implies a formal role assignment, such as teacher's aide.

one's motives are suspect; one's allegiance is questioned; one learns about proper etiquette after committing the *faux pas*. If we are very successful, if everyone cooperates, if the tape recorder works and we don't run out of tape, there is still the risk that ". . . the quantity of interview data . . . collected [is] almost unmanageable; we collected so much data that we left ourselves too little time to reflect on and analyze it" (Scott 1985:119). Compared to working in the lab or conducting research via standardized instruments, working in the field is *messy!* Sue Scott's candor is unusual; most published accounts leave out the false starts, the self-doubt, the errors of judgment and so on (but see Wax 1971; Lareau 1989b).[6]

However, the arguments which dictate that a good researcher get in direct touch with the phenomena apply with equal force to the need to get into the field. The volume of *prescriptive* literature on educational administration, the role of the principal, school governance and so on is voluminous. But in these millions of pages about what the elementary school principal should or shouldn't do, hardly a line had been written about how a real, live principal actually functioned until Wolcott (1973) undertook his two-year long study of *The Man in the Principal's Office*.

Two issues arise in connection with fieldwork: *sampling*—where does one go to do one's research, and *entry*—how does one get admitted and maintain the research role? In quantitative research (assuming one intends to use inferential statistics) the ideal sample is a random sample; any other kind opens the possibility that the researcher's bias might influence the selection process. In qualitative research the bias becomes purpose, as in *purposive sampling* (Bogdan & Biklen 1982). One chooses the site(s) that will yield the maximum information regarding the specific topic/issue one is investigating. Similarly, "sampling [adding sites, interviewing more informants, taking additional field notes] is terminated when no new information is forthcoming from newly sampled units . . ." (Lincoln & Guba 1985:202). Hence one chooses sites which are somehow "representative" for the phenomenon of interest. Peshkin studied "an exemplary Christian school . . ." (1986:12) and Wolcott an "average American Elementary School Principal" (1974:176). At the same time qualitative researchers are supposed to be opportunistic. Everhart (1983), on a team evaluating a federally funded instructional innovation in a junior high school, took an opportunity to pursue a topic (student resistance) largely unrelated to the evaluation. Some years ago, just prior to the onset of a new quarter, I noted with great interest an announcement for a "Rodeo Queen Clinic." Recalling that a horse-loving friend of mine intended to take my qualitative research course, I convinced her to do an ethnography of the clinic for her "class project." She started immediately under my supervision and was well into the study by the time the class started. Unorthodox perhaps, but I believe the results (Raitt & Lancy 1988) were more than satisfactory.

Margaret Raitt's affinity for horses gave her a considerable advantage in gaining entry as an otherwise obvious outsider in the clinic, and this problem is one of the most widely discussed in the methods literature. Education research often takes place in institutions that are under siege. Schools and families have, of late, been closely scrutinized for failing to live up to public expectations. This sense of vulnerability can throw up a wall of resistance to the qualitative researcher (e.g., Weiss 1985) who'd like "free access" but is unprepared to specify in advance what the findings might be. In fact, despite the researcher's careful speech to the contrary, most people assume that research equals evaluation—and yet I am always amazed at how welcoming students, parents, teachers, and school administrators are to my initial overtures and later queries. While much has been written on the subject of entry, perhaps the best advice is to "be prepared," as Fetterman (1989) notes: "The ethnographer enters the field with an open mind, not an empty head. Before asking the first question in the field, the ethnographer begins with a problem, a theory or model, a research design, specific data collection techniques, tools for analysis, and a specific writing style" (p. 11). Each situation is different, of course, and no matter how well prepared one is, being intrepid is an asset in the pursuit of one's research topic. Alan Peshkin, a Jewish professor at the University of Illinois, set himself the task of conducting an ethnography of a fundamentalist Christian school. Before eventually succeeding, he knocked on many doors and was repeatedly denied entry to study such schools (e.g., "You're like a Russian who says he wants to attend meetings at the Pentagon—just to learn . . . no matter how good a person you are, you will misrepresent my school because you don't have the Holy Spirit in you") (1986:12).

Observing and Interviewing Informants

Once data collection begins, the researcher has three principal data sources: observation, interviews, and artifacts. Observations are recorded in *field notes*, which can be free-form jottings that one takes down on the spot or lengthier, but perhaps less detailed, reconstructions after the fact. They are often written on two levels: the *facts*—very direct descriptions of what was observed and/or verbatim recording of what was overheard; and the observer's *comments* to provide context for the raw facts and/or to speculate on what it all means, how what was just observed relates to earlier observations, and so on. Aside from the blank note page, some studies call for more structured, precise observations that will be facilitated by the use of specially developed forms.[7]

One has several distinct interviewing formats from which to choose, beginning with the "non-interview." Although Margaret Raitt didn't formally interview any of the Rodeo Queen Clinic participants except the director, she created many opportunities to engage students, instructors, and parents in conversations that she led around to the issues in which she was interested. Individuals whom one is studying will often express more candid thoughts in a conversation than in an interview, though they are aware they are the objects of a research study. One can conduct a formal interview in a largely informal manner by using a series of very broad guiding questions. Lynn Meeks and I (n.d.) used such a strategy in interviewing ninth graders in an experimental composition class. We used such questions as "What is writing?" and "Tell me about this class." Although we had a list of "probes" that we each used, we varied the order; and if a student spontaneously mentioned a topic in which we were interested, we did not feel compelled to ask that particular question. One's goal in this type of interviewing process is obtaining information while removing any constraints on the interviewee's responses. This allows the interviewee to relate her own conceptualization of the phenomenon in a natural manner, as opposed to the investigator attempting to fit the interviewee's views into his or her pre-existing framework. Often one is rewarded by the interviewee presenting a view, or using a type of *phraseology*, which is completely unexpected (see Whyte 1984:97–101). In this particular study Meeks and I were not expecting students to tell us as much as they did about their previous writing experiences in and out of school, and these unanticipated forays provided us with the strongest analytical angle on our data.

Group interviews have their place. I found in my fieldwork in Liberian (Lancy 1980a) and Papua New Guinean (Lancy 1979) villages that group interviews were more natural than the typical face-to-face interview. Indeed, my informants often felt reluctant as individuals to respond to my queries about general aspects of their society, as they felt they lacked sufficient authority to speak on these matters. Also in schools, one can quickly dispel any mystery about one's role and purposes via a semi-structured group interview with teachers.

Then there at least two highly structured interviewing procedures that qualitative researchers use: the open-ended questionnaire, in which respondents have a great deal of latitude in composing their responses and which can be presented in verbal or written form, and the ethnosemantic interview (Spradley 1979). The latter procedure will be explained in some detail in the next chapter. Pre-constructed interview questions are incompatible with a phenomenological stance. However, there are strategies we can employ to increase the naturalness of this procedure (what Gorden [1980] calls "facilitators of communication"). For example, I completed a study of *Running Start* (a parent involvement/reading promotional program for first graders sponsored by the Chrysler Corporation) with Ann Zupsic, the teacher whose class constituted the research site. One item in the (meager) kit sent home to parents was a checklist of 10 activities that parents could initiate to promote literacy. We were, in fact, interested in the role parents play in promoting reading acquisition, so we used this list as a basis for asking parents about *their* practices. The list was, of course, familiar to them. With it in front of us, I asked, for example, "What do you think about item eight: *Share family stories with your children?*" (Lancy & Zupsic 1994).

Another interesting aspect of this particular case study was that, having spent a great deal of time interacting with the children in Ann's class, I was able to offer several observations about the child *before* beginning the interview with his/her parent. This helped to break down what was, in many cases, evident fear/hostility on the part of some parents. There are a number of comprehensive reference works available on the subject of interviewing (Gorden 1980; McCracken 1988; Churchill 1978; Whyte 1982), but the best designed interview is useless if the interpersonal "chemistry" isn't working. A slim volume by Jack Douglas (1985) is particularly helpful regarding the human side of this endeavor: ". . . small talk and chit-chat are vital first steps on the way to intimate communion" (p. 79).

Gathering Artifacts

Artifacts are the third major data source in field research. Typically they encompass various pieces of printed material.

> Thanks in part to the accountability movement, social institutions have become paper mills. Organizations produce written budgets, interoffice memos, market surveys, transcripts of meetings, personnel files, statements of policy or philosophy, and newsletters. Schools produce these and more: pupil case files, curriculum guides, test score reports, needs assessments, disciplinary codes, teachers' planning books, grade books, pupil essays, and student newspapers. Every piece of paper represents a poten-

tial source of data for the qualitative researcher. Added to the official records and archives of the organization are the writings of individuals— letters, diaries, autobiographies, and the like. (Smith & Glass 1987:269)

During Everhart's (1983) study of cognitive mapping in the social and formal organization of the school, he ". . . asked for and was assigned a mailbox in the school office, and received all announcements and material normally received by teachers" (p. 285). Another example is drawn from Leacock's (1969) study of racially segregated elementary schools in New York City: A study of twenty-three social studies texts that were being used at the time of the study

> . . . shows how serious were both the omissions in these books and the direct statements they made about other nations and racial and religious minorities . . . Missing from the texts was any mention of the consistent fight for freedom engaged in by the Negro people, or any discussion of the moral and physical injustices of slavery . . . Several books repeated the myth that Negroes were well suited to hard work in the hot sun. (p. 76–77)

As another example, I asked for, and was given, the New Year's Resolutions just after they were taken down from the bulletin board in one fifth-grade class because I felt they revealed something fundamental about gender stereotyping in the school. A sampling from the girls:

I resolve to brush my teeth four times a day. (several of these)
I resolve to stop biting my nails. (several)
I resolve to do better in my math and reading.
I resolve to do better in my schoolwork.
I resolve to stop fighting with my brother.

The boys' New Year's resolutions were different:

I resolve to stop talking. (several of these)
I resolve not to get any sentences. (as punishment)
I resolve to do my work and quit fooling around. (several)
I resolve not to play games before I am done with my work.
I resolve I shall not bug Thy [sic] teacher. (Lancy 1978:121)

Ray Rist (1978) conducted one of the earliest (1973–74 school year) studies of busing to achieve school integration (in Portland) and made extensive use of printed material, including newspaper articles, to provide historical perspective on the problem. Whereas these artifacts are usually given less attention than one's observation and interview records, they may become central to the aims of the study. Johnson (1980) used artifacts exclusively to study ". . . public schooling [as] . . . a mechanism for socialization and enculturation into *national* society and *culture*" (p. 174). Objects (*material culture*) in classrooms, especially posters and other wall decorations, were coded as reflecting local or national cultural values. Johnson found a near total absence of locally relevant material and concludes, "The nature of the setting in which elementary school children spend over 7,000 hours of their lives is primarily influenced by national rather than local mandates" (p. 185).

Triangulation

Printed material and other artifacts are combined with observation and interview records in a process that is widely known as *triangulation*. The qualitative researcher's most effective defense against the charge of being subjective is to buttress what she has observed with material that reinforces these observations from other semi-independent sources. Also, "The rationale for this strategy is that the flaws of one method are often the strengths of another" (Denzin 1970:308). Gibson (1987; 1988) creates a tightly woven net to support her argument that immigrant high school students from the Punjab were able to accommodate themselves to the demands of the school and achieve success without necessarily "becoming American." The fuel for her argument was made up of her notes from two years of participant observation; lengthy face-to-face interviews with students, parents, and teachers; test scores and report cards, and other sources. The major theme, "accommodation without assimilation," occurs throughout these materials. Contrariwise, she looked for and could not find material to support alternative themes (e.g., that the evident racism directed at the Punjabis had a depressing effect on their self-esteem and academic motivation).

Using multiple data sources also allows us to fill in gaps that would occur if we relied on only one source. For example, Peter Woods (1986) discovered that ". . . *punishment* books may not reflect all the punishment that has been administered . . . [a variety of minor punishments go unrecorded and] the '35 strokes of the cane administered to Stephen Winters by Mr. Gordon for persistently and deliberately refusing to bring his games kit' omits to say that the boy had to be held down shouting and struggling" (p. 91, italics added).

Analyzing the Data

Regardless of his tradition, the qualitative researcher faces the problem of systematically analyzing what is usually a substantial body of data. Unlike the quantitative researcher, however, he has relatively little idea at the onset of how to partition this continuous mass into discrete, perhaps even countable, *categories*. For example, with my colleague Steve Zsiray I developed a microcomputer-based robotics curricula for an eighth-grade class. Students worked their way through a series of interactive microcomputer programs that became increasingly challenging. The curriculum was trialed with a sample of 12 students who were "shadowed" and encouraged to "think aloud" (Ericsson & Simon 1984) as they explored each program. I read and reread the think aloud/interview transcripts, trying to find an analytical framework that best captured the patterns that emerged. Obvious candidates (computer phobic vs. hacker; smart vs. dumb) weren't useful. Ultimately, I found a developmental "stage" framework to be most effective (Lancy 1991).

Reviewing the transcripts and assigning students to stages based on their varied reactions to the programs didn't take very long at all compared to the lengthy time spent in creating the analytical framework. "There are no formulas for determining significance . . . no . . . tests for reliability and validity. In short, there are no absolute rules . . . [only] guidelines" (Patton 1990:372). Perhaps the best single source for such guidelines is Miles and Huberman's (1984b) handbook (see chapter 5 on case studies). By contrast the quantitative researcher usually *begins* the data analysis phase with categories, coding systems, and operational definitions *in hand*.

However, before one plunges into the nitty-gritty of content analysis, coding field notes, preparing case records, and so on, one must consider what the appropriate *level of analysis* should be.[8] One can envision two extremes. At one extreme there is relatively little analysis per se. The object is to provide a straightforward description of the phenomenon. DeWalt and Troxell's (1989) ethnography of an old-order Mennonite school is a case in point. Their goal was to provide a concise portrait of an unusual school. This is not to say that the task of summarizing their undoubtedly voluminous material in 17 pages was an easy one, but at least they didn't have to agonize over whether their *interpretation* of what they observed would seem credible. It may be that most people who are unfamiliar with qualitative research assume that these documentary pieces are its primary raison d'être, but as Schofield (1990) acerbically notes: "Unless the researcher chooses a very atypical site or presents an unusually insightful analysis of what is happening, the purely descriptive value of the study may be . . . discounted" (p. 205). Mischler (1979) discusses the other extreme—analysis to the nth-degree.

Very precise and detailed methods for analyzing qualitative data, especially naturally occurring discourse, are sometimes referred to as microanalysis (Green, Harker, & Golden 1987) or microethnography (Goetz & LeCompte 1984). As we will see, the level of analysis varies widely among the different qualitative research traditions. Among cultural anthropologists, description may predominate with relatively little analysis beyond what is necessary to prepare an organized and coherent report. By contrast, those engaged in cognitive studies may develop extremely elaborate schemes for organizing and representing their data (e.g., Leinhardt 1989). Finally, we can make a distinction between two different strategies (or two ends of a continuum) for analyzing qualitative data. On the one hand, Miles and Huberman (1984b), classics in the field like Becker, Geer, Hughes, and Straus (1961), and Glaser and Strauss (1967) suggest that one works from the bottom up, breaking the data into the smallest pieces possible; then systematically coding and collating all the lower-level (grounded) categories; and then moving upward to seek meaningful, larger aggregates. This contrasts with Lou Smith's (1978) "skimming the cream":

> During our last week of data collection we had to make a brief presentation of results to the several parties of the larger project we were investigating; these individuals were making decisions regarding the form the project would take in the succeeding years. The tactic we adopted was a simple one. In a local coffee shop, for a period of a couple of hours, we asked ourselves: "What are the major things we have learned from our

year in the field?" As we brainstormed these ideas, with no reference to our file drawer of notes, interpretive asides, or summary interpretations (some of which were still untyped on tapes because of organization resource problems), we gradually accumulated a list of ideas, findings. We pushed and pulled on these until they gradually fell into reasonable broader topics and differentiated outlines. (p. 337)

Reporting the Study

While it is easy to now find reports of qualitative research that resemble comparable reports of quantitative research, they more commonly employ a *narrative* format as opposed to a strictly expository format. Because of the enormous importance of description and context, as well as the growing importance of describing in very personal terms the researcher's *history* vis-à-vis this particular topic, the qualitative research report is written as a *story*. According to Van Maanen (1988), one expects the qualitative researcher to use a ". . . literary style that is . . . evocative and graceful" (p. 22). Also, the field worker disappears. He may introduce himself in a footnote or appendix, or reappear in an occasional "cameo" role, but "The voice assumed throughout the tale is that of a third-party scribe reporting directly on the life of the observed" (p. 64). Use of the vernacular, verbatim quotes, and precisely detailed observations all serve to convey that the author is merely a translator, and that the story is the natives' own.

However, if one goes too far in this direction one ends up writing what Van Maanen calls "Literary tales [which] are meant to provide an emotional charge to the reader. The reality is not sliced, diced, and served up analytically . . ." (p. 132). He refers specifically to authors Tom Wolfe, John McPhee, Joseph Wambaugh, and Peter Mathiessen, whose books ". . . are not written for tenure, grants or a Ph.D. . . ." (p. 134). Certainly the work that is most germane here is *Among Schoolchildren*, a best seller by Tracy Kidder (1989), which vividly portrays a year in Chris Zajac's fifth-grade classroom. Kidder is certainly all but invisible, his prose is graceful, and there is much we can learn from reading about Mrs. Zajac. However, *Among Schoolchildren* is *not* a report of qualitative research but a journalistic account.[9] It is almost purely descriptive, and when some kind of conclusion is drawn—"It is remarkable how much of the time of how many adults in a school a child can command simply by being difficult" (p. 166)—no empirical basis is provided to support it.

Hence, the essential problem a qualitative researcher faces is to combine description that is engrossing and convincing with analyses that go to the heart of the phenomenon. The analytical procedures must be made sufficiently clear so that the reader can follow the steps from evidence to conclusion. One can err on the side of so much description that the reader asks, "Where is this leading?" or so much analysis that the reader says, "I don't believe this, show me the evidence"; or a presentation of method so inadequate that the reader responds: "I don't follow this, how did we get to this particular conclusion?" Wolcott (1990) focuses on these kinds of issues (e.g.,

". . . qualitative studies in education . . . reveal a tendency towards heavy-handed or intrusive analysis . . .") (p. 29). He describes the writer's block that can occur when the author has a large volume of material, field notes, transcribed interviews, printed matter—and a weak or nonexistent analytical framework. It is this framework which guides one in deciding where to begin, how to organize the presentation of material, and what to put in and what to leave out.

Wolcott would also argue, and I agree with him, that one's framework should always be made explicit to the reader. As we will see, this dictum is not always followed. Indeed, far from reporting on their methodology for data gathering and analysis, some authors eschew the very idea of methodology (Suransky 1982). Among the items to be noted in the methods section, appendix, or chapter, Wolcott (1990) includes: the duration of the study, the setting, details about who was interviewed, the circumstances surrounding the interview as well as how questions were phrased, details on the use of recording equipment and so on. The overriding issue here is to provide sufficient information for the reader to judge the author's credibility as a research instrument and his/her astuteness as an analyst of social scenes.

EVALUATING QUALITATIVE RESEARCH

Particularly when studying the antecedents of student academic success, there's a growing disenchantment with an *exclusive reliance* on quantitative methodology. As McDermott and Hood (1982) point out, a major problem with many experimental tests of intellectual functioning is that even when we carefully select materials and language that are familiar to our subjects (e.g., Lancy, Souviney, & Kada 1981), the nature of the task environment itself is foreign in the sense that it does *not* represent a microcosm of real-world problem solving. In other words, humans use one set of reasoning strategies for everyday situations and another set for critical, test-like situations. When subjects use everyday problem solving in a test or laboratory problem-solving task, they will inevitably do poorly (Lancy 1989). The same arguments have been applied to standardized tests administered in schools (Cicourel et al. 1974). Cicourel (1968), McDermott and Hood (1982), and Hammersley and Atkinson (1983) are three of the best sources for critical analyses of the limitations of quantitative methods.

Another and closely related problem is the "definition of the situation." During my study of Longbranch, I spent a great deal of time observing in the science lab, which housed probably the most elaborate (and expensive) science curriculum ever developed for the elementary grades (e.g., Champaign & Klopfer 1974). A culminating activity in the program was the self-initiated independent activity (SIIA). Students were to apply the methods they had learned during the structured lessons in framing and carrying out their own investigations. Evaluated quantitatively the SIIAs were a total failure and cast doubt on the success of the entire program. However, when we look at the SIIA from the student's point of view, a different picture emerges:

> Because they must initiate the projects themselves, and because there are relatively few constraints on what they may do, they have redefined the SIIA so that it bears little resemblance to the curriculum developer's and teacher's model. A fourth-grade girl was interviewed about recent SIIAs she had done:
>
> > SALLY: Well, sometimes I make an experiment. Like my girlfriend and I once maked an experiment. We put 1/3 Dixie cup of lemon juice and sugar in it and we stirred it and then we put it in the freezer.
> >
> > D.L.: And what happened?
> >
> > SALLY: Then in three days we came back and it was frozen.
>
> This is a description of a fairly typical "mixture," and mixtures are the most common experiments. Girls seem to prefer mixtures that "turn out nice." When there was snow on the ground, a frequent activity was collecting a beaker full of snow and then adding various food color dyes until a pleasing effect had been achieved. Boys prefer making mixtures that either look or smell "awful." They delight in pouring unlikely materials (baking soda, honey, soap powder) together and then heating the whole thing until it boils. They also seem to relish heating things, in general, because they get to wear asbestos aprons, gloves and goggles (Lancy 1976b:18).

As the above example shows, quantitative research may oversimplify what is patently complex. Although one can detect a clear trend in educational research to move from simple univariate or bivariate designs to complex multivariate, nonlinear models (Barr & Dreeben 1983), all these procedures require *variables* that can be scaled—that is, numerically scored or rated in some way—whereas the qualitative researcher insists that not all of the reality that constitutes education is in fact reducible to variables.

Lincoln and Guba (1985; see also Edelsky 1990) provide a thorough analysis of perhaps the most damning charge against the dominance of logical positivism. They argue that, to a considerable extent, the persistence of bottom-up (phonics, vocabulary drill, syllabication) methods in teaching reading in schools as contrasted with what appear to be much more appropriate and natural "whole language" methods is attributable to the fact that the former methods isolate skills which can be *measured* by quantitative means. What they argue, in effect, is that research methodology cannot be opaque, especially with respect to theories of education. Put differently, the scholarly community is being held to account for the overreliance on what may turn out to be a misguided and potentially very damaging instructional technology (Hirsch 1987).

What many of the recent methods debates suggest, therefore, is that quantitative research (sometimes, often, always) obscures the very phenomena under investigation. However, I cannot endorse the extreme position taken by some (Lincoln and Guba describe "science" in the past tense: "Science was thought to be . . ." 1985:92) who would, I believe, throw the baby out with the bath water. Along with Mehan and Wood (1975), I am troubled by those who reject the scientific method because while they ". . . disparage science's absolute validity, they continue to embrace science's accomplishments in their daily lives. They reject science's philosophy but continue to turn to physicians when they are ill, to machines when they wish to travel . . . Few . . . have attempted to build alternative 'societies'" (p. 211).

The Transparency of Qualitative Research

Another major set of arguments in favor of qualitative research concerns its *transparency*: ". . . since the categories are discovered by examination of the data, laypersons involved in the area to which the theory applies will usually be able to understand it . . ." (Glaser & Strauss 1967:3–4). Woods (1986) talks at length about the value of ethnography to teachers, seeing them as "natural" ethnographers; this seems borne out by the easy collaboration between Lou Smith, a university researcher, and Bill Geoffrey, the classroom teacher (Smith & Geoffrey 1968). Patton (1990) reports on an evaluation of an "accountability system" in Kalamazoo, Michigan, in which the open-ended responses of the teachers—detailed, heartfelt and poignant—carried far more weight with board members than the systematically tabulated results of the "closed" questions on the opinionnaire.

There are several identifiable reasons for this transparency. First, qualitative researchers eschew variables and abstruse constructs (e.g., secondary circular operations; attention deficit disorder, learning styles) that only a specialist can be expected to understand. They usually speak and write in plain English rather than in "statisticese." They engage in face-to-face interaction over a prolonged period with "informants" whose opinions they value, thus building trust and credibility for their eventual findings. We are committed to *suspend judgment*; hence, rapport and cooperation may be more easily achieved. However, our proximal audience of teachers, students and so on are often disappointed when they find we have little practical advice to offer as we attempt to describe "how" things happen rather than "how well." Another source of disappointment lies in the relatively long time between the completion of a study and the appearance of the report. Ball's study of the Beachside school was done in 1973, and when his book appeared in 1981, several teachers were upset because it no longer accurately portrayed their school ("We don't do that anymore") (1984:90). On balance, however, the qualitative project should correspond much more closely to the lived reality of the individuals whose lives the research is designed to illuminate. We need to consider that, especially for the case study, a small-scale qualitative investigation of the problem may serve not as an alternative to a large-scale multivariate evaluation but as an alternative to "expert opinion." Or as Lawrence Stenhouse (1985) put it so well: ". . . the case study tradition may be seen as a systematization of experience within which interpretations are critically handled in the interest of preventing experience from becoming opinionated" (p. 266).

Undoubtedly, the apparent ease of doing fieldwork also contributes to the increased interest/volume of studies. One does not *need* to run the gaunt-let of statistical hazards, that confront most doctoral students, to do an eth-nography, for example.[10] More importantly, it is, I believe, much easier for a student to acquire a sense of "ownership" of a qualitative project—I have encountered many students who were never sufficiently proficient with quan-titative techniques to move their work beyond the "follow the recipe" stage and/or to escape from the ever-watchful eye of their major professor. At the same time, this very ease of access to qualitative research (especially if one finesses one of the "traditions") leads us to consider . . . .

SOME UNRESOLVED PROBLEMS

"Ethnography is becoming a mantle to legitimate much work that is shoddy, poorly conducted, and ill conceived" (Rist 1980:8). "The popularity of qualitative research . . . threatens to trivialize the approach. Researchers rush to join the bandwagon . . . without conceptualizing a sound research design . . ." (Noblit & Pink 1987:xiv.)

Strong words perhaps, but very timely. The major problem we face is not that there is poor work being done under the auspices of qualitative research, but that we still have no widely shared language to use in discussing the *worth* of a piece of qualitative research. Indeed, as Rist (1980) sarcastically notes: ". . . it is inappropriate for an outsider to challenge what, in the final result, was phenomenological and very personal experience" (p. 9). In Ham-mersley and Atkinson's (1983) text on qualitative research, for example, the authors take over 260 pages to review dozens of studies without writing a sin-gle critical word about a single one of them. There is, therefore, a pressing need to develop a set of standards that can be used to evaluate completed studies, guide neophyte researchers, and stimulate improvement in the qual-ity of research. One standard to apply is that the research should be unselfish. That is, it must satisfy something in addition to the authors' own selfish pur-poses. A doctoral student once came to me for guidance in carrying out a "History of the Deseret Alphabet." I asked him what purpose this work would serve, what question it would answer, what educational problem it would solve. He responded that its purpose was to fulfill degree requirements and that historians don't need a rationale for doing history. I said that I doubted the latter claim but that, in any event, the dissertation was being con-ducted in a College of Education. I further pointed out that as there were dol-lar costs associated with his dissertation (committee members' time for starters) and that taxpayers had a right to expect at least the attempt to relate the research to some practical matters. My pleas fell on deaf ears, and he car-ried on as planned (New 1985).

Then there is the "soapbox" problem, which occurs when the data are not commensurate with the analysis—that is, either there simply isn't enough data presented to carry the elaborate analyses and conclusions (e.g., Everhart 1983; Turkle 1984) or the data seem to have been selectively arranged to support what appears to be a preexisting thesis (Suransky 1982). Bengston's (1988) critique of Gershman's (1988) study of a high school drama production meets this issue head on: "Her focus is more in keeping with non-qualitative research which obscures contextual variation in its effort to find a superordinate principle that can be shown to operate across contexts. Had she been more qualitative—had she looked more precisely at what went on, we would have had a more accurate and substantial account of the proceedings" (p. 343).

Despite what I said a few paragraphs ago, the qualitative research literature is *not* devoid of convoluted language which, perhaps inadvertently, serves to shelter the author's work from critical scrutiny; for example:

> At certain times, it may be useful to gloss over a description of the work people do with each other in social events. In fact, the bulk of sociology does exactly this in centering its attention on social facts as adequate accounts of the constraints people have available in ordering their relations with one another. Such glosses can never be adequate, however, to the specification of how situations might operate to encourage the development and display of cognitive practices. (McDermott & Hood 1982:240)

Recent recruits to the qualitative fold can also be faulted for too readily applying the term "ethnography" to their work. As several authors (e.g., Wolcott 1980; Rist 1980; Howe & Eisenhart 1990) point out, ethnography is the methodology associated with the discipline or tradition of anthropology and carries it with a number of epistemological caveats that are blindly ignored by many who use it to describe their work (Miller, Leinhardt, & Zigmond 1988). Much the same can be said about the term "case study." More refined and restricted definitions for these terms will be presented in subsequent chapters.

THE NEED FOR STANDARDS

The field is slowly beginning to recognize the need for critical standards. Among other things, Howe and Eisenhart (1990) would like to see a good fit between questions asked and methods applied. They would like the author to relate his/her current study to previous research in the area, to attack previous arguments, and to offer new ones. They are concerned about the trade-offs between the quality of the data versus risks to informant confidentiality. Goetz and LeCompte (1984) have an excellent discussion of the problem with respect to ethnography but which can be applied, in the main, to all qualitative research. For example, they call attention to the length and intensity of the author's stay in the field as a check on the credibility of the findings. The investigator should demonstrate a high degree of self-awareness, so that he neither loses empathy for his informants nor "goes native."

The investigator must also balance the demand for fully describing the setting/culture under investigation without distortion while, at the same time, applying appropriate universal or pan-cultural constructs in the process of analyzing this material and constructing a theoretical model.

These authors are all striving to create a set of standards unique to qualitative research; however, there is now a lively debate as to whether the tools used to evaluate quantitative research can or should be applied to qualitative studies. For example, Kirk and Miller (1986) do an excellent job of defining *reliability* and *validity* in terms used by qualitative researchers. They argue that one way to assess internal consistency might be to have an outsider read the report and compare his/her conclusions with those of the original author. Unfortunately, field notes are not very accessible.[11] Wolcott (1975) suggests that enough raw data needs to be included in a report to permit a reader to form his/her own conclusions. Mehan (1979) makes a very strong case for the use of videotapes in qualitative research, which permits an independent investigator (or the original one, for that matter) to easily reanalyze the data.

Other writers seek to create alternatives to reliability and validity. Lincoln and Guba (1985) use "credibility" and "trustworthiness"; Patton (1990) would substitute *neutrality* for *objectivity*: "The neutral investigator enters the research arena with no axe to grind, no theory to prove, and no predetermined results to support" (p. 55). Cronbach and associates (1980) offer *extrapolation* in lieu of *generalization*. The issue of generalizability indicates just how difficult it will be to establish firm criteria for determining the value of a qualitative project.

> . . . what are the grounds—if any—for generalization? And if no generalizations are possible, how can knowledge accumulate? Thus, what does one make of an approach to the study of the educational world that depends on the unique aptitudes and proclivities of the investigator, that possesses no standard method, that focuses upon non-randomly selected situations, . . . indeed, are we justified in referring to the use of such a collection of procedures as "research"? (Eisner & Peshkin 1990:10)

Schofield (1990) argues that qualitative researchers are obligated to consider the generalizability of their results and suggests a number of steps, mainly revolving around careful sampling, to enhance generalizability.

I expect the "standards" problem will continue to receive a great deal of attention but, on a cautionary note, I'll let Phil Smith (1980) have the last word: ". . . while methodology should always be as rigorous as possible, it can be no more rigorous than the subject matter permits. A methodology might be extremely rigorous, but if it is not suited to the subject matter, it will not aid our understanding" (p. 6).

The Perspective Problem

Another persistent, but in many ways fascinating, problem is represented by the question, "Whose perspective should the qualitative researcher adopt?" It obviously should not be highly personal and idiosyncratic but unfortunately this is often the case.[12] Dobbert (1982) comments on the field-work report of one of her students done before the student had worked with her: ". . . she was not trained and not objective about her individual and cultural style . . . the data she could gather were merely personal and impressionistic. She could not achieve a cultural, holistic perspective . . . [but used] an approach [that] was deductive and predefined" (p. 18). Not only students go into the field with an ax to grind, however. James Spradley, who was one of the most widely respected methodologists in the social sciences, describes his own agenda for "strategic research" (1980:18–19) that would certainly flunk Patton's test for neutrality.

One of the most useful concepts in anthropological research has been the distinction between an emic (from phon*emic*) and etic (from phon*etic*) perspective. Emic represents the insider's perspective; etic, the outsider's (or objective). It is indeed a hallmark of qualitative research that the investigator must be able to describe the phenomena under study from an actor's (syn = native, participant, member) point of view. Lincoln and Guba (1985) offer as one test of the validity of a study the "member check" (p. 314), wherein one's conclusions must be screened by members of the group one has been studying. This strategy has been widely adopted in field studies of various kinds.

Taken a bit further, some authors (e.g., Woods 1986) state or imply that the *only* legitimate purpose of educational research is to work with teachers to resolve what *they* perceive to be problems. This is called "participatory research" (Lather 1986; Brown 1985). Fetterman (1989), on the other hand, makes the case that ". . . good ethnography requires both emic and etic perspectives" (p. 30).

Most qualitative researchers maintain a stance best described as *investigative*, where it is often taken for granted that "many of the people [the researcher] deals with . . . have good reasons to hide from others what they are doing . . . ." (Douglas 1976:55) and that the investigator ". . . learns things about the people he studies that may harm them, if made public . . ." (Becker 1970:105). One evident example of this state of mind is McPherson's (1972) study of teachers in a small town in New England. She herself was a teacher in the school, but she never made her fellow teachers aware of the fact that she was studying them for her dissertation. The resulting portrait is, perhaps, less flattering and more candid than had she done so.

The crux of the matter lies in the question of whether, in order to achieve an insider's perspective, one must personally *adopt* that perspective. In Everhart's (1983) ethnography of a junior high school, the principal and the teachers are presented in unrelieved negative terms while students, especially those who engage in creative and extravagant displays of what they call "goofing off," are portrayed sympathetically. Everhart (see also Willis 1977) clearly became "one of the boys." However, I would argue that this extreme identification with one's informants is neither necessary nor even desirable.

As we have seen, Malinowski has been held up to generations of student anthropologists as the model of the scientific, insightful participant observer, yet in his own diary (1967) he disdains any show of positive feeling for the people with whom he'd lived, as other equally talented scholars have done since (e.g., Hallpike 1977). Alan Peshkin's (1986) study of Bethany Baptist Academy represents an ideal balance between etic and emic perspectives. In the first chapter he lays out clearly his own etic perspective, but he also details his manifold strategies for suspending it while capturing the perspective of the school's participants. He actually set up house in the community for 18 months and returned to his own home only one day a week, for example. Then in chapters 2–10 he describes Bethany Baptist almost entirely in its own terms, using lengthy quotations. Hence, one is almost shocked when finally, in chapter 11, Peshkin reemerges and is ready to ". . . analyze the meaning of what I saw there from my own . . . perspective" (p. 270)—and this perspective is extremely *critical.*

Ultimately, an adroit student of the educational enterprise must deal with a multiplicity of perspectives.[13] First, there is one's own perspective, which reflects personal training and experience (e.g., allegiance to a tradition, prior experiences as student and teacher) and one's underlying philosophy of schooling (as a litmus test what one thinks of folks like Paulo Freire and E. D. Hirsch). Then there is the scientific perspective: "science" here means the accumulated wisdom on one's topic and not "positivism." Third, there are the obviously differing perspectives of teachers, parents, students and administrators (Lightfoot 1978). Fourth, no one of these groups' perspectives can be described as monolithic. Cusick (1973) was one of the first to demonstrate how varied the high school student's perspective could be. Ball (1984) discusses at length the problem of overly relying on the information supplied by a very cooperative but, perhaps, unrepresentative and even marginal teacher. But to represent these various perspectives is an ideal, something we should strive for but which has, in the literature published to date, been rarely achieved.

ENDNOTES

[1] I teach a class called Ethnography of Childhood, in which students do a brief study of children in a social setting.

[2] For a longer and more elegant answer to this question, see Smith (1986).

[3] There's a certain irony in Malinowski's use of the male pronoun as Weiner (1976), in subsequent research, found that he had ignored or distorted the role of women in Trobriand society.

[4] When I lived in Gbarngasuakwelle (Lancy 1996) I had to repeatedly fend off offers of marriage. It was unseemly for a man of my age and obvious means (I supplemented the local diet with canned corned beef and had a radio) not to take a wife; in this polygamous society the fact that I already had a wife "at home" made no impression. The "breach" caused no problems, fortunately, because I always felt I was among friends. I felt the same way in the Trobriand Islands—incidentally, *unlike* Malinowski.

[5] As Lareau indicates, being a *participant observer* can be a two-edged sword: "the few times when I forgot about notetaking and observing and just enjoyed being there, I felt a tremendous sense of relief . . . [but] the cost was a lack of carefully collected information" (1989:207).

[6] In quantitative research one is cautioned to *exclude* this kind of material. "Discuss . . . difficulties encountered in executing your study only if they might effect the validity or the interpretation of your results. Otherwise spare us your tales of woe" (Bem 1987:182).

[7] For a lengthy and thorough treatment of note-taking strategies see Dobbert (1982).

[8] Level of analysis is not synonymous with unit of analysis although there is a tendency to use broader, less precise analytical tools in working with larger units (e.g., school, community, district) and more precise, refined tools when working with smaller units (e.g., lesson, reading group, Sheila).

[9] Yin (1984) makes much of the same point about Kidder's (1981) earlier work, *Soul of a New Machine*: "Because the book is not an academic study, it does not need to . . ." (p. 32).

[10] But I am in complete agreement with Eisner and Peshkin (1990). ". . . Future scholars may find that being 'bi-methodological' is the true mark of scholarly sophistication" (p. 7). The authors acknowledge that Linda Grant coined this term at the University of Georgia.

[11] And this may not be all bad. Spradley (1980) tells of an ethnographer who was studying a school and was worried that his field notes would be subpoenaed in a lawsuit filed by the teacher's union against the district—they weren't.

[12] Among Smith and Glass' (1987) eight . . . issues to be raised about the qualities of [qualitative] studies:

> Researcher self-criticism. The researcher's preconceptions and biases can influence and perhaps distort the data. There should be evidence that these were acknowledged and controlled. If prior hypotheses or biases were evident, were they compensated for by the introduction of alternative hypotheses, multiple sources of evidence and observers, and a disciplined search for disconfirming evidence? (p. 278).

[13] A wonderful piece from Sara Delamont (1984) gives substance to this assertion:

> "I had a special gray dress and coat, the days when I expected to see the head [principal] and some pupils. The coat was knee-length and very conservative-looking, while the dress was mini-length . . . I would keep the coat on in the head's office and take it off before I first met the pupils" (p. 23)

2 The Anthropological Tradition

It is late in the afternoon and three women and a girl of seven are seated on the ground in front of the house. The head of the household is seated on the edge of a bench that adjoins the house. Two of his small children, a boy and a girl, age two to three, are playing under, around and on top of the bench. Of the women, two are wives of the man and a third, who lives nearby, is a sister to one of the wives. The women gossip as they shell and partially consume the peanuts. Fifty feet away, a third wife sits by the kitchen, her head cradled in her hands; she is ill, probably with malaria. The man watches and periodically he and his ten-year-old son, who has been sitting next to him, take pans full of shells to the edge of the town and dump them. The children play with a small pan that has a hole in the bottom. The little girl puts empty shells in the pan, then dumps them out—she does this repeatedly. Tiring of this, she bangs the pan on the little boy's head, he takes it from her and wears it as a hat. The little girl starts to scream and one of the women tells him to give it back, which he does. One of the wives scoops shelled nuts into a fanner and begins bouncing it up and down as shell-fragments fly out on the ground. This noise stimulates the little girl with the pan to mimic the bouncing action with the shells in her pan, which she does perfectly even though her back has been turned to the adults the whole time. In the kitchen a baby wakes up and starts to cry. The seven-year-old girl goes to fetch it and attaches it to her back with a length of cloth. The infant's mother takes the baby from its older sister's back and begins to nurse it. Another daughter joins the group, she's about ten. She brings her own pan and gets it filled with unshelled nuts, but does not sit down with the group. Instead she goes and sits down beside her mother, the sick woman, and begins shelling, the two exchanging no conversation. Just a short while later, it starts to rain and everyone prepares to retire indoors. The neighbor-woman holds out her hands, the headwife fills them with shelled nuts and she leaves.

The women carry their pans and stools inside and the man and his son make one last trip to dump the shells.

These notes were recorded in Gbarngasuakwelle, a village in the hinterlands of Liberia, during a project to document the process of education in a society without schools. Living in the chief's home, I gradually learned the ways of the village, experiencing the anthropologist's traditional rite of passage. I drew on this particular episode to illustrate how children of different ages carry out varying routines that prepare them to behave as adults (Lancy 1996). In this chapter, we'll take a look at a range of studies done by anthropologists, consider the kinds of settings in which they work, and the topics they find interesting. We'll look at how they conduct their work and how they arrive at their conclusions.

The image of the anthropologist immersing him/herself in a foreign society for a prolonged period of time to soak up the ambiance and then prepare a "verbal photograph" (Goetz & LeCompte 1984:238) of these obscure people and places resides, unfortunately, more in the public imagination than in reality. For one thing, the world is fast becoming homogenized, with wealth being the principal factor that differentiates people's lifestyles around the globe rather than the diversifying effects of culture. Second, it is no longer considered sensible or useful to attempt to study a people's entire way of life. One does topic-centered (Spradley 1980) studies of economy, kinship, or, perhaps, education. Third, there has been a marked shift in the attitude of the discipline to the conduct of inquiry.

As Van Maanen (1988) points out, "Until the 1960s, field work was with few exceptions simply done and not much written about or analyzed" (p. 96). Pelto (Pelto & Pelto 1978) echoes this refrain on a more personal note: "When I embarked on my first major anthropological research venture—the field work for my Ph.D. dissertation—I had had no formal training in the logic and structure of social sciences research" (p. xiii).[1] While the aims of the ethnographer have remained relatively constant, the methods employed to achieve these aims have received increased attention. The Peltos (1978) criticize much early anthropology on the grounds of ". . . the lack of specification of research operations that another investigator could use to replicate. Definitions and key terms are lacking, and the precise modes of observation (interviewing format, . . . etc.) are not generally specified by the ethnographer" (p. 34). Anthropology, chastised by its own (e.g., Harris 1968), has sought to shed its image as a highly personal, almost ad hoc endeavor (Eisner and Peshkin referring to qualitative research: ". . . there was about it almost a back door sense" [1990:1]).

THE UNDERLYING TENETS OF ETHNOGRAPHY

Ethnography is, or should be, the principal method of anthropologists. As such, the ethnographer seeks to describe the culture of a particular group of people, and "A culture is an historically developed, patterned way of life which includes beliefs and ideologies; formally and informally established interrelationships between persons and groups; and material goods and technologies, all of which are systematically related so as to form an integrated whole" (Dobbert 1982:10); but ". . . culture is never observed directly; it can only be inferred" (Wolcott 1987:50). Hence, the ethnographer must be prepared to interpret what she sees and hears, and ". . . anyone who has ever mistaken a blink for a wink is fully aware of the significance of cultural interpretation" (Fetterman 1989:28).

In Longbranch, fourth and fifth graders loved gym—it was one of their favorite subjects. I was therefore stumped by their furious reaction to the first couple of classes with a new gym teacher who arrived late in the year. But when they said things like "We have to learn skills . . . yeah, she makes us take tests!" I realized what had happened, in their view, was that a set of activities had been transformed from a rare and welcome commodity, "play," to a plentiful and unwanted commodity, "work," thus substantially affecting their enjoyment of school (Lancy 1976b).

The ethnographer gains increased confidence in her ability to interpret a particular culture if she has learned the native language or dialect; has spent an extended period of time in the field; and has systematically gathered materials, including notes from her observations, transcripts of conversations and interviews, and artifacts. She is expected, occasionally, to broaden her focus to achieve a holistic perspective which includes contextual information surrounding her topic. Further, we hope she has established sufficient rapport with a few of the participants so that they become key informants. They become virtual collaborators on the project and are able to assure that the ethnographer has captured their *emic* perspective to set alongside an *etic* perspective (Pike 1954) derived from the data and/or the scholarly literature dealing with this topic.

As a reader of her report we are inclined to find her interpretations credible to the extent that she shows evidence that she has done these things. We seek evidence of her training and experience and of her beginning the study without a lot of "baggage"—preconceptions about what she can expect to find.

> If a man sets out on an expedition, determined to prove certain hypotheses, if he is incapable of changing his views constantly and casting them off ungrudgingly under the pressure of evidence, needless to say his work will be worthless. (Malinowski 1922:331)

On the other hand, we would like to see that the ethnographer was systematic in seeking information regarding her topic and that she sought evidence to support her interpretation, as well as evidence which might support alternative interpretations. Her report should resemble Geertz's (1973) "thick description." "In order for a reader to see the lives of the people [she studies, she must show them through particulars] . . . i.e., not merely talk about them in generalities" (Spradley 1980:162). The reader ought to be able to second-guess the author by reinterpreting the data—much the way a well-written report of a quantitative study permits another scholar to accurately *replicate* the original study. But as I have stressed, we want to focus here not on what the novice qualitative researcher *should do* but on what real field workers do before, during and after their encounter with an alien culture.

In this chapter we will look at some of the major educational themes or topics that have energized anthropologists and will examine in depth several studies that address these themes. The reader should come away with a sense of the field of *educational anthropology*—both its substantive and methodological accomplishments.The first theme we consider is enculturation, the process by which culture is transmitted from one generation to the next in societies without formal schooling—in this case the Sisala and Kpelle societies of West Africa. We also look at societies that are just acquiring schools as a transition to a consideration of school-community relationships.

Another major concern of anthropologists has been the relationship between the public school and the surrounding community (Deyhle 1998). In many cases this relationship is a dysfunctional or hostile one. However, I go on to review, in depth, three societies where the relationship is more cordial, where communities have successfully adapted to formal education. These are the Amish, a Punjabi immigrant community in California, and a fundamentalist Christian community in the Midwest.

A major concern of educational anthropologists has been student culture, or the way in which students create their own society within the larger society of the school. We first review studies of student culture in the high school, including a mainstream school in the Midwest and a rural school in the Southwest serving a multiple-ethnic population, and then studies in schools serving younger children. We review Corsario's very thorough ethnographic studies of American and Italian nursery schools and then ethnography of student culture in an experimental elementary school. This last study incorporates a special type of ethnographic methodology called *cognitive ethnography* or ethnoscience.

EDUCATION AND CULTURE

The Study of Enculturation

Perhaps the earliest and still one of the most compelling topics in this field is the study of enculturation (see Middleton 1970 for a representative collection of studies). We've just had a definition of culture; in contrast, enculturation is the process whereby this "patterned way of life [and these] . . . beliefs and ideologies" are transmitted to the next generation. Margaret Mead, herself a student of Franz Boas at Columbia, made several extensive trips to the South Pacific to examine the experiences that children had from birth through adolescence. She was particularly interested in the role that parents and other adults played in guiding children's behavior (1928; 1930; see also Dennis 1943; Dubois 1944). As she made clear in her lectures as well as her writing she had been heavily influenced by prevailing Euroamerican theories of child development, especially B. F. Skinner's learning theory. As a student in her undergraduate Introduction to Anthropology class, I was assigned Skinner's *Walden Two* and Freud's theory of child/adolescent sexuality. However, heavily influenced by Boas, she sought to demonstrate that these theories did *not* hold up particularly well outside the culture that spawned them (as also happened years later when Piagetian theory was applied in Papua New Guinea: Lancy & Strathern 1981; Lancy 1983). For example, she argued, contra Freud, that adolescence was not inevitably a period of stress, especially vis-à-vis sexual activity. She based this on her observations and interactions with primarily female adolescents on Samoa, and the picture that she painted (Mead 1928) was of an almost idyllic life highlighted by open sexuality.

As we shall see, a hallmark of anthropological work in education and child development has been the "debunking" of prevailing wisdom. However, this study was later to come under attack (Freeman 1983) shortly after Mead's death, and the ensuing debate at conferences and in print totally preoccupied anthropology for years. Without taking sides, it is clear that Mead was determined to prove Freud wrong and that she probably was selectively attentive to evidence that supported her thesis. The debate about Mead's work notwithstanding, enculturation is still a lively topic of study. Like Mead and others, current students of enculturation are heavily influenced by a theoretical framework borrowed from psychology, namely, Vygotsky's social constructionist theory of child development (Wertsch 1985). However, unlike Mead, Vygotskians (Rogoff & Gardner 1984) seek to *support* Vygotsky's theory through the study of enculturation in non-Western societies.

Bruce Grindal's study (1972) in rural Ghana represents a fairly typical example of what was a real "growth spurt" in enculturation studies during the 1960s and early 1970s (see also Howard 1970; Jocano 1969; Leis 1972; Peshkin 1972; Read [1960] 1968; Williams 1969). He begins his account with a description of Sisala birth customs. This is a period that is fraught with danger and must be surrounded with precautionary practices and ceremonies: "A second ceremony must be performed for the protection and well-being of the unborn child. Called *wencheming,* or 'meeting on the road,' . . . it involves . . ." (p. 12). In the next section Grindal continues a stage-like description of development. His preoccupation with the details of toilet training belies the influence of Freudian theory; however, he, like others before and since who have studied village childhood, finds toilet training to be a rather casual affair. Indeed, the very term "training" has no real meaning in this society. "This emphasis upon situational observation and the lack of formal or structured learning is characteristic of all aspects of the enculturative process" (Grindal 1972, p. 31). Grindal does not report any sort of lengthy "bush school," which is found widely in West Africa and *is* associated with formal training designed to prepare young men (and, less often, women) and indoctrinate them into adulthood (Lancy 1975). Throughout, Grindal uses a Western lens to view his subjects in that he makes statements that can only have been motivated by implicit comparisons with "normal" practice in the West, e.g., ". . . the value often attached to children is based almost solely upon the criterion of usefulness" (p. 32).

Given the time frame of the study, it is not surprising that Grindal also had an opportunity to study "adaptation to formal schooling," another theme in the literature that we will take up shortly. Unfortunately, due to the slimness of his book, also characteristic of the majority of the works just cited, Grindal has no space to tell us about methodology.

My study of enculturation in a West African community was undertaken a few years after Grindal's but in a more remote and less acculturated area. Gbarngasuakwelle in 1973 had no school and very few other "benefits" of modernization. An occasional corrugated iron roof replaced the traditional thatch, and Western, store-bought clothes and cooking utensils were seen here and there. Although there were a few Christian converts in town, the traditional *Poro* secret society held sway, as masked figures literally terrorized the town twice during my stay.

Although a major objective of my study was the unadorned description of childhood among the Kpelle people—the largest of several tribes in Liberia—another prime objective was to explore an idea about child development that had its origin, unlike other theories referred to so far, in studies of non-Western societies—namely, that play contributes in significant ways to enculturation (Roberts, Arth, & Bush 1959; Lancy 1980b). Hence, from the start I narrowed my observational focus to activities to which people (children themselves or nearby adults) would point and label *pele,* or play. Additionally, I used a special set of interviewing techniques collectively known as cognitive ethnography (or ethnoscience) to *elicit* the entire taxonomic domain of *pele*. In this way I could either observe activity X and ask what was going on or, in the case of more complex play forms like *Malang,* ask to be included as a novice player. Alternately, I could take a named play form from my interviews and ask to have it demonstrated. These procedures yielded a total of 101 distinct play forms. I also reasoned that there might be links between particular play activities and particular work activities, so I used the same observation and interview procedures to elicit descriptions/demonstrations of *tii* (work), yielding a total of 128 work activities (Lancy 1996).

A variety of procedures were used to probe links between play and adult skills, values, beliefs, and so on, on several occasions including learning-type experiments (Lancy 1977). Not surprisingly, among the richer areas for exploration proved to be *neé pele,* or make-believe. Because Kpelle adults conduct their work in the out-of-doors for the most part, these activities serve as a prolific source of themes for *neé pele*.[2] One of the most elaborate episodes I witnessed was a make-believe enactment of the work of the blacksmith (Lancy

1980a:271). This put me on the alert for similar episodes, and I also conducted a rather thorough analysis of the process whereby a youngster eventually becomes a blacksmith. This analysis involved my hanging out at the forge and informally interviewing two elderly blacksmiths and their helpers.

These studies of enculturation have immensely enriched our understanding of the nature of child development (Cole & Cole 1989). In general, we find that in non-Western, non-industrialized societies, there is little formal teaching; much learning may occur in play; and parents don't "push" children's development—they are expected to observe the behavior of those older than themselves and, when the time comes, glide easily into more responsible roles in the community. The guidance and nurturing of one's biological parents is supplemented by the watchful eyes of the entire community, which shares child-rearing responsibilities. This literature provides a corrective to our Eurocentric view of children and suggests that there are different endpoints to development, and different pathways to get to those endpoints. However, the spread of formal, Western education provides a common endpoint. There is a growing consensus, internationally, on the need for universal literacy and numeracy. The intrusion of elementary schools into villages has, therefore, provided a challenge to traditional enculturation practices.

Schooling and Transition

The *U.S. Agency for International Development* was busy building rural schools in Liberia in the 1960s. They were staffed by U.S. Peace Corps volunteers until Liberia could train its own teachers. This pattern prevailed throughout much of what came to be called the third world, and many researchers studying enculturation also availed themselves of the opportunity to study the impact of recently introduced public schools. Grindal's (1972) work is representative. The one-room schoolhouse in "his" village is crowded and ill equipped (see also Baker 2000). The teacher is rigidly authoritarian; instruction is teacher-centered (see also Tabulawa 1998). This heavy-handed approach is reinforced by parents (see also Wolcott 1967) because "The . . . villager who sends his child to school regards education as an investment: a child who attends school will someday be able to earn good wages with which to help his father . . ." (p. 81). The informal, casual nature of instruction characteristic of the village no longer applies in school. Now, in a very short period of time—six years rather than the life-long education of the village—students must master whole volumes of new information, and in a foreign language. The result, I argued from observing in a school similar to the one in which Grindal observed, was "indoctrination without education." Students become indoctrinated with Western values and aspirations, rejecting the traditional values of the village, but the quality of instruction is so poor that they don't learn enough to succeed at increasingly higher levels in the education system (Lancy 1975). Interestingly, a similar process occurs in a totally different educational milieu: ". . . for the vast majority, the West

Point education is what it is meant to be—a socialization process. Most cadets have been trained rather than educated . . ." (Ellis & Moore 1974:121).

This scenario was repeated a decade or so later in Papua New Guinea, where Australia played the patron's role, building and initially staffing rural schools throughout the country. My colleagues and I had an opportunity to observe this process firsthand in several different villages (e.g., Carrier 1979; Lancy 1979; Wohlberg 1979). Unlike studies of enculturation, these studies of villages in transition (see also King 1967; Modiano 1973) forced ethnographers to become cognizant of government policies and initiatives. We had to take into account the multi-tribal, multi-cultural nature of these post-colonial "republics" as the school teacher was often (in Papua New Guinea, *always*) from a different ethnic group than that of his/her students. In short, the patterns established by Malinowski, Boas, and Mead for conducting ethnography would no longer suffice.

The added burden of taking these multiple perspectives into account also yielded a valuable dividend in that we were able to *compare* the dynamics of adaptation to schooling cross-culturally. Ali Pomponio and I took advantage of the fact that, in Papua New Guinea, the spread of formal education had been gradual, thus permitting us to look at three communities that had, relatively speaking, long, medium, and short histories of Western-style formal education. What we found was that community support, while initially quite high (with consequently high levels of academic investment on the part of students), dropped precipitously after a five- to eight-year period if the expected *economic* returns were not forthcoming (see also Hanks 1973). That is, villagers expected that students who completed their six years of schooling in the village would continue their education in boarding schools in urban centers, would eventually land high-paying white-collar jobs, and would remit funds home regularly. These expectations were, increasingly, unfulfilled, as the white-collar workforce became saturated and the central government shifted to a policy of "education for rural development," whereby school leavers were (unrealistically) expected to work to transform the subsistence-based local economy via cash-cropping and various entrepreneurial schemes (Pomponio & Lancy 1986). Our study fell under the heading of *ethnology*—we took three separate ethnographic studies and compared them. Although ethnology has a long and respectable history in anthropology (e.g., Frazer 1900/1922; Murdock 1967); it has not been particularly popular in educational anthropology. However, Noblit and Hare (1988) introduced the concept of *meta-ethnography* to describe research that involves the comparison or synthesis of two or more ethnographies.

These studies of adaptation to public schooling in Africa and Papua New Guinea were paralleled by studies of schooling among Native American and Black communities in the United States (e.g., King 1967; Wax, Wax, & Dumont 1964; Rosenfeld 1971; Ward 1971). Some of these ethnographies focused exclusively on the school or even on the classroom and relied on the pre-existing ethnographic record to flesh in details of the culture of the surrounding community (e.g., Gallimore, Boggs, & Jordan 1974), while others were more truly *holistic* and extended the study to the community (e.g., Ogbu 1974; Phillips 1983; Wolcott 1967). All the ethnographies document persistent "failure," in the sense that one sees little pleasure in either the teaching staff or the children—nor is there evidence that students are making satisfactory academic progress, enabling them to "climb out of the ghetto," "leave the reservation," or "become self-sufficient." Increasingly, anthropologists who study minority education now take student failure as their point of departure (see special issue of *Anthropology and Education Quarterly* on "Explaining the School Performance of Minority Students," 18 (4), 1987).

Dysfunctional School-Community Relations

One obvious explanation for these students' lack of success can be located in the differing values, beliefs, and practices (e.g., *culture*) of the community and those of the school. A recent statement of the culture-conflict theory has been provided by Trueba (1988), but it was a central issue in Howard Becker's dissertation study in Chicago in 1951: "We had one of the girls [first-year teacher] who came to school last year . . . she'd never had anything to do with Negroes . . . almost in tears she said, 'But they don't even want to learn. Why is that?'" (p. 148).

Similarly, Chilcott (1962) saw trouble looming ahead for immigrant children from rural Mexico: "Transferred from the rural villages to the United States and placed in the modern classroom the children . . . appear frightened, bewildered and quiet" (p. 46). As he noted, the experiences of a child growing up on a *rancheria* ill prepare her for the hectic, information-rich life of the modern classroom. Again, we see evidence of relaxed child-rearing practices. "The [toilet training] methods are as variable as the starting age . . . [also] . . . a child may eat whenever he gets hungry" (p. 43). "Toys and games are rare, . . . a girl is 9–10 years old before she is assigned definite duties . . ." (p. 44). On the other hand, "Usually, by the age of 13–14 a girl will have learned all the household skills . . ." (p. 45). There is no formal education and little emphasis on, say, oral history: "The history of the rancheria is learned mostly through listening to the conversations of parents. Few children, however, could give an accurate account if asked" (p. 46).

Burton, Obeidallah and Allison (1996) find that inner-city Black children don't really get to be children very long (see also Kotlowitz 1991). They bear responsibility for their younger siblings, they engage in sexual relations at a relatively young age, and they must seek employment to sustain the family. However, in the context of the public school, they are expected to behave like children in relation to their adult teachers—which sets up a direct conflict.

Erickson and Mohatt (1982), Heath (1983), Phillips (1983), and others have shown that children acquire communication styles at home which are different than those expected in the classroom. For example, Sarah Michaels and Courtney Cazden (Cazden 1988) have made videotapes of and studied

"Sharing Time"—that part of the K–first grade class called "Show and Tell," "Sharing," or "News." These narratives have distinctive patterns: they are topic centered; there is an opening with information about time, setting and central actions; and the child uses rising intonation. However, only about one-fourth to one-third of African-American children's sharing narratives look like this—they are more often "episodic." Michaels and Cazden find that teachers are less accepting of episodic narrative and try to steer children around to topic-centered narratives. Cazden (1988) argues that teachers use sharing time as an opportunity for students to ". . . construct an oral text that is as similar as possible to a written composition, . . ." (p. 14). Aside from problems with the form, episodic stories don't have natural stopping places and tend to "run on," which provides further frustration for the teacher.

ADAPTIVE STRATEGIES IN SCHOOL-COMMUNITY RELATIONS

When a community finds its values in conflict with those of the school, open hostility and "failure" are not inevitable, as is shown in three studies to be reported in this section on Punjabi immigrant, Amish/Hutterite/Mennonite, and fundamentalist Christian adaptations to public schooling. All three studies show again the anthropologist's penchant for studying the culture of people who are perceived as "different."

The Amish

The first study is actually a composite of several studies stretching over several years on relations between North American descendants of radical Swiss Protestants and public schools. One of the first reports on enculturation and education among these people appeared in 1971 as *Children in Amish Society* (Hostetler & Huntington). The "Old Order Amish . . . reject much of modern technology and new cultural developments" (p. 2); further they espouse "separation from the world" (p. 5). Their dress is distinctive; they practice "shunning" and arranged marriages, and they speak a distinct language. Throughout this report, the authors (p. 17) adopt a *normative* stance ("Amish babies are rarely alone. . . . During the first year of life the baby receives solicitous care from a large number of Amish of all ages") and the *ethnographic present* is used throughout. There is the assumption of a relatively unchanging world reflective of the anthropologist's interest in small-scale, isolated and essentially conservative societies like the Amish as well as an interest in documenting those particular aspects of culture that seem most resistant to change.

However, in this and other works (Hostetler 1974) the authors describe the growth and resolution of conflict between the Amish and related groups and the *in loco parentis* authority of the public school system. "Acquiring literacy and skills for their young without subjecting them to a change in world view confronts the Amish community with a fundamental problem" (p. 124).

The Amish have fought court battles to win exemptions from mandatory schooling laws, and migrated to other states when these were not successful. "The high school is viewed as a system that prepares the individual for living in the 'world' not in the Amish community" (p. 127). Today, no Amish child is required to attend school beyond the eighth grade.

A second problem arose during the 1960s with the school consolidation movement, which wiped out one-room, locally-controlled schools and replaced them with large, modern schools whose curricula were set by anonymous committees. The response to this problem was typically forthright: the Amish and similar groups opened their own local schools. The curriculum range was narrow and conservative. "Some . . . schools substitute agriculture for history and geography" (p. 44). *McGuffey Readers* over one hundred years old are still used. The Amish object to fairy tales and fantasy, abjure stories from other countries and cultures, and so on. Children are expected to become fluent in High German, the language of their religion; Pennsylvania Dutch, the language of the home; and, less importantly, English, the language of the outside world. Teachers are "called" from the community and seldom have more than an eighth-grade education themselves and no teacher training. Teachers are inevitably female. One notable difference in instructional practice is that accuracy and thoroughness are emphasized over speed. A final contrast between Amish educational philosophy and that of the public schools is "education for persistence" versus "education for change" (p. 106).

These observations about early attempts by the Amish to establish their own schools were nominally based on a study of one school that had been in operation just three years. But Hostetler and Huntington have devoted their entire professional lives to the study of these peoples; hence it is often difficult to trace in their writings the origins of a particular insight. This sort of blurring of various distinct bits of "data" is commonplace in much anthropology, as is the tendency for an anthropologist to invest his/her entire career in the study of one particular society (towards which they may show such a proprietary attitude that other investigators may be reluctant to "invade" their territory).

Hence, a more recent account (DeWalt & Troxell 1989) represents an interesting contrast methodologically. It is a study of a single "old-order Mennonite" one-room school, one of approximately 750 operating in the United States. Not only are the authors quite explicit about their methods but create a convincing rationale that these methods contributed to enhanced "rigor." The essential theme of the DeWalt and Troxell study parallels the work done 25 years earlier[3] by Hostetler and Huntington, namely, that in this case Mennonite communities reduce the conflict between their own values and those normally associated with public schools by vigorously managing what goes on in the school. The only unusual subject is German, as noted; texts are often cast-off public school texts valued as much for the absence of modern information as for their obvious economy. In social studies, references to war and environmental problems are OK—they provide a positive contrast with the pacifist, environmentally conservative practices of the Mennonites—but references to TV, evolution, and other seductive topics is taboo. New "Text books in use are written for old order Mennonite and Amish Schools and are designed to portray the ethnic values of hard work, anti-materialism, nonviolence, and honesty" (p. 322). The teacher upholds community values; her salary is $22.00 a day, which she considers "too high" (p. 320). She ". . . teaches as she was taught. Innovative ideas are not expected or encouraged" (p. 215). Students rarely leave their seats for any purpose and are rarely off task. "Student work habits are automatic. They know what to do and when to do it" (p. 317). Not surprisingly, parents visit the school often and are responsible for cleaning and maintenance.

Bethany Baptist Academy

Interestingly, as Hostetler (1974) observes, when the Amish established their own schools "The intent was not so much to teach religion as to avoid the 'way of life' promoted by a consolidated school system" (p. 125). This provides a nice point of departure as we turn to look at Peshkin's (1986) brilliant study of Bethany Baptist Academy. The Baptist congregation in Bethany faced some of the same problems faced by the Amish, but their conflict with the public schools was, if anything, more acute because, unlike the Amish, they do not live in complete isolation from modern society. They, and more importantly their children, interact daily with the mass media and others who don't share their culture. The Amish economy revolves totally around nonmechanized agriculture, so they have no compelling need for higher or vocational education. Bethanyites don't have this luxury; their children must be educated in order to insure themselves gainful employment. Bethany Baptist Academy, therefore, was established by the community to insure that their children do not stray from the faith. The curriculum at BBA is not only heavily censored, as it is in Amish schools, but teachers and the curriculum actively proselytize the students at all times. For example, these comments come from an interview with the librarian: "I look for evolution . . . I look for swear words . . . We take those out . . . I just sealed the pages together and it didn't bother the reading on the other side . . . If I find a naked person, I draw a little bathing suit on them. . . . One of the books sort of made light of discipline and so we, instead of having a little frowning boy . . . that had been punished and he didn't accept it, we put a sticker on there with a smiling face" (p. 263). However, we also learn that the goals of the science class are . . . "To develop a Christian mind so that kids see everything from God's viewpoint . . .; and the purposes of speech and drama. It's not to put students on the stage but to get them to be more effective witnesses for the Lord" (p. 80). All of the teachers quite consistently infuse Christian dogma into their classes at every opportunity.

Peshkin's study of Bethany Baptist Academy is noteworthy in two respects. First, it represents an extraordinary level of commitment. He actually moved to Bethany for the (18-month) duration of the project, commuting home to visit his family one day a week. He had to invest a great deal of time just finding a Fundamentalist school that would admit him as a researcher. The second extraordinary aspect of *God's Choice* is Peshkin's handling of his own perspective vis-à-vis that of the pastor, the principal, teachers, and others. He spends most of the first chapter delineating these differences, revealing a great deal about himself, arguing that the ". . . more he reveals of his personality and motives, the better able readers will be to . . . make their own judgements about what I saw, what I missed, and what I misconstrued" (p. 15). Using very long verbatim transcripts of his interviews, Peshkin lets members of the Bethany community speak for themselves, even quoting the pastor's attempts to convert him. In chapters 2–10, Peshkin proceeds to chronicle a thorough description of the Bethany Baptist Academy, convincingly, from an emic perspective. Finally, in chapter 11, Peshkin sheds his participant observer cloak in order to ". . . analyze the meaning of what I saw there from my own [subjective] perspective" (p. 276). Clearly Peshkin has found a way around the perspective controversy I discussed in the previous chapter.

The school is remarkably successful in its own terms. "If most school statements of philosophy and goals are misleading guides to what actually happens in schools . . . the converse is true at BBA" (p. 38). Students do well on standardized tests. Enrollment is stable and the budget is balanced. Staff turnover is light, and their dedication to the school is phenomenal. More importantly, raising children to be "true believers" is clearly the primary aim of the school; secular education is secondary. Teachers' fondest hope is that graduates will become preachers. "We think of scholarship as an avenue of service [to Jesus], as opposed to scholarship for its own sake" (p. 58). Peshkin's (1986) research shows that the school *is* very successful at enforcing conformity of dress, behavior, beliefs, politics, specific attitudes about gender roles, racial separation and so on. The reader is convinced that Peshkin was sufficiently immersed in this setting to allow him to penetrate the "facade," if any. Even when "anonymous" questionnaires were used, hidden opposition or nonconformity on the part of either teachers or pupils was almost nonexistent. Further, like the Amish practice of shunning, students are summarily removed from school for offenses, and the principal brooks no interference from individual parents. ". . . [W]hen parents send a check to us each month they feel they're buying a service. This makes them think they can criticize us, just like they would poor service at Kroger's . . . They either accept our view or remove their child" (p. 95).

The fact that Peshkin presents what is, essentially, a sympathetic[4] portrait of BBA is all the more remarkable given the very grave reservations he has about the school, as we learn in his concluding chapter. In the first chapter he notes the steadily rising enrollment of students in Christian academies (as contrasted with the steady decline in traditional parochial schools) and the rising influence of the religious right on public schools (e.g., school prayer, creationism, book censorship). He considers BBA an ". . . exemplary Christian school" (p. 14) and is troubled by what he has seen there. Peshkin decries the hypocrisy of BBA's support for notions like diversity and plural-ism when it comes to arguing for freedom from interference by government agencies seeking to regulate or control them (e.g., an unsuccessful attempt to deny tax-exempt status to schools that practice racial segregation), while teaching students that diversity and plurality are inherently wrong, evil (e.g., "We are the way. Mormons don't have it" [p. 133]).

Peshkin is also disturbed by the inroads that the emphasis on indoctri-nation makes into the student's education (see also Ellis & Moore 1974); "Christian students reside in a cognitively limited environment. . . . The price they pay is what they do not become, what they cannot enjoy, what they fail to comprehend" (p. 286). Peshkin concludes, "I confess to seeing Bethany's doctrinal yardstick poised like a guillotine to lop off dissenting heads, mine and others" (p. 290).

The Punjabi

The third ethnographic study of successful community/school adapta-tion contrasts with the previous studies along several dimensions. Margaret Gibson (1983; 1987; 1988) undertook to study the process whereby a recent, and still very poor, immigrant community manages to socialize its children for success in a typical American high school. Sikh immigrants from the Pun-jab (Northern India) experienced a great deal of conflict with the schools but did not, or could not afford to, establish their own school. Like the Baptists and Amish, this conflict centered on religion, values, dress, customs, or life-style, but they also experienced overt racism and had to communicate and learn in what is for them a second language. In other words, Gibson con-fronted a considerably more complex nexus of social and cultural issues than is typical.[5] The "community" in this case consists of at least two minority "subcultures" (Punjabi and Mexican American) and a White, largely agrar-ian majority. Further, among the Punjabi, she found that girls experienced schooling in ways very different from boys. She also found herself ". . . in the midst of Punjabi community factionalism, with one group trying to oust my co-investigator and, to bolster its position, sending letters to the funding agency to say that we were misappropriating money" (personal communica-tion 9/9/90).

To present a complete and credible account of this complex phenome-non, while at the same time addressing a theoretically important question, took an enormous amount of time. Gibson spent two years in Valleyside (Stockton, California) as a participant observer and rarely missed an impor-tant school or community event, even if it meant bringing along her nursing infant. She was aided by three assistants, two of whom were hired from (and one paid for by) the local community (Gibson 1985). Among other things the assistant carried out interviews (in Punjabi when necessary) with the parents of the 44 seniors who were the focus of the study. Similar structured inter-views were conducted with students and Valleyside educators, and Gibson

(1983) reported that: "Altogether the database for the project exceeds 5,000 typed pages, plus computerized data on school achievement" (p. 16). Finally, and I think this is remarkable, Gibson and her family also spent a year in the Punjab region of India, where she gathered additional background material that she uses extensively in her analysis (Gibson 1987; 1988).

She draws on this material to trace the cultural "roots" of the Punjabi community in California and to illustrate their motives for immigrating. The Sikh reputation for aggression, for example, stems from the fact that Sikhs were originally a group of Hindus who eschewed a passive response to Mughal invaders in the sixteenth and seventeenth centuries. Initially, immigrants have to work just as hard as they did as farmers in India. However, in California they can acquire farmland (particularly orchards) with their savings, there are opportunities for factory employment, and students who proceed with their education often end up in high-paying jobs in technical fields.

The study demonstrates that adaptation to the demands of formal education is not easy for these students. Their English is often very poor, and ESL classes appear to be a mixed blessing. They look and act differently and are the subject of racially motivated harassment. Their society teaches them to respect authority, and yet teachers demand that they express and defend their own opinions, and this is just one of the many subtle and not so subtle ways that teachers and students attempt to force the Punjabis to conform to "American ways" (Gibson 1988:142). And yet, on a variety of measures of academic success, Punjabi students do better than Anglo students. The parental/home/community view of what it means to be a student appears to be a major factor.

Among Anglos, only 12 percent take college prep courses, and parents and students seem to share a low estimate of the value of schooling. Similarly, ". . . principals observed that the Mexican American children seemed to have less sense of purpose and direction in school than the Punjabis . . . Mexican American parents . . . looked to the schools for assistance in helping children develop and maintain their Spanish skills, while the Punjabi parents favored all-English instruction" (p. 107). This and other evidence from her study suggest that parents in the three groups view schooling quite differently and convey their differing values to their children and to the school authorities, and that these values significantly influence student/school interaction patterns.[6] On the other hand, in rural Punjab there continues to be a feeling that "too much education can 'spoil' a girl" . . . Valleyside Punjabis were worried, too, that if a daughter went away to college "she might . . . wish to arrange her own marriage or . . . find it difficult to take up her proper role within her future husband's family. She might say . . . 'I've just finished college; how can I make the roti?'" (p. 112).

"Parents were not naive about the difficulties their children faced in school. They simply brooked no excuses for poor performance" (1988:293). They couldn't blame their failure on teachers or the "system." If students fell out of line they were forced into early marriage and/or put to work in fruit orchards. The primary method by which Punjabi parents facilitate their children's success is by insisting that they conform rigidly to the academic demands imposed by the school; they ". . . directed their children to do as teachers [say], to follow the rules . . . to acquire the skills and credentials necessary for competing in mainstream society but warned them at the same time to do nothing that would shame their families" (p. 128). Like students at Bethany Baptist Academy, the Punjabis implicitly accept their parents' views. They work hard, do homework before watching TV, stay out of fights, and obey and respect their teachers. Students do not want to follow their parents into the orchards but aspire to well-paid white-collar occupations. The Punjabis feel that "American" kids have too much freedom and too little responsibility. Punjabis students don't engage in extracurricular activities, sports, jobs; they don't date since marriages are arranged.

Gibson (1988) argues that the Punjabi community has achieved "accommodation without assimilation." They have managed to transmit their culture intact to the next generation while insuring that their children acquired sufficient education to permit them to participate in the economic mainstream. Unlike the Amish and the Bethany Baptists, they have done so without being able to exercise any control over the teachers or the curriculum.

Another issue that Gibson addresses at length in her work is cultural discontinuity. "The comparative success of American-educated Punjabi Sikhs and other immigrant minorities forces us to take a fresh look at some of our theories and assumptions regarding the school performance of minority students. Many of these theories have originated in an effort to explain minority failure and have been generated without sufficient attention to cases of minority success" (p. 168). Arguments that minority student failure can inevitably be traced to the fact that children who are poor, don't speak English, or are culturally different[7] are inevitably given *prejudicial* treatment by public schools must be reexamined. Various theories (e.g., Bempechat & Drago-Severson 1999) have been offered to explain the differential success/failure of minority students in American schools, notably by John Ogbu (1987).

A third and related theme in Gibson's work is the process whereby the Punjabi students band together to reinforce for each other their community's model for appropriate action in the high school. "There is increasing evidence that the peer group can act as a force for resistance to school authority, but among immigrant students the peer group more frequently serves to reinforce a positive school adaptation pattern and to support compliance with school norms" (p. 178).

The peer group has attracted the persistent attention of qualitative researchers, including ethnographers. Scholars have been particularly interested in the way in which youth create their own society that stands in contrast (or outright opposition) to the dominant or adult society. Prominent consideration should be given to Gary Fine's (1983) study of *Dungeons and Dragons* players and Frederick Thrasher's (1927) early and Ruth Horowitz's (1983) more recent studies of adolescent gangs. Our focus in the next section will be on ethnographic studies of the operation of the peer group in school, or student culture.

Student Culture in High School and College

Willard Waller's ([1932] 1961) somewhat misnamed *The Sociology of Teaching* is perhaps the first descriptive work on the high school which evinces understanding and sympathy for high school students.[8] Waller had trained at the University of Chicago, where some 25 years later a group of the faculty (Becker, et al. 1961) went off to Manhattan to study the student culture at the University of Kansas Medical School. They also ". . . used an interview guide, asking each student 138 questions . . . but we left room for the free expression of all kinds of ideas and did not force the students to stick to the original list of questions or to answer in predetermined categories" (p. 29). They followed students from class to class and dictated their observations at the end of the day. What they found was that the student culture was organized around the requirements for succeeding in medical school. That is, students used whatever freedom and autonomy they were granted by the school to develop their own institutional practices which, while self-serving, also served the ends of the school. This finding is very consistent with the Punjabi students studied by Gibson (1988) and the West Point cadets in Ellis and Moore's (1974) study, but strikingly at odds with many studies of student culture, as we shall soon see.

Historically, a third benchmark was established by Phil Cusick's (1973) ethnography, done while he was a faculty member at the University of Chicago, *Inside High School*.[9] Cusick very clearly played a *participant's* role without actually trying to pass as a student. In his study of a Midwestern high school, he found that school life was organized almost entirely around several well-recognized student groups, including "athletes," "power clique," and the "music-drama group." Every classroom situation was filtered through the particular group to which one belonged and defined accordingly. For the "hood" group, to which Cusick attached himself, all classes were profoundly boring, and members put forth as little effort as possible. They tried to get away with as much as they could, and they constantly trod the borderline of expulsion (see also MacLeod 1987). The loyalty to one's group and its view of the school was unswerving: "I asked one of the athletes, Greg, about associating with those not in his group. The thought just did not make sense to him. 'You know, like if you came here and didn't hang around with us, I wouldn't even know you'" (1973:67).

Cusick's use of student argot and his ability to view the school through their eyes goes far in convincing the reader that he is describing student *culture*. However, it is likely that by overly associating with one group (compare Varenne 1976; 1982) his portrait may be unbalanced, something that Deyhle (1986) freely acknowledges in her study of ethnically mixed Border High School. "I also marked myself . . . by publicly identifying with a particular group, and perhaps forfeited access to the 'opposing' student groups" (p. 115). She vividly describes the work she does to "present herself" and "manage the impression" (cf. Goffman 1959) students have of her.

> During my first few weeks students were polite, curious, but hesitant about my presence. I was clearly an adult (I did not try to act 15), but I was also somehow different from the other adults in their school. I dressed closer in style to the students; they called me by my first name and they could use "slang" and profanity around me without fear of repercussion. I did not judge their academic work, nor did I interfere with "fights" in the class, and they often interacted with me out of school, in the local teenage fast food restaurant, and on the town streets. (p. 114)

Deyhle (1986) carried out her ethnography of student culture during intermittent (and often lengthy) visits to the school in 1984 and 1985, facts that we don't learn at the outset. Very effectively she arouses the reader's interest by beginning with a lengthy anecdote, and it is only in the middle of the second page that she tells us, "I had come to this border community to do a study of . . ." (p. 112). This strategy is not at all uncommon in writing ethnography. The crux of the opening anecdote is summed up in the following quote from one of the students: "Yeah, we don't hang out there; it's for the jocks and preps. Us breakers don't hang out at the end of the hall" (p. 112). This is a study of student cliques in a high school, and of one low-status, marginal clique in particular, Ute and Navajo "breakers."[10]

Deyhle goes on to analyze the purpose of break dancing: "Break dancing formed a powerful support group for these Indian students. The clique dictated clothing and social stance. It offered its members both self-confidence and a means for expressing success in an otherwise indifferent or negative school and community environment" (p. 112).[11] However, her "telling" the reader would have been far less believable if she had not also "shown" us using quotes like the one above.

As Gibson did, Deyhle faced an extremely complex social scene at Border High School. She uses *quantitative* data very effectively to help "set" this scene. Since her focus is on a group of students, her observations don't end at school. For example, she notes that break dancers offer a defiant "side-show" at football games, demonstrating simultaneously their indifference to one of the more cherished rituals of the popular students, while also showing off their own formidable physical/athletic skills. Indeed, she clearly shows that school is not one but several different places, depending on the perspective of a particular group of students. Indian students: ". . . were academically marginal, finding very little in the classroom that was of interest to them or relevant to their lives out of school . . . [they] . . . saw school as a place to organize socially, . . . class activities . . . interrupted the pleasant times with their friends" (p. 117). As Michael Agar (1986) points out, this is the essence of ethnography: "Ethnographers set out to show how social action in one world makes sense from the point of view of another" (p. 12).

A study by Lois Weis (1985) of the Black student culture[12] in an urban community college makes me wonder about Ute and Navajo students at Border High School who *didn't* associate with the "breakers." Weis (1985) adopts a critical theory perspective (see also Willis 1977; Everhart 1983; McClaren

& Giarelli 1995) to argue that the Community College, ostensibly established to open additional avenues for upward mobility, instead aids in *reproducing* the existing social order (Bourdieu & Passeron 1977) (see next chapter). Weis had to overcome a great deal of initial hostility to gain access; the college had been experiencing a run of bad press—a not uncommon situation in urban schools. Eventually she was able to play a participant observer role. Her observations were complemented by open-ended interviews and a highly structured student opinionnaire. Not surprisingly, Weis found hostility between different student groups. In particular, White students wanted "efficiency," maximum learning or career advancement for the dollars and time they invest, and therefore resented Black students' efforts to make classes more casual and informal, "rapping," bringing along their children, eating, and socializing. The Black student culture is cohesive; there is a high degree of conformity because it is a culture that has been incorporated almost unaltered from their own community. This culture promotes active resistance to the norms of the school and to attempts by the school to change student language use, reading, study, and attendance patterns. Thus, we see this student culture operating in a manner quite different from that of the Punjabis at Valleyside High but quite consistent with Border's "breakers." Where Weis breaks new ground is in her analysis of the few Black students at Urban College who are academically *successful*. These students forgo membership in the Black student culture and embrace mainstream values and habits. They "act white" (Fordham & Ogbu 1986). They actively seek out faculty support. The faculty respond in turn, almost without exception; they seem willing to spend an inordinate amount of time assisting Blacks who demonstrate that they are willing to begin learning the dominant culture.[13]

Increasingly, the study of school social structure revolves around *ethnicity* as high schools take on a "rainbow" hue (Patthey-Chavez 1993). A very interesting study in this regard was done recently in a San Francisco area multiethnic school. Goto (1997) found: nerds (hardworking, serious ethnic Chinese students); normal people (similar students who hid their academic success in order to fit in, compare Fordham's [1995] high achieving group); homeboys (Black and Chicano students who resisted conformity to school requirements); and Wannabes (Cambodian and Vietnamese students who sought acceptance by the homeboys).

Another prominent theme in the more recent literature, unfortunately, has been school violence. John Devine's long-term study (1996) of "lower-tier" schools in New York City is a comprehensive analysis. While the nation was appropriately shocked by the Columbine killings, the culture of violence has been pervasive in our inner-city schools for years. The extent of the problem can be grasped in the following statistics: Devine (1996) states that there were over 3,200 uniformed officers in the New York City Division of School Safety—a contingent larger than the entire Boston Police Department. Beta school had a total of 110 "security personnel"; by comparison, the size of the teaching staff was 150 (pp. 76, 78). Devine points out that reform policies actually exacerbate the problem because they are a form of *tirage* (my term). That is, the more promising students are routinely pulled out of the lower-tier schools to attend magnet public schools. Lower-tier schools become a kind of "dumping ground" and even serious, conforming students who've recently immigrated from outside the United States (especially from the Caribbean) quickly acquire an (anti-school) "attitude" from the entrenched African- and Hispanic-American students. Devine (1996) maintains that the heavy-duty security apparatus is as much part of the problem as it is a solution, and he consistently faults the *teachers* for failing to take a stand to enforce standards of dress, etiquette, and academic integrity. However, in view of the teacher murdered recently in Florida for enforcing rules, it's not hard to excuse the teachers from this responsibility. As Devine reports, "When I ask teachers in these schools how they maintain classroom control, their response is, 'I can always call security if the kids get too rough'" (p. 2).

Some Methodological Issues

The study of student culture presents several interesting methodological paradoxes. We can clearly see the potential value of close identification with the "natives" in a study of student culture. Moffatt (1989), who conducted a field study of student culture at Rutgers while on the faculty, offers a convincing defense of participant observation (p. xv) but then: "In 1977, on a whim, I decided to try passing as an over-age, out-of-state freshman for the first few days of the fall semester at Rutgers College" (p. 1). The facade, however, cracked after a few days. For example, his roommate told him that his ". . . vocabulary had been too advanced . . . and he had thought it odd that I read the *New York Times* every day . . ." (p. 11). Nevertheless, his "discovery" of the overwhelming preoccupation that Rutgers' students have with sex suggests the depth to which he was able to penetrate the student culture.

And yet one must ask, if the goal is to maximize one's similarity to and affinity for one's informants, how one can "make the familiar strange" (Erickson 1973/1984). Harry Wolcott, widely regarded as *the* authority on the ethnographic method, has written about this problem as faced by his students:

> Requiring my students to select informants or scenes from societies radically different from their own . . . enhances the likelihood that the differences students identify will be associated with aspects of culture . . . On a grander scale, that same argument has obtained in the strongly voiced preference for having anthropology (and anthropology and education) students do their first major fieldwork—typically the dissertation study— in a distant society, or at least with a dramatically different microculture. (1987:50)

A potentially serious problem stems from the overidentification with one's informants noted by Deyhle. Willis' (1977) *Learning to Labor* is a widely admired (e.g., Everhart 1983; McClaren 1989) description and analysis of the pattern whereby the working class (male) student culture in a *comprehensive* high school in Britain actively "resists" school authority. It demonstrates an extraordinary degree of rapport with a widely scorned and misunderstood group. However, as Davies (1985) points out, Willis so fully accepts the "lads'" perspective that his work comes across as blatantly sexist and anti-female. Hymes (1977) suggests that "the conditions of trust and confidence that good ethnography requires (if it is to gain access to . . . meanings) make it impossible to take . . . the role of impartial observer . . ." (p. 21).

Wolcott (1987) laments that school ethnographers in the United States lack a comparative or cross-cultural perspective, rendering it all the more unlikely that the investigator will experience what Agar (1986) calls "breakdown." This occurs when something unexpected happens, it doesn't make sense, and the ethnographer has to talk to his/her informants seeking "resolution." Ideally, the ethnographer should read other ethnographies dealing with his/her topic to gain a comparative perspective. But they often fail to do this, and the following "pledge" by Ellis and Moore (1974) indicates why this might be so: "The purpose of this book is to describe and analyze the operation of the United States Military Academy. . . . Our research was begun as a concentrated effort to withhold judgement until we felt that we understood how West Point viewed itself" (Ellis & Moore 1974:vii). Moffatt's (1989) work is one of the most recent studies of *student culture*, and yet he cites only one (Varenne 1982) of the many antecedent studies cited here. Like Ellis and Moore, Moffatt wanted to see how Rutgers' students view themselves. Evidently they do not feel they are participating in a student culture; hence, he saw no need to review literature on the topic. On the other hand, by not reviewing this growing body of work, he may have missed a chance to make the familiar seem strange.

We have, then, this double paradox. Ethnographers are urged to take great pains to identify with and blend into the culture they are studying, while also being urged to study that which is most foreign and strange. Likewise, they are advised to tease out unique aspects of the culture and to adopt a posture of cultural relativism, while at the same time they are advised of the value of a comparative perspective and exhorted to conduct a thorough review of prior research on their culture/topic. There are other pitfalls for the novice ethnographer.

The growing popularity of qualitative research has meant that the researcher is faced with a new and fortuitous problem—how to review and synthesize several ethnographic studies on his/her topic. We have just identified one problem associated with this enterprise, namely, the emphasis on the uniqueness of culture precluding the use of etic terms and categories. Hence, while a quantitative researcher interested in student "motivation" can quickly find a welter of current and appropriate sources through ERIC, searching for qualitative studies on "student culture" would have turned up less than half of those cited here. Indeed, I would still be ignorant of Moffatt's work if my colleague David Bergin hadn't called it to my attention.

Another problem is identified by Noblit and Hare (1988) in their innovative work on meta-ethnography. As they point out, ethnographers use a wide variety of analytical frameworks, from the traditional structural/functional analytic approach (Burnett 1969) to the more recently employed Marxist or critical theory framework (Everhart 1983), thus making it difficult to compare across studies. Agar (1986) also addresses this problem: ". . . ethnographies of similar groups, or on similar topics, differ from one another. They differ because of differences in the audience addressed, in the background of the ethnographers, or even the groups themselves" (p. 15). Nevertheless, if one focuses on the *descriptive* part of the ethnography as Noblit and Hare (1988) advise, one can carry out a ". . . reciprocal translation of studies into one another . . ." (p. 11), as they have done for several studies of school desegregation (Collins & Noblit 1978; Metz 1978; Rist 1979; Schofield 1989) and as I have done here for student culture.

Nursery School Ethnography

While the ethnographic study of student culture has been dominated by works that focus on adolescents, there have been a few studies of younger children, and these illustrate several noteworthy aspects of epistemology and methodology (e.g., Tammivaara & Enright 1986). William Corsario (1985) conducted an extremely thorough analysis of student (or peer) culture in American, and more recently (1988a; Corsario & Rizzo 1988) Italian, nursery schools. Corsario faced a number of methodological challenges, at least partly because, unlike Phillip Cusick (1973) in Horatio Gates High School, he could not ". . . easily check his perception by asking [students] to describe and explain a particular event or asking them to verify his perceptions for accuracy" (p. 5). Further, he tells us that ". . . it was essential that the children perceive me as different from the teachers and other adults in the nursery school setting, so that they would not suppress certain behaviors for fear of negative reactions" (p. 27). He also needed to be sure not to act like other adults; he noticed that adults were active, they initiated contact, so he decided to be reactive: ". . . of all the many hours observing in this setting, these were the most difficult for me. I wanted to say something ('anything') to the children, but I stuck with the strategy and remained silent" (p. 28).

Although Corsario (1985) is eventually granted full access to the student culture, getting an emic perspective was difficult. He explains that it took him a very long time to notice ". . . how deeply concerned the children were for the physical welfare of their playmates" (p. 177), and that ". . . young children are deeply concerned with physical size" (p. 179). Hence, most of his constructs are etic, derived from the literature (e.g., *secondary adjustment* from Goffman 1963) or grounded in his data. He began with non-participant observation, observing through a one-way mirror, a common feature of the kind of university-sponsored nursery school (or child study lab) in which he worked. He worked back and forth between his notes and the literature to gradually sharpen his focus until he had a workable unit of analysis, the *interactive episode*.

Once he was confident that he had a workable strategy for making sense of activity in the nursery school, Corsario negotiated entry into the student culture (see also Knupfer 1996). Later still, after he had been accepted, he began videotaping.[14] The videotape record would permit him to achieve a more fine-grained analysis (he describes his method as "micro-ethnography"). He goes so far as to identify quantifiable variables, e.g., "coefficient of variation" (V), which ". . . is a way of estimating how widely each child spreads his contacts" (p. 156) and uses inferential statistics to compare "V" for the morning and afternoon nursery school sessions.

Data collection and analysis proceeded simultaneously within a "constant comparative" (Glaser & Strauss 1967) or "reflexive" (Mehan & Wood 1975) framework. The reader is made aware of shifting hypotheses: ". . . children were primarily concerned with control over play areas and used friendship as a device to gain control and exclude others" (p. 39). ". . . A further analysis of field notes in initial videotaped episodes suggested that they were more concerned with *maintaining the stability of the interaction* than with the *control of territory or play materials* (p. 40).

Among his major findings is a vivid picture of the emergence of the concept of "friend" that we see when children ". . . used the *denial of friendship* as a basis for exclusion [from interaction]" (p. 150, italics added). He also observed the beginnings of "resistance" (cf. Willis 1977): ". . . one of children's most cherished desires: *to defy and challenge adults, share the experience, and not be detected*" (p. 261).

George Spindler (1983) is critical of studies of "youth culture" in the United States because ". . . there is no explicit and very little implicit cultural comparison" (p. 71). Corsario (1988a) remedies this problem with his study of a *scuola materna* in a major northern Italian city, using nearly identical methods as in his initial study. In this article he focuses his attention on several recurrent "routines," such as the construction and maintenance of an interactive play area. In general, there were many commonalties between the two peer cultures. "The fact that there were so many analogous routines in the two data sets provides some evidence for the possible 'universality' of certain elements of the peer culture of young children"[15] (p. 5). However, he found that Italian children's fantasy play is much more "permeable" than that of the Americans. They are more tolerant of other children joining in their play activity even if just temporarily passing through. They seem able to maintain the fabric of their play activity intact despite interruptions. Corsario relates this to the northern Italian's noted ability to maintain several conversations at once.[16]

Ethnoscience in the Elementary School

As documented by the Peltos (Pelto & Pelto 1978) anthropology in the 1960s was shaken by an epistemological earthquake. A number of scholars, notably Frake (1964) and Goodenough (1971), challenged the accepted view of both the purpose and methods of ethnography: the focus should shift from documenting the patterns of human behavior and interaction and interpreting their meaning to discovering culture as manifested in the learned and ordered beliefs of members. Methods would change from the relatively unstructured and ad hoc participant observation, key informant interviews, and the like, to highly structured and precise "elicitation" procedures. Adherents were not modest in their claims: ". . . ethnoscience shows promise as the New Ethnography required to advance the whole of cultural anthropology" (Sturtevant 1964:101). Widely employed in non-Western societies, the late James Spradley stands out as the dominant force in the application of cognitive or ethnoscientific methods in the study of U.S. urban culture (Spradley 1979; 1980; Spradley & McCurdy 1972). Not surprisingly, not all anthropologists "heeded the call," and there have been vigorous counterproposals (Harris 1968). Consequently, today we can identify a materialist stance associated with those "materials" (including human behavior and speech) one can *observe and record*, and a cognitive stance that treats as primary data the schemas people use to make sense of their social world.

It is rare for an ethnographer to maintain one stance to the exclusion of another; however, sometimes there are special circumstances. Often, the group of interest presents formidable problems as potential informants, forcing one to focus more exclusively on behavior and achieve a primarily etic description. Such certainly was the case in Corsario's work, as we have seen, but was also the case in Gleason's (1989) long-term study of a residential facility for severely retarded individuals (see also Bogdan 1980).

Another special circumstance occurs, I would argue, in studying the student culture in an elementary school. For 18 months during the 1974–75 school year I conducted an ethnography of Longbranch, an otherwise typical elementary school that had been used for nearly ten years as an experimental school to field-test the federally funded curriculum projects developed at the Learning Research and Development Center (LRDC) in Pittsburgh. Two issues led me to employ the ethnoscientific (Jacob [1987] refers to this tradition as *cognitive anthropology*) methods. First, the method forces the investigator to act as a stranger, asking *naive* questions. I was very concerned that my familiarity with U.S. elementary schools would blind me to taken-for-granted aspects of the student culture. Second—while the nursery students are given a great deal of autonomy and much of their activities are not directly managed by the teacher; and the student culture in high school is readily apparent in dress, speech, seating and class participation patterns and so on—I assumed that elementary student culture would be at least partly hidden to conventional participant observation. As I will show, ethnoscience specifies a set of interviewing and analysis techniques (Spradley 1979) that greatly increase one's chances for getting an emic (or in this case, the students' rather than teachers' or the participant observer's) view of this experimental school. Indeed, researchers had already gathered a great deal of test data on students at the school and had also interviewed teachers regarding their attitudes towards the (individualized) curricula (Glaser 1976).

Before beginning ethnosemantic interviews with students, I did spend four months conducting more conventional participant observation.[17] As much as anything else, this period allowed participants to get to know *me*. I also began learning the students' "language." I did this by openly eavesdropping but also by listening to tape recordings I made in areas where students habitually gathered. One such place was a large metal storage cabinet in the hall that contained hundreds of audiocassettes used in language arts lessons. Students would go and get the appropriate tape when instructed to do so in their individualized lesson; permission from the teacher was not required. When, as frequently happened, two or more students arrived to get or return a tape at the same time, a conversation would take place, recorded by the machine sitting plainly in view on top of the cabinet. These conversations were invaluable in helping me to create an initial portrait of the student culture and, more importantly, teaching me the appropriate vocabulary to use in talking about it.

Following this initial period, I conducted ethnoscientific interviews with several fourth and fifth graders:

D. L.: What else do you do in the library?

JOHN: We throw things.

D. L.: What kinds of things do you throw?

JOHN: Oh, spit balls, pencils, paper airplanes.

D. L.: What kind of activity is it when you throw things?

JOHN: That's when we're fooling around.

D. L.: How else do kids fool around in the library?

JOHN: They bug people.

D. L.: What does that mean?

JOHN: Well, when someone is working, you bother them. You steal their pencil, or call them names. Anything to get 'em upset. (Lancy, 1976a:15–16)

Earlier I had determined that "library" was indeed a term students used, ditto with the term "activity." Notice that "What else . . ." elicits additional terms at the same level in the taxonomy (or "cognitive map," as I referred to it in this study), while "What kind of . . ." elicits subordinate categories. I continued in this vein until I had an exhaustive taxonomy (Lancy 1993: fig. 2.1). Students' view of school was organized around "activities" and not "groups." They more closely resemble nursery school children (Corsario 1985) than junior high students (Davis 1972; Everhart 1975). I will come back to this issue shortly.

One of the bases on which ethnography in general, and ethnoscience in particular, has been criticized is that we generalize about an entire society on the basis of intensive study of only a few informants (Harris 1968). As the Peltos (1978) point out, studies show that core values and beliefs may be widely shared, but one must be extremely skeptical of the cherished assumption in anthropology of *cultural homogeneity* (for an early, critical study of the homogeneity principle, see Roberts 1951). Consequently, techniques were developed that permitted me to measure quite precisely the degree to which this particular worldview is shared. In this study (Lancy 1976a) I designed a *similarities judgement* instrument that could be easily scored and analyzed by a process called multidimensional scaling. The analysis yields a taxonomy that displays the distance (i.e., very similar, very different) between any two activities and provides a measure of consistency. In this case the taxonomy generated from data on eighty students very closely resembled the taxonomy elicited from the few students I had interviewed at length.

Another concern has been the failure to relate the participants' thoughts about the situation or setting to their behavior in that setting. Ethnographers are exhorted (Fetterman 1989) to seek both etic and emic perspectives. Hence, I used my interview material to construct a *behavior observation checklist* to use in conducting systematic observation of the children's behavior throughout the school. Each of the eighty students was observed in six different settings in the school, and observations were distributed so as to obtain a representative sample of all combinations of students/settings/activities. I (and a second observer) had no difficulty identifying each of the activities, and only one activity not supplied by students ("waiting") had to be added to the checklist in order to make it exhaustive of all observed activities. This suggests that the cognitive ethnography I had obtained was accurate and comprehensive.

At the time the Longbranch study was conducted,[18] there were relatively few extant studies of student culture. Cusick's (1973) study suggested that student groups or cliques were central to understanding student culture. Davis (1972), in a study of a junior high school, also found cliques—Troublemakers, Goody-goodies, Brains, Cool Kids, Colored Kids, Loners, and others—although these were probably less stable than those in the high school. She also found that junior high students, unlike students in Horatio Gates (Cusick 1973), were extremely conscious of the adults in the school, especially teachers, talked about them a lot and had shared views on everything from their "strictness" to their "picking on kids." Finally, and again unlike the high school students, "activities" occupy a prominent place in the view of school held by junior high students. Many of their activities are analogous to those I found at Longbranch but there are interesting additions, including "trying to act cool."

With this background, I probed for evidence of these additional elements in Longbranch students' view of their school. Students utterly refused to acknowledge that there were different groups or kinds of kids in school. They freely used epithets with each other but were unable to generalize a trait or collection of traits to a group. Indeed, aside from loose-knit, small, and shifting friendship clusters, this school did not have cliques—nor did I find any evidence that "teachers" or "types of teachers" figured prominently in this student culture. Obviously, they were present in the school but must have been as static and unremarkable as items of furniture. Whether this is a function of the unusual curriculum or characteristic of student culture in the elementary school is an open question. However, one thing does seem clear: while activities dominate the student culture in nursery and elementary school, gradually student groups appear and, increasingly, occupy the dominant position. The few studies of post-secondary student culture suggest a weakening of the clique system in many cases and a reassertion of "activities" as the principal organizing rubric for student culture.

THE FUTURE

Despite the decline in opportunities to study enculturation and acculturation in non-Western societies, the field of education and anthropology is thriving. Membership in the Council on Anthropology and Education has climbed steadily, and CAE is now one of the largest subdisciplines of anthropology and occupies a large part of the landscape at annual meetings of the American Anthropology Association.

I find it interesting that it has become harder and harder to identify educational anthropology on the basis of topical foci. Educational anthropologists now study issues that historically have been the provenance of sociologists, social psychologists, and political scientists. Increasingly, it is the ethnographic method (an all-encompassing concern for the entire culture of a group of people) that serves as the hallmark of an anthropologically oriented study.

Nevertheless, the topics identified in this chapter deserve continued attention. The study of enculturation has received a boost from renewed interest in the developmental theory of Lev Vygotsky. His work directs our attention to the role of parents and the larger social group in assisting the child to become a competent member of society. Another robust source of inspiration for enculturation studies is the voluntary organization, such as the street gang, 4-H, catechism class, Karate lessons, learning to manage a paper route, and so on (e.g., Raitt & Lancy 1988).

While globally more and more children are becoming "schooled" and the culture of the school is becoming more standardized, interest in alternatives to regular schools is growing in the United States. Home schooling and magnet schools are two recent alternatives, but there are many others. We very much need ethnographies of these new kinds of schools and schooling which, among other things, relate their programs and practices to the culture of the community that sponsored them.

Studies of student groups show no signs of abating but student groups in vocational schools and community colleges (London 1978, a rare case) are underrepresented in the literature. I would also like to see us rapidly rectify the relative neglect of female student groups (but see Finders 1997) at all levels of the education system.

RECONSTRUCTING THE WEB

Most anthropologists use the ethnographic method, which in many ways is the prototype for the qualitative method. However, anthropologists have a unique concern for culture, a term subject to a variety of interpretations. Think of it as a spider web—as this strong, multifaceted, but nearly transparent structure. Classical anthropologists attempted to capture the entire web; modern anthropologists focus on a particular topic or section, but—and this is the key—they are bound to trace, at least cursorily, all the silk threads leading away from the little area in which they've chosen to work. They do this in order to get some sense of what the total web looks like, but also in order to hazard a guess as to what happens in other parts of the web when there are perturbations in their area. Notice the way Corsario traces aspects of Italian children's play to adult communication patterns. Notice the way investigators consider the impact on culture of foreign elements like the school. For some societies schools are like juicy new bugs that are pounced on with relish by the spider; for others the school is an inedible, even destructive substance that disrupts the delicate harmony of the web.

Tracing the patterns formed by all these filaments takes a great deal of time; hence, ethnography is characterized first and foremost by prolonged engagement and participant observation. As the chapter progressed, we moved from the relatively unstructured and intuitive methods of the traditional ethnographer to the more and more refined, precise and redundant (or triangulated) methods of the contemporary ethnographer or ethnoscientist. It's as if the modern ethnographer wants to move beyond describing the surface appearance of the web and examine its molecular structure. Now participant observation is supplemented by systematically interviewing samples of informants, casual observation is buttressed by structured observation procedures, and computer programs aid in the analysis of massive amounts of text—notes, interview transcripts and printed materials. One reason for this escalation in the use of a greater variety of techniques and the supplemental use of quantitative data to enhance credibility is the need to capture several different perspectives on the phenomenon of interest. It is not enough to study and report what *we* think the spider's web looks like, how it is structured and how it functions. We must also describe it from the spider's point of view, from that of its victims, and from the perspective of the birds which prey on the spider. Is it any wonder that anthropologists return again and again, over the course of their careers, to study the same people, as Deyhle (1998) has done with Indian adolescents in Southwestern Utah?

However, as we attempt to enhance reliability and become more focused, more rigorous and more precise in analyzing specific aspects of culture, there is the danger that validity will be sacrificed, that we will fail in our mission to adequately describe the culture with all of its fascinating nuances. After all, most spider webs command respect for their sheer beauty. Ethnography without rich narrative description isn't worthy of the name. This detailed, recorded-for-posterity quality of ethnography comes through in the use of the present tense and the use of a static framework (Grindal describing the *Wencheming* ceremony) and in the tendency to offer a collective portrait of group members (Gibson's Punjabi) and gloss over inter-individual variation.

The best time to study the spider's web is in the morning, as heavy dew throws it into sharp relief. Otherwise the web, like our own culture, is all but invisible. This is the primary reason anthropologists study societies markedly different from their own, as Peshkin did at Bethany Baptist Academy. One can also *contrast* two or more distinctive cultural responses to a particular situation, as Pomponio and I compared Ponam, Mandok, and Imbonggu adaptation to government schools. One can contrast what one observes with descriptions of the same or similar societies in the extant literature. One must somehow make the familiar strange, as my pat understanding of what a spider's web should look like was shaken upon moving to Arizona and encountering the black widow's "web."

Ultimately the anthropologist's primary identification is not with a particular research methodology (psychology departments advertise for *experimental* psychologists, anthropology departments do not advertise for *ethnographers*); nor, usually, with a specific topic, but with the culture associated with a particular group of people. The anthropologist represents a living archive of material on these people (all-knowing, like E. B. White's Charlotte) capable of speaking authoritatively on many aspects of their culture. She continually adds to her archive through reading others' research reports and returning to the field to collect additional data. Even in the absence of new data, she will reanalyze old data in the light of new theoretical ideas. Painstakingly, sometimes over many years, the anthropologist studies the web of culture by reconstructing it over and over, getting it better each time, until even the spider herself would be fooled.

ENDNOTES

[1] "I really did not know much about field work. The course on methods that Professor Boas taught was not about field work . . ." (Margaret Mead, 1972:147). "I think it is complete nonsense to say that [anthropologists] have a method" (Jean Lave as quoted in Kvale 1995). ". . . training has been very much a matter of the transmission of a craft and of learning by doing . . . it has not helped that some people talk as if the key to ethnography were a personal psychological experience, rather than the discovery of knowledge" (Dell Hymes 1977:5).

[2] However, I must agree with Corsario (1985) that ". . . role play is not simply imitation of adult models, but is often an innovative expansion of the adult model" (p. 105).

[3] About as close as we get to "replication" in anthropology.

[4] Fred Erickson (1973/1984) earlier had argued that ". . . much of the ethnography of schooling in our own society has fallen short on this point . . . we give in to our rage too self-indulgently and present schools, teachers, and students as essentially . . . inhuman . . ." (p. 61).

[5] Ogbu (1982; 1993) argues that many cultural discontinuities are "natural," learning in context versus decontextualized learning, for example. Or, Corsario's (1988b) observation that, at home, such items as toys are owned, whereas in nursery school they must be shared. Ogbu's point is that not all cultural discontinuity is bad. Also, he identifies "primary" discontinuities—for example, of the sort I found in Papua New Guinea between the indigenous

counting system and that taught in school (Lancy 1983). Then, there are "secondary" discontinuities—associated with caste-like minorities such as Blacks and Indians in the United States, Bunraku in Japan, and Maoris in New Zealand where members of these groups and their children actively resist conformity to the norms of the public school, which is seen as an extension of the dominant, oppressor society.

6 Recent Russian immigrants to the area seem to have a very similar attitude: "Although the immigrant families are unfamiliar with the new system of education, they are, nevertheless, eager to do whatever it takes for their children to succeed in school" (Delgado-Gaitan 1994:150).

7 No doubt this study also benefited from her work on a very similar project, a comparison of native and immigrant student adaptation patterns in a high school on St. Croix (Gibson 1982).

8 "The present writer feels that the gang makes an indispensable contribution to personality and a contribution that adults sometimes overlook. One learns morality in the gang, and one learns to take punishment. Even a vicious gang is better than no gang at all" (Waller 1932/1961:180).

9 Notice that the term "ethnography" is used to describe a particular kind of methodology *as well as* the end product of the study that used the ethnographic method. This, as well as the title of his book, conveys the kind of finality and completeness that anthropologists strive for in their work. It implies that they tend to view the world as rather static; it also suggests a degree of arrogance or at least great self-confidence. Further, Cusick (1973) has almost no discussion of methodology. However, subsequent studies (Palonsky 1975; Eckert 1989) have added to but not substantially challenged Cusick's ethnographic portrait.

10 Interestingly, Varenne (1982) did not find students using clique labels to refer to themselves in their own group, only to others.

11 While Deyhle can see the importance of break dancing for these students, she frequently makes the point that teachers/administrators utterly fail to see how important break dancing is to Indian students and fail to understand or acknowledge what it says about the Indians' "attitude" toward school.

12 It says something about the "culture" of the anthropologist tribe that none of us has seen fit to do an ethnography of a country club, and when educational anthropologists do an ethnography in a school they rarely study those in positions of authority like teachers, administrators, and high-status student cliques.

13 An interesting confirmation for this finding comes from the University of California at Berkeley. A mathematics instructor was puzzled as to why Asian students did so well in his calculus class while Black students did so poorly. He discovered that the Asian students studied in groups while Black students studied alone. Probing further, he found that these academically successful Black students had to divorce themselves from Black student culture in order to succeed in high school. While being a loner was an adaptive strategy in high school, it became dysfunctional in college. The professor helped the Black students form mutual support groups and achieved the hoped-for effect on their calculus grades (Treisman 1983).

14 Actually, he had a research assistant do the videotaping so he wouldn't have to step out of character. He signaled to her what to record and when to start and stop taping.

15 We will take up the universality issue in the fourth chapter.

16 I can personally verify this pattern, as I vividly remember having a heated interchange with a submanager at the Fiat factory in Torino (as to why my new car wasn't ready) while he kept three other conversations going—two via telephones and a third with one of his office assistants.

17 The reader should be aware that this study, like many others in this chapter, including Corsario's initial study, were generously funded by organizations like the National Institutes of Education. During the 18 months that I worked on this project I had virtually no other assignments (the salary was commensurate), and I had access to computer-assisted data analysis, graduate research assistants, audio and video recording equipment, typing, and so on. While straightforward participant observation may be relatively "inexpensive," assuming the researcher has some source of salary, as soon as one complicates the research by trying to triangulate field notes with more systematic data collection and analysis, the costs for human

and machine "assistance" can quickly become prohibitive for the "unfunded" or "small grant" researcher. Compare these remarks to Lareau's (1989b) discussion of the difficulties encountered in doing an unfunded field study (pp. 208–209).

[18] As an aside, about a year after I completed my study, management at Longbranch was turned back over to the local school district. They refused to provide funds to continue purchasing the consumable lesson materials; hence, the entire individualized curriculum was dropped in favor of traditional textbooks and whole-class instruction. The fate of similar educational innovations will be discussed in the case study chapter. I should also note here that Everhart's (1983) study of student culture in a junior high school in "Jefferson" district was initiated as part of an evaluation of a federally funded program to individualize instruction. However, he concludes, ". . . student life was not significantly altered by the project" (p. 279).

3 Sociological Traditions

> Twenty-two of 37 of the East Asian parents reported that they had spent time teaching their children reading, writing, and simple arithmetic skills before entering kindergarten. Four out of 25 Anglo parents indicated that they engaged in similar types of activities. . . . In comparison to Anglo parents, more East Asians paid tuition for . . . private lessons in music, computer science, martial arts, or languages. (Schneider & Lee 1990:372–373)

This is a brief excerpt from a lengthy, meticulous point-by-point comparison of the support structure for academic achievement provided by East Asian immigrant and native Anglo parents. Schneider and Lee (1990) were interested in the role that parents might play in accounting for the greater academic success (as measured by grades, test scores) of East Asian students. In effect, what they are asking is how children from poor low-status families gain high status in school, their theme *stratification* in school and society. From an initial pool of 30 schools they selected a suburban and an urban school in the Chicago area and studied 46 East Asian and a matched group of 49 Anglo students from the sixth and seventh grades. Families in the two groups had similar income levels, but East Asians had lower occupational status; they made up the income differential by working longer hours or holding multiple jobs as compared to the Anglos.

"Eighty percent . . . of the East Asian parents compared to 13 percent of the Anglo parents stated that their children studied at home at least an hour a day . . ." (p. 372). This very thorough description of Schneider and Lee's methodology and the precision with which they report the results should alert us that, in sociological studies, there is a blurring of the distinctions between qualitative and quantitative research. At least one reason for this is that, in contrast to the anthropologists' wide compass, sociologists are overwhelmingly united in their pursuit of a narrow range of interlocking questions: (1) How does schooling affect one's economic and social status (= stratification)? Is it enhanced, or do students end up with roughly the same status as their parents?[1] (2) How do class, ethnicity and gender interact with schooling to create stratification in society? (3)What role do parents, students and teachers play in creating stratification *within* schools? This study clearly resonates to all these questions.

Of these three general questions, researchers interested in pursuing the first tend toward the quantitative end of the continuum, and the last question is more often studied qualitatively, while the second gets attention from scholars of both persuasions. Further, how one approaches these questions (and the range of answers considered reasonable) depends on which of several *grand theories*[2] one has chosen to embrace. We turn now to a brief discussion of a couple of these theories.

GRAND THEORIES

Schneider and Lee (1990) relate their findings to Ogbu's (1987) education and caste model, which posits that members of minority groups in the United States who have suffered a history of economic discrimination withhold their investment in education because they believe it will not pay off. They see this theory as inadequate because "Even though East Asians receive relatively low economic returns from additional schooling, they encourage their children to acquire more education . . . it would seem that non-economic cultural values such as self-improvement and upholding family honor may mediate the perceived economic benefits of education" (p. 362). Mikelson (1989) also challenges this "investment" theory of education. Based on their far lower returns, *women* should invest far less in education than men, but just the reverse is true. She says, "Abstract attitudes . . . cannot predict achievement behavior . . . [all groups of students hold positive attitudes toward school and believe] . . . that schooling is a vehicle for upward mobility and success" (p. 48).

In Ogbu's theory some groups (see the discussion of Punjabis in the previous chapter) *do* take advantage of the opportunities for upward mobility that schooling may provide. But, in classical Marxist (now called *critical*) theory, such mobility is just not possible: ". . . power is in the hands of dominant classes or groups who control all wealth and capital, and who maintain and reinforce traditional class, ethnic and gender inequalities" (Bennett & LeCompte 1990:14). In this chapter we will review works by Anyon and Suransky that are written from the Marxist perspective. Bourdieu (1977) is a theoretical descendant of Marx who argues that, contrary to popular wisdom, public schooling reinforces the existing social class structure. Bourdieu refers to "cultural capital" as information and habits that one generation passes on to the next. Success in school and, by extension, in the world of skilled or professional employment, is much more likely for students who start with the appropriate cultural capital—always assuming they chose to use it and not fritter it away (Lareau 1989b).

Juxtaposed to these reproduction theories is the theory (Mehan, Hertweck, & Meihls 1986) that drives much of the quantitative research in the sociology of education. In this view, schools are charged with the responsibility of developing *human capital*. Students show up on the school's doorstep possessing various resources, knowledge, intelligence, "educability," and so on, and schools aid the student to make the most of these resources. Along the way schools also evaluate students' worth in human capital terms by awarding *symbolic* capital, grades, diplomas, placement (e.g., high reading group, vocational track), and designations (gifted, learning disabled). Finally, once the student leaves the education system he or she has an opportunity to convert this symbolic capital into "real capital": by obtaining a wage-earning job, marrying a wage earner, collecting welfare, and so on. Bud Mehan (1979) has for years been a critic of the purely quantitative, mechanical analysis of these "variables." Instead Mehan argues that, "If we want to know whether student-teacher ratios, classroom size, teaching styles, and all the rest actually influence the quality of education, then we must be able to show how they operate in pragmatic educational situations" (p. 5). Qualitative researchers in sociology focus, therefore, on "descriptions of actual processes." Think of this approach as similar to a doctor's clinical assessment of a patient.

It would be instructive to consider what implication each of these theories has for improving education. The strong version of Marxist or critical theory would posit that nothing can be done about education, until the class system itself is dismantled by changing the relationship between society, capital, and the means of production. A weaker version (e.g., McClaren 1989) posits the need for a redistribution of resources. That is, schools for the poor must receive drastically more resources than schools for the rich in order to achieve equity. Additional resources could be invested in shrinking class sizes, improving physical facilities and the supply of materials, attracting better-trained teachers via higher salaries, and so on.

Those who base school reform on considerations of cultural capital have proposed two drastically different alternatives. Hirsch (1987) would insist on the infusion of "high culture" throughout the curriculum and would hold schools accountable for *all* children regardless of race, class or gender becoming *culturally literate*. By contrast, here is a proposal circulated in England (Hargreaves 1982): "A grammar school academic and cognitive-intellectual curriculum, which is partly defined as 'high culture,' is not suitable for . . . working class pupils. Instead, they must be provided with a 'popular education' which is closer to their own culture, life style and capacities; it will be a curriculum which is oral rather than literary, concrete and practical rather than theoretical and abstract" (p. 118).

Followers of the human capital model would embrace any proposal which promised to make schools more "efficient" at evaluating and developing students' potential. Obvious contenders are those who labor to improve the validity of I.Q. and other tests to measure "capacity" as well as standard-ized tests of achievement and other measures of "competency." Indeed, the I.Q. test was developed in the first place as a means to make selection for schooling more efficient (Gould, 1981). Currently popular constructs like *effective schools, academic learning time, magnet schools, career ladders,* and *voucher systems* all derive from an underlying model of the school as searching out, developing, and certifying human talent.

Notice that while anthropologists can, according to their traditions, conduct their work from a dispassionate, neutral, scientific perspective, soci-ologists—especially those working with children, families and schools—don't enjoy a similar freedom. They must wrestle with issues that show up on the cover of *Newsweek*. Note also that, because of shared views on the nature of the "problem space" and a relatively ecumenical attitude toward methodol-ogy, sociologists are more likely to draw on both qualitative and quantitative studies in synthesizing material on a topic.[3]

Thus far we have seen that sociologists are concerned with the study of how society comes to be stratified. Qualitative sociologists may use quantita-tive indices in their pursuit of this issue, and they tend to invoke broad, all-encompassing theories to account for this phenomenon. In the remainder of this chapter we will see these issues addressed in the course of reviewing research under several major themes. First we will consider the role of the family in mediating the child's relationship with his/her school. Then we move from the home to the pre-school, contrasting the pre-school curricula available to children from different social classes. A similar comparison is undertaken for the elementary school, and then we review "tracking" in the secondary school, another pervasive form of stratification in education.

In the second half of the chapter our focus shifts more drastically. We now zoom in to scrutinize very closely the ways in which social structuring actually happens. We consider the interactions among participants in social settings. A pervasive feature of educational institutions is the task of testing, selecting and placing students. We review several studies of these processes from intelligence testing, to selection into first grade, to designation as learn-ing disabled. We then move into a regular elementary-school setting to observe the way classroom social competence is defined and developed in the interactions among teacher and pupils. Our lens moves into even closer range as we consider a very special, and highly stratified, area of the elementary school classroom: the reading group. Investigators have carefully revealed the very subtle prosodic and semiotic cues which structure interaction in the reading group. Then, we take a close look at power relations displayed in the interaction between pairs of individuals, students and guidance counselors and students and writing center tutors.

In the remainder of the chapter we return to the wide-angle setting to consider some more general issues raised by this body of scholarship.

THE ROLE OF PARENTS:
PRESCOTT AND COLTON SCHOOLS

As much as anything else, growing interest in the role of parent/family in facilitating/hindering school success stems from the disappointing results of numerous government-funded research and development efforts in the 1960s and 1970s. However, as McNeil (1988) suggests, we must look beyond simple markers of ascribed status (e.g., parental education, family income, number of bathrooms in the home) and study more dynamic and instrumental aspects of parental influence of the sort identified by Schneider and Lee (1990). This was precisely Annette Lareau's (1989b) objective in her two-year-long study (her doctoral dissertation) of a working-class and a middle-class community in Northern California.[4] As her goal was to study the impact of social class on family/school relations, she chose her two schools and two first-grade teachers carefully. Both Colton and Prescott were considered to be "good" schools, as were the teachers. While Prescott served a mainly White upper-middle-class community, Colton served a working-class, ethnically mixed (50 percent Anglo, 33 percent Hispanic, remainder African- and Asian-American) community. Lifestyles were not, however, vastly different—the Colton community was not troubled by massive unemployment, widespread drug abuse, violent crime and the like, and it was reasonably stable, a "good place to live."

Lareau acted as participant observer in the two first-grade classes the first year, selecting five children from intact families and one from a single-parent family in each school for in-depth study during year two. She indicates the "typicality" of her sample with statements like: ". . . the Colton families I interviewed were somewhat more active in their children's schooling than the average parent" (p. 199). Also, "There were no glaring omissions in terms of discipline problems, achievement levels, temperament, popularity, and parent involvement in schooling" (p. 200). Lareau shares precise details reflecting the quality of her database, e.g. ". . . I succeeded in interviewing only three of the five fathers . . . I only interviewed . . . once rather than twice" (p. 201). She encountered numerous minor problems like the fact that, with working-class parents, she had great difficulty defining herself—"graduate school," "research," "field study" were all foreign to them. They thought she was studying to become a teacher or working for the school.

After she began the study Lareau discovered that straightforward description (of the sort found in an ethnography) is unlikely to lead to answers to the question, "*How* does social class influence children's schooling?" Fortunately she was taking a research methods class at the time, and her instructor's comments on her initial write-up ". . . made it clear that I could not continue to conduct a study that posed no problem and articulated no argument . . . an unfocussed 'thick description' would not do" (p. 212).

Lareau describes at length her procedure for analyzing interviews. Each interview was transcribed, a process that could take up to fifteen hours depending on tape quality.[5] Interviews were segmented, with each segment cut out and pasted on cards. The cards were ". . . sorted by basic category . . . 'parents' views of their role'. . . 'teachers' expectations of parents'. [She] . . . ended up with over a thousand cards . . . all over the living room floor" (p. 205).[6] She made "data displays," for example, ". . . matrices with the children listed in rows and various types of parental involvement in columns (i.e., reviewing papers after school, reading, attending open house . . .)" (p. 206). All this effort pays off as Lareau achieves a balance between analysis and data—*at no time does one feel that her interpretations are unsupported by evidence, nor does she provide excess description that goes unanalyzed.*

The value of long-term, painstaking, qualitative research is borne out by the "cumulative nature" of Lareau's findings. No *single* factor sharply differentiates between Colton and Prescott—for example, "When I went into the field I thought I would find evidence of institutional discrimination . . . I thought . . . that the teachers were going to differ significantly in their interaction with parents on different social classes. I did not find evidence to support this position" (p. 218). Prescott parents were conscientious about reading to their children. They also helped them see the practical value of their education by integrating ". . . educational goals into virtually all aspects of home life" (p. 74). Parents selected toys and presents with a view toward their education value, and they enrolled children in ". . . supplementary enrichment activities including art and French classes, soccer, and Indian guides" (p. 67). On the other hand, Mrs. Morris is typical of Colton parents in that "When Tommy entered first grade, she turned over responsibility for his education to the school" (p. 41) (a very widespread finding, e.g., Ngana-Mundeke 2000). Teachers resist taking 100 percent responsibility for children's education: "During this twenty-minute conference Mrs. Thompson suggested at least five times that Tommy's mother keep her son reading during the summer" (p. 21). Colton parents have only a vague idea of what goes on at school, and Mrs. Morris is surprised when Mrs. Thompson recommends that Tommy be retained in first grade.

Prescott mothers, without exception, are intimately aware of their children's progress in school. Mrs. Harris observes Alan's (lack of) progress in spelling as she serves a volunteer stint in the classroom. She asks for and is granted spelling materials to (successfully) work with Alan at home. As Lareau notes, ". . . parents' activities shaped the degree to which children received a 'generic' or a 'customized' educational experience within schools" (p. 123). Another family found out that their son needed occupational therapy for fine muscle control, which they willingly paid for, and the child experienced ". . . dramatic improvement in his posture, his handwriting, and his motor coordination in soccer" (p. 117). Indeed, this is one of Lareau's most striking findings, that ". . . the most intense family-school relationships were not for the highest achieving students in upper-middle-class families. These occurred in families whose children were at the *bottom* of their class" (p. 129).

Mary Lee Smith (1982), in a study of how students come to be designated "learning disabled" in a suburban Denver district, which we will consider shortly, seems to offer additional support for this finding. She reports several cases at length. For example, John was not doing as well in school as his parents thought he should. His mother bought him educational games, drilled him with flash cards, and observed in his classroom. ". . . she was . . . frantic . . . she said . . . 'reading is so *central* . . . if you can't read, you can't learn anything'" (p. 38). Despite his teacher's claim that "I'm not worried . . . he is a little behind grade level; there are several children lower than he is in this class" (p. 40), his mother asked to have him "referred." The evaluation and placement process determined that he was not qualified for special education services. The parents hired a tutor for the child and continued to press the school to have him placed in the resource room. They threatened litigation, and finally the school acquiesced to their wishes.

Prescott parents' high status and substantial education give them the confidence and resources to intervene very directly in the school experience of their children (see also Baker & Stevenson 1986). They address teachers on a first-name basis, enter classrooms without preamble, and freely criticize teachers among themselves and to the administration. "Parents felt that Mrs. Walters' expectations were too low, the discipline was lax, the class was too noisy, and the children were not required to work consistently or finish their projects" (p. 79); and they could speak knowledgeably in *academese* about their children's problems—"His attention span is short. He has auditory reception problems . . ." (p. 77). Colton parents, by contrast, felt inferior to teachers—"If they start using big words, you think, 'Oh God, what does this mean?' You know, it is just like going to the doctor's. And it makes you feel a little insuperior [sic] to them. But I don't have the education they do" (p. 108). "Colton parents lacked educational *competence*, and they were aware of their shortcomings" (p. 107). "A lot of the mothers [who came to school] felt they would grade a paper wrong . . ., even in the first-grade level, to even spell the words" (p. 109). They feel particularly inadequate at E and P (Evaluation and Planning) conferences: "She put that paper in front of me with all this stuff, and you know, half of it I didn't understand" (p. 108). While some Prescott parents had used schooling as a means to dramatically alter their social status (from son of barber to Harvard M.B.A.), Colton parents had less positive experiences. Several had not graduated from high school, and some claimed to have reading problems.

While Colton teachers continued to solicit parental involvement and assistance at every turn (and there was evidence of a positive relationship between student achievement and parental involvement), Prescott teachers were sometimes resentful at the lack of respect offered them by parents. Clearly the ideal is high parental involvement that is *directed by the teacher* (see also Van Galen, 1987).

Many other studies in the United States (Lancy 1994) as well as in Israel (Ninio 1979), Australia (Goodnow, Cashmore, Cotton, & Knight 1984), and elsewhere *replicate* Lareau's basic findings. Taken all together, this research suggests the need to modify Bourdieu's theory of cultural capital, at least as applied in the United States. The transmission of knowledge about "high culture" appears not to be sufficient to insure the academic success of one's offspring. On the contrary, ". . . not all resources associated with upper-middle-class life were salient. Teachers appeared to be relatively indifferent to the size of the children's homes, the quality or quantity of house furnishings, the distribution of family vacations, parents' taste in music, and the style of clothing worn by children and parents" (Lareau 1989:145). Rather, it is the middle-class parents' vigorous monitoring of the child's at-home and in-school learning environments and knowledge of strategies to enhance and modify those environments when needed, including a willingness to purchase materials and supplemental educational services, that explains why schools reproduce social stratification.

SOCIAL CLASS

While these preceding studies have tended to focus on the parents, in this section we will review two very similar projects that consider the ways in which the very character of a school might reflect the sorts of expectations held by parents from varying socioeconomic strata.

Classroom Instruction: Preschool

Lubeck (1984) carried out parallel field studies in an all-White pre-school and all-Black Head Start program located about one mile apart in an integrated suburb of a major Midwestern city. Although her study lasted only two months, she had previously taught in a preschool and was easily accepted as a participant observer. She freely shared her notes with the staff who ". . . found it remarkable that [she] could record information they thought trivial" (p. 221).

Differences between the two programs were pervasive. In the preschool the curriculum was richer and more varied. It included science—there was much discussion and several activities to teach "raw" vs. "cooked," for example. On the other hand, in Head Start ". . . school days were composed of activities that were repeated day after day . . ." (p. 224). At Head Start a great deal of time was taken up with catering to the nonacademic needs of the children ". . . van regularly picks up groups . . . during the school hours for their medical, dental, and lead poisoning check-ups" (p. 22). Head Start children are served two meals a day, there are many holidays, and sessions are held on only four days per week. "The sum total of these policies, procedures, and contingencies means that the Head Start children have considerably less *school* time than their preschool peers" (p. 222).

At the same time, in Head Start but not in preschool, there was a lengthy period each day for "group time," where children learn how to behave in a group. They are taught their names, addresses, the calendar, the alphabet. Group time is seen as ". . . getting the children ready to listen to the

[Kindergarten] teacher" (p. 223). In other respects there was a clear demarcation of the children's space/activities from the staff in Head Start, whose ". . . primary focus of attention appeared to be on other adults . . ." (p. 225), and during free play ". . . teachers tend to other duties" (p. 268). By contrast, the White preschool teachers interacted directly with children in the various centers and assisted them in carrying out chosen activities in a process referred to in the child development literature as "scaffolding" (Rogoff & Gardner 1984). Lubeck (1984) creates a "local" as opposed to "grand" theory and relates the teaching/learning environments in the respective programs to home life/parenting styles associated with the White middle-class and Black underclass cultures (see also Heath 1983). However, we can see how well her study complements that of Lareau, in that the preschool teachers are clearly augmenting the cultural capital their pupils own at the outset. By contrast, Head Start teachers themselves are "uneducated" and lack the requisite cultural capital; hence they are unable to offer a truly "compensatory" experience for their charges. So, it's the preschoolers who're getting a genuine "head start."

A book by Valerie Polakow Suransky (1982) entitled *The Erosion of Childhood* provides some interesting points of comparison with Lareau and Lubeck's work. Suransky, as her title suggests, is concerned with the tendency to overly structure and regiment children's lives in preschools in the name of academic preparedness. Further, she sees her theoretical perspective not as something to be tested or modified, as we have seen above, but *as a given*. As Patton (1990; see also Anderson 1989; McClaren & Giarelli 1995) notes, Marxist or *critical* scholars like Suransky and Anyon (1980; for critique, see Lancy 1993:82–83): ". . . aim to describe and explain *specific* manifestations of already presumed general patterns . . . confirmation and elucidation rather than discovery" (p. 86). There is, characteristically, no presentation of methods. Indeed, Suransky dismisses the very notion of methodology in what she describes as a "hermeneutical undertaking."

She provides brief portraits of five centers for the care of preschool-age children. The "Golda Meier Nursery School" and "Busy Bee Montessori Center" most closely resemble Lubeck's preschool. However, where others might see the continuous pressure on children, scaffolded by adults, to develop cognitive and social skills and a sense of efficacy in a positive light, Suransky sees teachers "interfering" with children's natural tendencies. The "Martin Luther King Child Care Center" and "Pinewoods Freeschool" (of mixed race but taught by a Black mother of five) closely resemble Lubeck's Head Start program. Here children are left alone to do their own things, fighting and rough play are not tightly controlled and, like Lubeck, Suransky sees the extended family style of parenting characteristic of the Black community at work in these programs. Suransky is unconcerned that some preschoolers aren't acquiring the information and skills valued by the dominant culture. In her view, cultural differences must be respected and, as a Marxist, she believes that resources should be distributed according to need.

Tracking in the Secondary School

Willard Waller ([1932] 1961) is widely acknowledged as the first educational sociologist and, not surprisingly, class and stratification attracted his attention: "Many children attain an easy and unhealthy leadership through the use of economic resources of their parents. . . . It is upon the basis of such distinctions that many of the cliques and social clubs of high school children are formed . . ." (p. 37). However, another University of Chicago sociologist, A. B. Hollingshead (1949/1975) conducted the first true *field study*[7] of stratification in the public school. Hollingshead and his wife (who evidently was a co-investigator, although not a co-author) lived in Elmtown, a medium-sized Midwestern town between 1941 and 1942. Their goal was to study the ". . . relationships existing between the behavior patterns of the 735 adolescent boys and girls who lived in the community and the positions occupied by their families in the community's social structure" (p. v). Simultaneously they studied families and student culture. They became extremely active in various community organizations: "I was invited into the rotary club and attended all meetings . . . we skated and bowled with them, shot pool. . . . our policy was to be with them whenever and wherever possible" (p. 15). Their notes from fieldwork were supplemented by lengthy interview "schedules." This was a highly stratified society, and respondents had no difficulty identifying and labeling the various strata.

In the second part of the study the Hollingsheads attempted to determine how a student's social class influenced her high school experience (including those who had dropped out). There were, for example, college prep, general and commercial tracks, and "Enrollment in each [track] is related very significantly to class position" (p. 122). Parents acted to guide children into what they considered to be appropriate tracks. For example, Nellie (whose family occupied class IV, or second from the bottom) had enrolled in the college prep track because a friend had done so. As a result, her mother reprimanded her and ordered her to change to the secretarial (or "business") track. The upper-class parents extended subtle pressure on the school, and their children were treated deferentially. They were more likely to get scholarships and less likely to get detention.

Reaction to the publication of *Elmtown's Youth* was quite sensational. Despite Hollingshead's attempts to conceal the town's identity it attracted national media scrutiny, and he was the recipient of angry letters from townspeople and educators who felt the book had tarnished their reputation. Nevertheless, the Hollingsheads found a welcome on their return for a lengthy "restudy" in 1972. Although the town's population had grown by a third, it was still ethnically homogeneous and the class structure very much intact. A great deal of additional money was being spent on schooling, and school governance appeared to be much more democratic.[8]

Metz (1978) examined tracking in two junior high schools during the 1967–68 school year, but she goes well beyond establishing that social class and tracking are linked. She studies the process whereby teachers and students collaborate to create distinctly different educational climates in the different tracks.

> High track students wanted "liberal" teachers who would provide opportunities for discussion where students could express themselves. When a teacher simply expected the students to incorporate the contents of a textbook, to "memorize" as some of them complained . . . they characterized these teachers [as teaching] "straight from the book" . . . [they] were quite capable of carrying on debates with teachers who disagreed with them about educational goals. (p. 76)

On the other hand, lower-track students

> . . . took the school as they found it and did not question the administrators' and teachers' right to define what they should learn, how they should learn it, or how they should behave. However, . . . they frequently failed or refused to cooperate in the activities the definitions implied . . . they held themselves apart from it . . . these students considered adults to be people really very different from themselves. (pp. 81–82)

Nor surprisingly, "In the daily rhythm of classes, the lower-track groups were far more restless and subject to collective activity distracting from the lesson at hand than the top-track ones were. It was harder for the teacher to simply get their attention" (p. 96). Teachers "dummied down" material accordingly:

> I have found, of course, that dictionary work with [lower tracks], particularly, has been successful. They love it. They like to be busy. Isn't that strange? They like to be able to sit down, open a book, and work on something . . . Discussion—they have not been able to handle too well. (Hesitation) Because it's still, "Let's outshout one another." I tried discussions with them and found them unsuccessful. I keep trying a little of it but cutting it down, making it pretty short to get kids to express their ideas. (p. 102)

Metz's (1978) findings regarding differences in the nature of instruction in the various tracks are supported in large-scale observational studies of secondary schools (Goodlad 1984). One of the investigators (Oakes 1986) reports, "Students in high-track classes were exposed to 'high-status' content, literature, expository and thematic writing, library research, and mathematical ideas. Students in low-track classes were not expected to learn these topics and skills. They rarely, if ever, encountered them. They worked in workbooks and kits and practiced language mechanics and computation" (p. 63). Gamoran and Berends (1987) note, in a review of these and other studies on tracking, that qualitative studies consistently find differences in the way instruction is organized in different tracks; however, quantitative analyses suggest that the actual *effects* of tracking on achievement may be minimal. Quantitative studies *control for* initial achievement levels, so tracking has to exert an influence *over and above* the influence of the student's knowledge base, his or her commitment to school, parental influence, and so on. Nevertheless, "de-tracking" has now become quite popular, and schools can get grant money to undertake this change (Datnow 1977).

The peer group is also a factor. Hollingshead (1949/1975) discovered that student cliques do not cut across tracks to any appreciable degree. Indeed, as we have seen in the last chapter, the influence of the student culture in high school may be so pervasive that it can create a "track-like" experience for students even in the absence of a formal tracking system.

Two contrastive studies are worthy of note. Lewis (1996) has conducted a prolonged field study in Japanese elementary schools. She finds that the Japanese go to great lengths to avoid tracking or ability grouping. In harmony with important cultural values, they promote group-building activities that reduce the likelihood of social comparison and ranking. Harklau (1994) has shown that highly motivated Chinese immigrants to the United States can crack the tracking barrier. Assigned to a lower track because of their poor command of English, some immigrants eschew the boring, slow pace of instruction and successfully negotiate reassignment to a higher track.

We turn now to a major divide in the sociology-of-education landscape. To this point, the unit of analysis or object of focus was the school or several schools. Although we have seen researchers peering inside the black box, their middle-range focus has allowed them to see the results of stratification but not to really capture the processes that operate to *create* stratification in the school. In the research to be reviewed in the remainder of the chapter, investigators have zoomed in on the single classroom, or, even more narrowly, on testing, tutoring, and counseling sessions involving only two individuals. Where earlier we saw authors using snippets of interviews to illustrate a particular point, in the work that follows natural language samples as well as interview transcripts will be the subject of intense analysis.

ETHNOMETHODOLOGY AND
THE STUDY OF ROUTINE ACTIONS

Ethnomethodology has a somewhat similar history to *ethnoscience* (Leiter 1980). It developed in California as a reaction against the mainstream of the discipline of sociology: "Early ethnomethodologists claimed that sociologists, in their search for regularities in social structures, had ignored participant's structuring activities . . ." (Mehan 1978:60). Ethnomethodology was originated by Harold Garfinkel (1967) to describe the *ethnographic study of the methods* people use to accomplish everyday tasks. Garfinkel's earliest studies were concerned with how juries reached verdicts and how medical decisions were made.

As Mehan (1978) notes: ". . . one of Garfinkel's seminal contributions was to . . . exhort . . . researchers to find in the interaction between people, not in their subjective states, the processes that assembled the concerted activities of everyday life" (p. 60). Garfinkel and his followers discovered that, contrary to the Aristotelian view of man and society, there are few hard and fast rules; people do a great deal of "ad hocing." So-called objective criteria, like test scores and grades, are always subject to interpretation—they are social accomplishments. Further, "Ethnomethodologists stress that the social world is made up of shared meanings and shared viewpoints. So much so that if actors changed places they would quite likely see the world in much the same way and that our knowledge of the world is generated through interpretations" (Hitchcock & Hughes 1989:158). George Payne's (1982) analysis of how a secondary history teacher "puts down" a latecomer to his class is a model application of this research tradition.

If Garfinkel (1967) invented ethnomethodology, Aaron Cicourel and his students deserve credit for applying it in education. However, in considering their contribution, we immediately encounter a serious difficulty in trying to make sense of it all. We have almost the opposite problem of the overuse of the term *ethnography* to describe studies that bear little relation one to another. Here, the problem is that a great many studies that I see as sharing a common concern for the description and analysis of reoccurring social situations, are identified by a great variety of different labels. Cicourel (1974), while freely acknowledging his intellectual debt to Garfinkel, refers to his work as *cognitive* sociology, perhaps to show a parallel with cognitive anthropology (see previous chapter). Bud Mehan, Cicourel's student, close colleague, and co-author of the definitive text on ethnomethodology (Mehan & Wood 1975), calls his own work *constitutive* ethnography. Among the scholars Mehan (1978) cites as sharing his view of methodology is Fred Erickson (1982), who refers to his own work as *micro-ethnography*. Others (e.g., Cazden 1988) refer to this tradition as *sociolinguistics*. Finally, in Jacob's (1987) article on traditions, she uses *ethnography of communication* and *symbolic interaction* to refer to work which, I argue, shares a single tradition. Although some of these terminological differences do reflect important epistemological and/or methodological differences, I hope to show that the similarities outweigh the differences and that, in time, scholars will see the need to unite under a common banner. "Ethnomethodology" would get my vote.

HOW EDUCATORS MAKE PLACEMENT DECISIONS

Cicourel and Kitsuse's (1963) *The Educational Decision Makers* is widely cited as a classic in the field and provides a bridge between the community-oriented research of Hollingshead and others and the more narrowly focused studies of Mehan and his colleagues. Done in 1958, the study was designed as an antidote to quantitative studies that sought to relate collections of "background variables" to the decision to attend or not attend college. Working in Lakeshore, a large high school serving predominantly White, middle-class Evanston, Illinois, it was their ". . . wish to investigate how the *routine decisions* of the guidance and counseling personnel within the high school are related to the college/non-college decisions and, by implication, to the occupational choices made by students" (p. 6, italics added). Their methodology depended heavily on lengthy, unstructured interviews with parents. They found that: "[A]mong the middle and upper social classes, parents routinely expect their children to go to college, and their children consistently reflect such expectations . . . independent of whether the student's tested capability is high or low and irrespective of his prior school performance as recorded in his grades" (p. 35).

Grades and Test Scores

While Cicourel and Kitsuse (1963) relied primarily on interviews, most subsequent studies have used more direct observation. Cicourel (Cicourel et al. 1973) undertook a series of studies of educational testing and the ensuing placement decisions, utilizing videotaped recordings and interviews to capture with fidelity the "methods" people used in "constructing" test scores and grade placements, in order to demonstrate that these ". . . are institutional facts and not brute facts" (Mehan, Hertweck, & Meihls 1986:85). Mehan (1978) videotaped five sessions where a psychologist administered the Wechsler Intelligence Scale for Children (WISC). On 21 of 65 questions the tester deviated from standard procedure: he ". . . either repeated the question or prompted the student with cues. . . ." (p. 52). Analysis showed that ". . . a student's score could increase as much as 27 percent as a result of the tester's cueing" (p. 53). "The testers' puppeteering practices contribute to the assembly of student answers . . . Testers may emphasize key words, compliment correct replies, or cut off students after they have completed an answer . . . [and] these . . . are not the result of sloppy test administration but are inevitable aspects of the social interaction that comprises testing encounters" (p. 55).

Roth (1973) also focused on intelligence testing, but his attention was drawn to the way the tester adapted to the behavior of the testees, African-American children who had not yet learned the "proper" way to behave in such situations: "Pe was as difficult to work with in the testing situation as An was. He was playful and talkative, though much less noisy than An, and never defiant. The main trouble with Pe was how easily he reached the verge of tears . . . the tester couldn't probe as deeply as she wanted for fear Pe would break down" (p. 205). Roth observes, "It is unreasonable to expect that a tester or teacher can maintain a strictly standardized procedure while probing children's unstandardized background knowledge and while managing the children's feelings" (p. 215).

Leiter (1976), as part the same project, interviewed kindergarten teachers as to their reasons for placing students in first or "junior first" grade. Among the background information teachers used was information on the child's language. A Hispanic girl got a better evaluation than her placement test score warranted: "Now on the phonemes, the auditory part, she was low but a lot of this could have to do with language, you know" (p. 61). A Black child with low scores was given a higher placement because ". . . the mother wants badly for her children to achieve" (p. 62), indicating the importance of perceived family background. Finally, teachers take into account emotional handicaps, as with an immature, inattentive child: ". . . he answered the questions by himself. I didn't answer them for him but I had to sit there and point my finger just to keep his attention on the right line and to make sure he was in the right place" (p. 63).

Special Education Placement Decisions

Mary Lee Smith (1982) undertook a study of the evaluation and labeling of elementary students as "learning disabled." She spent three months negotiating access to Belleview, a suburban district near Denver. Then "Six months were spent full time in direct observations of staffing conferences, meetings, and other relevant interactions, in-depth interviews with . . . [all participants] . . . and analysis of documents such as files of pupils identified as learning disabled. Two months were spent analyzing the data and writing the preliminary report for the district" (p. 230).

An ethnomethodological study allows one to compare informal, socially constructed practices with the formal procedures and criteria that are to be followed. Prior to the enactment of PL 94-142 in 1975, the determination of assignment to special placement was subject to the whim of the principal. "The laws were intended to make the decision-making process—the 'staffing' process as it is called—standard throughout the nation. They have taken the powers of decision out of the hands of teachers and principals and turned these powers over to staffing committees . . ." (p. 3).

It is not clear how many "staffing" meetings Smith attended altogether, but she presents three cases in some detail. The staffing draws on a large cast of characters (6 to 18, average of 10)—the teacher, nurse, special education supervisor, the principal, speech therapist, psychologist, and parents. Not all of the people are present at every meeting, and no one role holder dominated consistently, although "The wishes of the parents were powerful and only resisted when the data and wishes of the staff were extreme in the opposite direction" (p. 100). Meetings lasted about 90 minutes, longer when parents were present (75 percent of the time), as more "explaining" was necessary, and circumlocution was used ". . . so that feelings could be spared" (p. 96).

Smith makes clear that the underlying premises of PL 94-142, indeed the premises underlying the entire field of special education, are faulty[9] and that this is a major reason for the protracted meetings and complex negotiations: "It was almost possible to see alliances building as one person's eyes sought those of another. There seemed to be a need for each side, not just to present data, but to build a case and sell the others on it" (p. 24). She points out: "The handicap of learning disability has always been controversial and difficult to define . . . requires an *inference*, a leap, based on several separate characteristics . . . [however,] these same characteristics are shared by many normal children" (p. 5).

As a consequence of this lack of fit between the rational, medical model PL 94-142 imposed on special education and the complex-lived reality of teachers, students, their families, less than half of those designated learning disabled actually met the official criteria. Instead, there was an implicit definition: ". . . children [who] needed more help than a teacher could give and were behind their peers" (p. 232). Smith (like Cicourel & Kitsuse 1963) finds that "data" like test scores and grades, far from being the determining factor, were used selectively to justify a decision that had been reached on other grounds. Furthermore, the federal dollars allocated to the district to pay for these special education services were fixed, so there was an optimal number of cases that could be handled, and ". . . definitions of learning disabilities seemed to be loosened or tightened to maintain this steady state" (p. 100).

Smith's (1982) initial report was filed away and forgotten—"a fate common to many evaluation reports" (p. 234) but it found its way into the hands of a state legislator, who successfully pushed for a ". . . statewide evaluation of identification practices" (p. 234). Smith (1982) conducted this study as well, which included a total of 790 cases, 10 of which were examined in depth. She was, essentially, able to replicate her initial study.

Mehan and his associates replicate and extend the study of Belleview in their analysis of the entire cohort of 157 students referred for (special education) evaluation and placement in one school year in a working-class district in Southern California. Like Smith (1982), Mehan, Hertweck and Meihls (1986) find that: "Disability . . . is . . . a function of the interaction between educators' categories, institutional machinery, and students' conduct" (p. 164). They also describe the formal, impossible-to-fulfill procedures mandated by PL 94-142 and the informal practices the district employed to remain in compliance. For example, they were unable to process referrals within the government's mandated time frame, so they "stopped the clock" and ". . . the clock did not start until the case had actually been heard by the committee" (p. 64). The main reason the process dragged on is because the law requires the presence of a number of designated individuals at SAT (School Advisory Team) and E&P committee meetings, making them extremely difficult to schedule. Teachers were reluctant to be gone from their classrooms or to prolong the school day by coming early or leaving late. Hence, ". . . they just tried to get meetings over with—an attitude that is not conducive to careful and reasoned consideration of complicated referral cases" (p. 59).

In addition to studying the entire process, Mehan's team conducted a fine-grained analysis of three points in the decision-making process, the initial referral by the teacher, the testing by the psychologist, and the E&P meetings. In the case of referrals, they videotaped 55 referred children in their classrooms and asked the 27 teachers to review the videotapes. These *viewing sessions* show that the "reasons" for referral did not completely correspond to the "reasons" listed on the referral form. Also, there is a blurring of the distinction between a referral category and examples of behaviors that fit the category. This is borne out by the fact that the behaviors teachers noted as being linked to referrals were not noted when they were displayed by children who had not been referred. "Because the teacher is attending to organized configurations and not discrete elements, a piece of behavior is not the same when it is conducted by different people in different contexts" (Mehan, Hertweck, Coombs, & Flynn 1982:313).

The team also videotaped 20 testing sessions. It was immediately apparent that the tests were not administered according to the manual or in a standardized manner. Aside from the referral and the test results, other issues came into play in E&P meetings. Again, as in Belleview, there was an optimal number of children that the system could handle, so early in the year ". . . teachers reported to us that they received strong recommendation to find more children in order to meet the quota" (p. 61), while later in the year they were discouraged from making referrals. However, unlike Belleview, or perhaps because they were able to make more careful analyses with the aid of videotape records, they did find evidence of an authority hierarchy in the E&P meeting. High-status participants—psychologist, nurse—have technical expertise and "present" their information, whereas low-status participants—teacher, mother—". . . had information *elicited* from them" (p. 126). Especially interesting is the apparently more passive role of parents, as contrasted with that of Belleview parents ("This is a school district with sophisticated parents who know their rights and demand them" [Smith, 1982:9]). Taking the Mehan et al. and Smith studies together we can, again, see the influence of social class and parental involvement in children's educational careers.

What the Mehan et al. (1986) study does not show is any evidence of systematic bias or prejudice such that children are selected for special education (about two-thirds of those referred are actually placed) on the basis of race, ethnicity, or social class. On the contrary, they found that Mexican-American children who exhibited referral behaviors were not referred because they were in *bilingual education* classes and their teachers felt they could better deal with the students' problems in the regular classroom. Indeed, as Palincsar (1986) points out in her review of *Handicapping the Handicapped*, "the serious indictment implicit in the title is never actually supported in the book" (p. 192). In other words, while the special education system undoubtedly does contribute to stratification within the schools, it is not clear from this study whether it alleviates or exacerbates stratification in the society at large. However, as Lareau (1989) points out, ". . . with a few dramatic exceptions, research has found little evidence that teachers apply standards unequally" (p. 104).

Participation Structures in the Classroom

While academic achievement, or underachievement, does entail quite open labeling of children with self-evident consequences for their status, classrooms provide other, less obvious opportunities to rank students vis-à-vis one another. An earlier, groundbreaking study by Mehan (1979) explored something called *participation structure* (cf. Phillips 1972). In this book he makes a case for the use of video- and audiotape recording in qualitative research. As we will soon see, the fine-grained analysis that a videotape record affords is absolutely essential in studying something as subtle as participation structure.[10]

Mehan (1979) studied an ungraded primary classroom in a school serving a poor African/Mexican-American neighborhood in San Diego. He and his team ". . . videotaped the first hour of school every day for first the week of school, and one hour a day approximately every third week until April" (p. 25). They had a total of 13 hours of tape to work with, not all of it usable because much student talk was lost, but they ended up with a corpus of six complete lessons. In this study the verbal and nonverbal behaviors of students and teachers is examined in very fine detail—an extremely expensive, labor intensive process. Their general goal was to study ". . . socialization of students into the academic and normative demands of the classroom" (p. 26). However, Mehan is particularly interested in *social competence* ("the skills and abilities that people must employ to be effective as members of a particular community") (1978:48). As he points out: ". . . participation in classroom lessons involves the integration of academic knowledge and social or interactional skills" (p. 34). In the report we are provided with transcriptions of portions of the discourse segmented and analyzed to reveal participation patterns or structures. Further, the transcripts include examples of children appropriately responding to the teacher's discourse demands as well as examples of inappropriate responses.[11] I refer here not to correct or incorrect answers per se but to the (in)correct use of various classroom sociolinguistic conventions.

However, in this classroom the teacher seems to be adept at socializing children so they learn the proper rules for participation. For example, in the six lessons there were no examples of negative evaluations; the teacher provided either a positive evaluation or no evaluation at all. The transcripts are coded using variables like "accepts," "prompts," "ignores," and so on and frequenciers are tallied, allowing Mehan and his team to show that while 70 percent of student initiatives in early fall were ignored (suggesting that they were inappropriate), by mid-January the figure drops to 30 percent. Unfortunately, Mehan (1979) does not indicate whether this improvement in social competence was true for *all* students. Again, while we can see that the participation structure has the *potential* to contribute to stratification, there is no evidence presented to affirm that it actually does so.[12]

Another study of participation structure (Morine-Dershimer 1983; 1985) more directly addresses the stratification issue. Methodologically this work, conducted in 1978–79[13] is quite similar to the study just described. Morine-Dershimer videotaped six classrooms (grades 2–4) in an urban, ethnically mixed, working-class school in the San Francisco Bay area. Twelve minutes (beginning, middle, end) of each of 36 language arts lessons were taped. She also interviewed a sample of the children she had videotaped. The results indicated that by the third grade, students not only know and can follow participation rules (but they may choose not to, see Hanna 1988) but can articulate them as well. Students' reading achievement scores at the beginning of the year was the only variable that seemed to affect participation. Anglo children did participate more, but they also had higher reading scores. Mexican-American children had lower rates, but "Their . . . deficit in entering reading achievement was not reinforced by . . . deficits in status with teacher (expectations) or participation in class discussion" (p. 166).

Participation and Reading

Reading groups are to elementary schools what tracks are in the high school: an instructional "adaptation" to differing levels of skill and interest that also confers social status. As such, interaction in the reading group has attracted a great deal of attention from those interested in stratification (McDermott 1976; Piestrup 1973). A study (Eder 1982) that closely parallels the previous two compared participation by students in four ability-linked reading groups in a single first-grade classroom. This time four lessons in each group were videotaped at intervals during the year. These data showed that the teacher used a much stricter regimen in the high ability group: "When students in the high group talked or read during another student's turn, they were often reprimanded . . . when students spoke out of turn in the low group, however, the teacher did not reprimand their interruptions, and often acknowledged them" (p. 256). Eder argues that "If teachers perceive academic tasks as being more difficult for low group members, it is not surprising that they allow more turn-taking violations" (p. 262). However, a consequence of this was that while interruptions declined drastically from fall to spring in the high group, they stayed constant in the low group. Hence, children in the low groups would fail to learn "proper" participation rules and would appear "less competent."

James Collins (1988) analyzed 16 lessons (part of a larger corpus), five drawn from the high and 11 from the low reading group in a first-grade classroom. His report indicates just how versatile videotape is in terms of affording the opportunity to conduct multiple analyses on the same database. The low group is given primarily low-level, decontextualized "skills" instruction whereas the high group gets more opportunity to interact with real text (cf. Edelsky, Draper, & Smith 1983). ". . . the different instructional emphases were evident in the first weeks of school and continued throughout the year" (p. 315). Collins then proceeds to the next level of analysis where the children's "reading aloud" was carefully analyzed: ". . . the staccato quality was more noticeable with low group readers. They read with pauses between words . . . high-group readers, on the other hand, were more likely to have some of the intonational characteristics of a fluent adult reading aloud . . . [On the other hand, in analysing teachers] . . .With the low group, corrections concentrated on low-level linguistic instruction about phoneme-grapheme correspondences [and 'correct pronunciation']. With the high group . . . information about clauses, sentences, and textual inferences were also brought into play" (p. 316–317).

Collins' analysis illustrates the way well-intentioned teachers, imbued with a *bottom-up* view of reading acquisition, keep dragging poorer readers down to lower levels by focusing their attention on sound-letter correspondence and correct pronunciation, thereby denying them the scaffolding effects of story, picture, and syntactic cues to aid decoding. Far from being enabling, bottom-up instruction becomes crippling. Collins suggests that children come to school with varying levels of reading "readiness" but also with ". . . prior tendencies to focus on reading as an exercise in meaning extraction or an exercise in correct utterance" (p. 320).

Indeed this is precisely what my colleagues and I found with parent-child interaction in early reading (Lancy, Draper, & Boyce 1989). We videotaped 32 parents (in two cases, grandparents) reading to their children and listening as their children read to them for thirty-minute episodes that were designed to simulate or reconstruct what happens at home during "bedtime stories" (Heath 1982). Like Collins, we "passed through" the data several times, each time seeking a more fine-grained view. We found parents of early fluent readers acting much like the teacher in the high reading group: they emphasize context, meaning, and pictures; they enhance fluency by assisting children with words they hesitate over, making it fun and not a chore. We called their general strategy "expansionist" (Lancy et al. 1989). By contrast, the parents of late, nonfluent readers used a "reductionist" strategy: they read straight through the book, and when listening to their children read they provided little help beyond reminding the child to "sound it out." They reduce fluency by forcing the child to stop and correct minor errors that do not affect meaning. In a second pass through the data, we developed a measure of fluency (Bergin, Lancy, & Draper 1994) and were able to show, for example, that the parents of fluent readers encourage questions whereas nonfluent readers tend not to ask questions and/or are discouraged from asking questions.

These last studies move the zoom lens in close to focus on interaction in a dyad, or "face-to-face interaction." Here the videotape comes into its own, so to speak, as one does not so easily lose children's voices as in a classroom setting. One can also capture subtle aspects of communication, body position, gesture, and other forms of nonverbal communication.

Face-to-Face Interaction

As indicated earlier, many sociologists are concerned with the way in which class, ethnicity and gender interact with schooling processes to effect the nature of one's education or career as a student. The studies reviewed to this point have been primarily about class. These last two investigators looked at ethnicity and gender.

Erickson and Schultz (1982) filmed a series of counseling sessions at a community college in Michigan (using both 16 mm film and videotape). Prior to filming, they spent ". . . 3 or 4 days . . . sitting in the counselor's office doing interviews with students, having lunch with the counselor and asking about his work—the organizational routines involved in it . . ." (p. 55). Within two weeks of filming, they found an opportunity to have counselors and students view the videotapes and identify points that were salient. For example, often as the counselor or student watched his or her video, ". . . it was at moments of conversational stumbling that the counselor or student would stop the videotape and say that something had gone wrong in the interview" (p. 104). They concentrated their analysis on what they came to call *co-membership* and its role in structuring the counseling session. To begin with, they looked at ethnicity. Among the 25 sessions, they had at their disposal various combinations of Italian-American, Irish-American, and African-American counselors with students of the same ethnicity, as well as Polish-American students.

The conversation began by attempts to establish co-membership, and while this process was clearly facilitated by similar ethnic background, high co-membership was not synonymous with shared ethnicity. For example, an Italian-American counselor who was a former coach and used sports as a basis for constructing co-membership had no luck establishing rapport with an Italian-American student who was overweight and a music major. When things are going smoothly (the norm for high co-membership), there is a great deal of synchrony: ". . . conversational partners are literally completing one another's action in and across time; they are forming behavioral environments for one another in real time" (p. 96). The audio portion of the tapes was subject to a voice print analysis and the video portion studied for nonverbal and kinesic patterns. These analyses ". . . show clearly . . . extreme points of emphasis—those points marked by both volume and pitch shifts on the verbal channel, and also by simultaneous kinesic shifts in a number of body parts on the nonverbal channel . . ." (p. 92). Also, arrhythmia or asynchrony occurs during "uncomfortable moments," which occurred in some of the sessions of low co-membership.

In cases where counselors were able to establish co-membership, they accepted the student's goals and did what they could to facilitate, including suggesting courses the student should take that would transfer to program X at college Y. Therefore, "In the high co-membership context, solidarity with the student and distancing from the official role of counselor was appropriate . . . [However,] in the low-co-membership context less solidarity with the students was found, and the counselor embraced the official role of institutional gatekeeper" (p. 161). Gatekeeper here refers to the counselor's imposing the school's goals on the student, urging him or her to complete course work in the most expeditious manner to earn an associate degree and graduate. As Erickson and Schultz (1982) note, gender seemed to play a role as well, in that cross-sex sessions seemed different than same-sex sessions.

This study, like many others reviewed in this chapter that involve the analysis of discourse and kinesic patterns, is characterized by an enormous demand for resources required in collecting and analyzing the data. The tighter one zooms in the lens to focus on more finely detailed aspects of behavior, the costlier will be the analysis and the longer it will take to complete. Hence, my last word of advice is, don't do it unless you are reasonably certain you'll find something worth writing about. Many topics in the sociology of education can be adequately covered by thorough and meticulous participant observation without the need of audio- or videotape recordings.

PERSPECTIVE TAKING

One of our themes has been that qualitative research must be viewed as emerging through various distinct "traditions"—e.g., anthropology, sociology, biology, history, and so on. However, within each of these traditions there is considerable diversity as well. In anthropology, we have seen that the emic-etic distinction[14] is helpful in understanding some of this diversity. In sociology this dimension also holds true but is cross-cut by another dimension that we might call *description vs. interpretation*. This second dimension is nicely illustrated by a selection from a group discussion that Willis (1977:198) had with some of the working-class youths—after they'd had a chance to read a draft of his report on their adaptation to school and work. Students understood and agreed with Willis' descriptive material; it was the "analysis" they couldn't follow. Nevertheless, from the students' comments, Willis is able to confirm that he was not viewed as an authority figure but rather was seen as being sympathetic towards the lads' lifestyle and was, therefore, deserving of their trust. His descriptive material is accurate from their (emic) point of view. On the other hand, it is equally clear that his interpretation was externally imposed, as the lads were unable to penetrate his analysis.

Willis (1977) does not conduct a parallel "member check" with teachers and/or figures of authority. He is apparently unconcerned as to the accuracy of his description from *their* point of view. Further, other *critical theorists* (Anyon, Suransky, Everhart), while obviously attuned to a student's perspective, give no indication that either their interpretation or their description had been subjected to members' scrutiny.

While Beynon (1983) makes much of his previous experience and credentials as a teacher to break the ice and increase the candor of his teacher-informants in a London High School, Metz (1978) and Lareau (1989b) attempt to distinguish their role from the teacher's. "I also had the status of a sociologist. Here it was more important that I *lacked* certain other statuses. I had never taught in elementary or secondary school, and I was not in the field of education. I also was not (yet) a parent. All of these nonstatuses made me credible as someone who came without an ax to grind" (Metz 1978:257). However, she is careful not to set herself above the teachers. "Since I genuinely needed a good deal of basic information about the functioning of school, I embraced the role of learner. In my observing classes and interviewing teachers more than one person who was initially wary grew comfortable in undertaking to inform me" (p. 258).

Lareau (1989b) draws another distinction. "Educators are trying to change social behavior; sociologists are trying to understand it. As part of this investigation sociologists have a duty to examine a wide array of social variables, including those that cannot be easily changed through school programs and policies" (p. 13). This view contrasts with that held by those conducting case studies (see chapter 5) who *do* make common cause with educators.

Lareau (1989b) also quite explicitly rejects the obligation to cast her interpretation within an emic framework. ". . . I do not want to restrict myself to 'folk explanations.' It does not trouble me if my interpretation of the factors influencing their behavior is different from their interpretation of their lives" (p. 213, see also Sleeter 1998). Silverman (1985), provides a very neat analysis of the problem: ". . . second-order sociological accounts will have an analytic purpose that may be irrelevant to members' first-order concerns. Instead of relying on direct comparison of these two accounts, the aim is to discover whether members understand and accept the researcher's account" (p. 44).

Mehan's work exemplifies the way in which the researcher can move back and forth between the scientific and the participants' perspectives, slighting neither. In his analysis of classroom lessons, the IRE model is clearly etic in the sense that neither the model nor its constituent parts are supplied by the teacher. Indeed, as Courtney Cazden, a Harvard Professor on leave who served as the teacher in this study, observes in her forward to Mehan's (1979) book: "Where the researcher sees order [e.g., IRE], the participant may have felt impending chaos . . ." (p. ix). Mehan (1979) constructs his interpretation with the assistance of participants, the aim being to describe ". . . the social organization of classroom lessons in such a way that the researcher's model captures the participant's actual practice [in a way] . . . the participants themselves already 'know' but may not have been able to articulate . . . [revealing] . . . patterns of interaction that surprise participants or scientists" (p. 173).

Sociologists appreciate the value of an emic perspective but, as their goal is to elucidate the workings of society and not just a description of culture, their analyses will ultimately reflect a commitment to a universal or an etic framework.

ISSUES FOR THE FUTURE

Mehan (1978), in reviewing his own and other ethnomethodological work, says that these ". . . studies point to stratifying practices within schools that produce differential treatment and may result in differences in later life" (p. 671). Yet, with the possible exception of the reading group studies, there is little evidence that links stratifying practices in schools to one's later socioeconomic status. That schools are suffused with opportunities to classify, rank, and differentially treat students is clear. But we simply don't know whether such actions are a help or a hindrance, or neither. I anticipate great interest in magnet schools, and voucher and other choice systems on the part of sociologists. Given what we have seen here, we could expect such systems to accentuate the influence of parents on schooling practices. We should expect to find that schools that serve children of active, concerned parents will focus their energy on enhancing each child's potential, whereas schools that serve the remainder will fulfill a largely custodial function.

The influence of community on the character of schools might also be fruitfully investigated within a contrasting qualitative research tradition, via personal accounts (see chapter 6). It would be fascinating to interview experienced teachers who have taught in different communities (urban vs. suburban) and get them to reflect on how their classrooms differed in the different circumstances.

The concept of cultural capital suggests a related notion that bears investigation, namely, the redistribution of cultural capital. Lareau's (1989b) case contains one example. Another, to be described more fully in the case study chapter, had parent volunteers who read storybooks to their children at home, come daily to kindergarten classes, and read storybooks to pairs of students—including, inevitably, many who are not read to at home (Lancy & Nattiv 1992). Two more recent cases (Mehan et al. 1996; Romo & Falbo 1996) provided otherwise low-achieving Latino high school students with the cultural capital to move from lower to upper tracks and greatly enhance their academic success. These examples only suggest what may be a widespread and understudied phenomenon.

DECODING THE COLONY

If anthropologists study the spider's web of culture, then the ant colony with its workers, slaves, soldiers, and queen provides a model of the sociologist's domain. Sociologists are interested in how society comes to have these different "types"; how people in different roles or classes relate to each other; how rank, status, and power are manufactured and displayed during these encounters; and how individuals go about constructing and maintaining their own "face" or status in their own and in others' eyes. As we have seen in this chapter, they're particularly interested in the way in which social status is transmitted from one generation to the next.

To be sure, there is much overlap between the anthropologists' and sociologists' perspectives. For example, sociologists study the *culture* of working-class youths while Ray McDermott, trained under educational anthropology founder George Spindler, was the first to study *stratification* in the reading group. There is also much overlap in methodology, ethnography being almost indistinguishable from field study. Ultimately, however, their foci are different. U.S. anthropologists have tended to document the unique culture of particular student groups—e.g., Deyhle's breakdancing Utes—whereas British sociologists like Jenkins, by contrast, have focused on the *interactions* of varying status student groups in the secondary school.

This concern for interaction has led to the growth of a distinctive methodology. The interview is far more central in sociology than in anthropology because the private, face-to-face interview is the only way to elicit members' views of the other parties in a social setting. While the anthropologist studies the tightly scripted routines of the ritual or ceremony, the sociologist studies informal encounters where social ends are negotiated. Even when studying supposedly routine events like the E&P meeting, the sociologist seeks to discover the ad hoc, unscripted activities that actually structure the meeting. For this reason, audio- and videotaping can be essential. Otherwise it would be impossible to capture the moment-to-moment unfolding of the event to discern, for example, the way high-status persons manage the meeting, or to establish that the nature of counselor-student interaction varies as a function of shared ethnicity. Further, because language is so central in human interaction, the ethnomethodologist is almost by definition a sociolinguist. In addition to the mechanical tools of videotape recorder and word processor, she must draw on a panoply of conceptual tools as well as the analysis of prosody, turn-taking, notation systems, backchanneling, and so on.

Of course not all sociologists choose to focus on the interaction process itself. Their attention may be drawn to more stable and static aspects of intergroup relations such as family-school ties. Here, participant observation is the preferred technique, because it is necessary to obtain a large quantity of basically descriptive material to provide sufficient context to turn social class from an abstract label or category into the lived reality of a group of people. Hollingshead and Lareau provide hundreds of details to illustrate the distinct lifestyles and values of Elmtown, Colton, and Prescott residents. Metz offers a comparably rich description of life in a junior high school and shows, compellingly, the way in which the curriculum and the atmosphere changes across the various tracks. These field studies most closely parallel ethnography in method and substance.

Sociologists, to a much greater extent than anthropologists, tend to draw on quantitative data in their analyses. This occurs in one of two ways. In the field studies of social class, they may collect various quantitative indices to buttress the normative portraits achieved from the fruits of participant observation. Schneider and Lee's comparative study of Asian and Anglo-American parental investments is a case in point. A second source of quantitative data are the audio- and videotape records made in the course of doing ethnomethodology. These qualitative data can be converted to quantitative indices in partitioning the behavior stream by the use of a code derived from grounded theory. These variables can be aggregated and used descriptively, as when Mehan compares indices of classroom competence at the beginning and in the middle of the year.

Lastly, there is a pronounced tendency in sociology to locate one's study within the framework provided by one or another grand theory. This is especially so in the sociology of education. Schools in the United States operate implicitly from the theory that their role is to aid in the location and development of human capital that is distributed randomly throughout the population. Each student should be afforded the opportunity to develop inherent abilities and talents to their fullest. An individual born into an impoverished family but with talent and drive should be able to use the school as an avenue of upward social and economic mobility. Most sociologists would agree that this scenario is idealized. There is disagreement over just how often it happens and, more importantly, why the school is unable to achieve this ideal. It is in the ferment regarding these issues that theories are constructed, modified and brought into contention. For some theorists, human society is dynamic—under the right circumstances the pauper can become a prince. But, for others, it is analogous to the ant colony, where it is as unlikely for someone born into the working class to ascend to middle-class status as it is for a soldier ant to become a worker ant.

ENDNOTES

[1] One perspective views schooling as the central channel of social mobility. Evidence in support of this position is obtained from intergenerational mobility studies ". . . which show education is largely independent of social origins and is a strong determinant of occupational status . . . the other perspective puts more stress on schooling as a transmitter of the existing status advantages of a group from one generation to the next. Support for this position comes from studies that claim attained socioeconomic status can be predicted better by background socioeconomic variables than by education achievement . . ." (Cicourel & Mehan 1983:5).

[2] Grand theory here means a theory that goes beyond trying to account for why it is, say, that children from a particular ethnic group do well or poorly in school. Grand theories take in all members of society and all of society's institutions, the family, the schools, places of employment, government bureaucracies, etc.

[3] Annette Lareau herself suggested I review the Baker and Stevenson article in this chapter, which prompted a discussion as to whether it was qualitative (Lareau) or quantitative (Lancy).

[4] Lareau's 1989b effort is also noteworthy because she offers one of the most detailed and honest accounts of methodology in the literature. Methodological issues are discussed throughout the text, but there is also a lengthy appendix entitled "Common problems in fieldwork: A personal essay." She discusses aspects of her own background, including a long-standing interest in education (both her parents are teachers) and her qualifications to do this research (lengthy apprenticeship as a paid interviewer). We also learn a great deal about her sampling procedures.

[5] Based on painful prior experience, I recommend against using "built in" microphones on either audio- or videotape players. Hock your pearls if you have to, but use a lapel-pin wireless microphone.

[6] Specially designed word processing programs for analyzing qualitative data (Pfaffenberger 1988) would facilitate this process.

[7] What makes this a field study rather than an ethnography is more its purpose than its methods. Hollingshead is very clearly motivated by specific theoretical concerns, and he seeks to answer a very specific question. Yet, his thoroughness, lengthy residence in the field, and

willingness to let his informants and events guide his inquiry make clear the fundamentally qualitative nature of the study. And, although the methods may be similar, the sheer volume of data—especially interview data—collected is noteworthy.

8   Hollingshead (1949/1975) never quite comes out and says this in so many words, but he suggests that in the 1940s the upper classes maintained a stranglehold on school finances to keep schools from functioning effectively in enabling children from lower classes to get a "good" education and enhance their status. The high school lost its state accreditation, for example, but even this drastic blow failed to convince community leaders to spend money on the school and its underpaid staff.

9   Indeed, Smith uses an even broader brush: ". . . those who advocate centralized programs to reform education and those who preach positivist social science find common cause . . . Federally-imposed programs, no matter how well conceived, are inevitably modified by local circumstances. Positivist research and evaluation models designed to study these programs overlook these local circumstances and therefore are bound to fail" (p. 229).

10 *Learning Lessons* is an excellent source of ideas for researchers interested in videotaping classroom activities. However, scholars have begun to debate (Raymond 1991) the need for constraints on the use of videotapes obtained in a research study. Often tapes are used subsequent to the original research without the consent of the research participants.

11 As mentioned in the previous chapter, Susan Phillips' (1983) study shows that Native American children are placed at a distinct disadvantage because of their lack of competence in what to them are alien participation structures in the public school classroom.

12 Note the "production cycle" from the onset of research in 1978 to publication of the report in 1985. The time involved in developing and applying a coding scheme, using it to code thousands of discrete behaviors on the videotape, transferring these coded data to the computer for analysis, and so on, means that "micro" ethnography takes even longer from start to finish than "regular" ethnography. This study was one of several studies of language use in the classroom funded by the federal government in the late 1970s (Wilkinson 1981). A study by James Collins, to be discussed later in the chapter, is another.

13 Erickson and Schultz (1982:57–58) have an excellent description of the origins of the emic/etic contrast.

14 For similar methodology see: Csikszentmihalyi, M., & Larson, R. (1984). *Being Adolescent: Conflict and Growth in the Teenage Years*. New York: Basic.

4 Traditions Derived from Animal Behavior and Psychology

"Rough-and-tumble play," as I shall call it . . . consists of seven movement patterns which tend to occur at the same time as each other and not to occur with other movements. . . . These are running, chasing, and fleeing; wrestling; jumping up and down with both feet together ("jumps"); beating at each other with an open hand without actually hitting ("open beat"); beating at each other with an object but not hitting; laughing. . . . There seems to be a common facial expression in this play . . . an open-mouthed smile with the teeth covered which morphologically resembles the "play-face" of *Macaca* and *Pan* [primate species] . . . (Blurton-Jones 1967:357–358)

The quote is taken from a landmark study of children's play carried out by Nick Blurton-Jones (1967) while a student of Nikko Tinbergen's at Oxford. Tinbergen, along with Konrad Lorenz, had been the founder of the field of *ethology*—the naturalistic study of animal behavior. One hallmark of the field is the use of the qualitative paradigm—"Lorenz had always argued that to understand a species you must go through a prolonged period of acclimatization, 'just watching,' leaving behind one's preconceptions and entering into the *Umwelt* of the species being studied" (Smith 1990:192). And, like sociologists, ethologists are preoccupied with a limited set of questions—what Tinbergen (1951) called the "four whys." For example, when observing a piece of behavior—some act—they would like to know what its proximal cause was, what released or triggered it. In a broader sense they would like to know what the function of this behavior is, how it helps the animal in its fight to survive and reproduce. How did this behavior develop over time in the species (evolution)? How does it develop in the life cycle of the individual (ontogeny)?

However, Tinbergen and Lorenz had limited their research to animals with relatively simple behavioral repertoires, dumb creatures with neither speech nor "intelligence." Blurton-Jones originally studied birds, specifically the great tit (Blurton-Jones 1968), when in 1963 he began the first study of human ethology—of British nursery school children. As he says, "My approach is best described by reference to ethological studies of bird behaviour . . ." (1967:348). Beyond this he ". . . used no special observation techniques, but simply visited the school repeatedly, and sat on a chair in the corner with a notebook" (p. 349).

Several things are worth noting in the opening passage. First, there is the focus on easily observable behaviors—"running, chasing . . . openmouthed smile with teeth covered" (pp. 357–358). Ethologists avoid making inferences based on the animal's imputed cognitive or affective state, e.g., "angry," "sad," "eager." Second, one object of this open-ended, descriptive stance is to uncover sets of behavior that go together in some integrated, purposeful fashion. Here Blurton-Jones teases apart rough-and-tumble play from aggression, a very similar complex. Imagine the proverbial traveler from Mars visiting an elementary school classroom and gradually distinguishing "math" from "reading." Third, note that Blurton-Jones compares what he observes with what is reported in the literature for other primate species. This comparative perspective is essential in addressing the perennial questions already alluded to as well as the question as to whether the behavior at issue is instinctual or learned—an issue we will take up shortly.

The first section of the chapter is an overview of the basic techniques employed by a human ethologist, especially the various sampling procedures available. Then we consider several prominent themes in the human ethology literature, including rough-and-tumble play and the dominance hierarchy and density, with one short digression to discuss "natural experiments." Density is also a theme one encounters within the tradition of ecological psychology, an area of scholarship in which the physical spaces that constrain human interaction are a paramount concern.

CONSTRUCTING THE ETHOGRAM

McGrew (1972a, b), following closely on Blurton-Jones' heels, conducted a series of ethological studies in nursery schools between October 1966 and September 1969. He identified many of the topics that have held investigators' interest to the present day, including the response of the group to the addition of a new member, dominance hierarchies, and the effect of varying density. However, his most significant contribution was the development of very precise *definitions* of commonly observed behaviors that have since become part of the basic tool kit of ethologists who study children. In chapter 4 of *Elements of Behavior*, which runs to 76 pages, McGrew (1972a) identifies over one hundred distinct behaviors, including the *eyebrow flash*:

> . . . a rapid raising of the eyebrows, which remain elevated for 1/6 second, followed by a rapid lowering to the normal position. It may occur

singly or in short series, and it results from the contraction of the frontal belly of the *occipito frontalis* muscle . . . Like adults, children appear to use eyebrow flashing in friendly greeting, for example, when glancing up at passing and approaching individuals. (p. 43)

The first human ethologists saw themselves as radicals in methodology: "At that time [early 1960s] simply watching and recording behaviors seemed a dangerously new idea compared with the laboratory traditions in which we had both been educated" (Smith & Connolly 1980:xi). McGrew (1972a) boldly challenges the prevailing wisdom of the behaviorists who ". . . held that the origins of behaviour could be wholly accounted for by postnatal individual experience" (p. 18) in arguing for the importance of the genetic blueprint. His goal in this series of studies is ". . . a tentative attempt at defining an ethogram for the young *Homo sapiens*" (p. 36). An ethogram is the behavioral equivalent of anatomy and physiology—that is, a description and mapping of the behavioral repertoire of the species where the frequency of behaviors and their temporal relationship (e.g., two behaviors occurring simultaneously or sequentially but unrelated) are depicted. McGrew (1972a) finds, for example, that, among nursery schoolers, most interaction occurs in pairs and that the mean length of an interaction is 12.9 seconds. Many of these interactions share a common pattern—they are "possession struggles." Not only do these have clear winners and losers, but over time a pattern emerges: ". . . most interactions involve the more dominant males engaging in possession struggles with each other . . . [others have obtained] similar findings for adult male langurs . . ." (p. 122).

Keeping this catalog of behavior in mind, McGrew (1972a) unobtrusively ". . . recorded observations on a portable tape recorder. . . . [These] were later transcribed, timed by stopwatch, and coded onto a standardized sheet. Two percent of the data were rejected because of . . . data were punched onto cards and analyzed using conventional electronic data processing methods" (p. 178).[1] Indeed, computerized data processing is virtually a prerequisite to the attempt to produce a human ethogram. The outcome of the analyses consists of tables of figures that permit various comparisons among the behaviors of interest.

McGrew (1972a) demonstrates his skill as a natural historian or field biologist by taking advantage of climactic conditions to conduct a natural experiment (Tinbergen and Lorenz were also masters of this). He wanted to know how density would affect behavior. Three differing conditions were possible: during bad weather, children had to play indoors, producing high density; just after it had been raining, the children could play indoors or on the paved areas, producing medium density; and during fine weather, play could extend from these areas onto grassy areas, producing low density. Of the many changes that were noted, this was typical: "The amount of time children spent in arm movements increased significantly with higher group densities . . ." (p. 179). We shall return to the topic of density shortly.

As comprehensive as McGrew's (1972a) lexicon of behaviors is, there is an interesting omission, namely, speech. Ethologists are primarily concerned

with nonverbal behavior because of the desire to make cross-species comparisons; and because they are interested in universal or pan-species aspects of
behavior, and the content of conversations is likely to be heavily influenced
by the child's experience. With an exception to be noted below, ethologists
don't talk to their subjects, either, at least partly because to do so would inter-
fere with the naturally occurring behaviors they are trying to record.[2] Instead,
they have devised a variety of means to observe and record the behavior of
individuals in groups. The major problem to be faced, of course, is that the
observer can't possibly record *everything*—he or she must *sample* from the
available behaviors. Janet Altman (1974), a primatologist, has prepared the
definitive work on the subject, describing seven basic sampling procedures.

Rough-and-Tumble Play

As we have seen (Blurton-Jones 1967), children's rough-and-tumble play
(R & T) was one of human ethology's discoveries, and it remains an extremely
popular object of study. Pellegrini (1988; 1989) and his students observed kin-
dergarteners and second- and fourth-graders from a public elementary school
on the playground during recess. Tabulations were made of R & T and aggression as a function of grade level, location on playground, and gender. Of the
behaviors noted, about 11 percent could be reliably coded as R & T, but boys
were three times more likely than girls to engage in R & T. Aggression
occurred very rarely. Further, ". . . popular boys often engage in r/t. They do
so to have fun and to interact cooperatively with peers . . . aggressive behavior
. . . was negatively correlated with popularity . . ." (p. 257).

Peter Smith and his colleagues have also conducted a thorough investigation of rough-and-tumble play in children. They note the distinctiveness of
play and aggression: "Twelve out of 325 rough-and-tumble bouts observed
(3.7 percent) led to an injury. In eight of these, the partner comforted the hurt
child . . . only three fights were seen throughout the whole study . . ." (Humphreys & Smith 1987:205). In this research observers often work from videotape recordings of schoolchildren on the playground.

Two methodological issues are raised here that pervade the human
ethology literature. First, there is a concern for the quality of one's *operational
definitions*. To the naive observer, behavior occurs in a continuous stream. The
challenge for the ethologist is to partition this stream in sensible ways—that is,
in ways that correspond to some objective reality (e.g., chase vs. flee) and that
taken together reveal predictable patterns. A videotaped record allows one to
continuously rework these definitions so that particular segments of behavior
can be reliably coded as one thing and not another (e.g., flinch vs. duck). A
second problem concerns the perceptual filter of the *observer*. Despite training,
different observers will still see different things. Consequently, all studies that
involve the analysis of observational data mandate multiple observers.

An exception to the rule noted above (that ethologists do not interview
the individuals whose behavior they have recorded) occurred when Smith and

Lewis (1985) had eight (of 26 in the study) nursery school children view videotapes made on the playground. The children were asked to judge whether a given episode was playful or aggressive. The children's judgments corresponded closely to that of the researchers, demonstrating the congruence of emic and etic views—although Smith and Lewis do not use these terms.

Empirical study of rough-and-tumble play is invariably accompanied by speculation on its *function*. Smith (1974; see also Smith 1982), perhaps reflecting on the pervasiveness of R & T reported for juvenile *canids* and *felids* (Aldis 1975) as well as on human R & T, theorizes: ". . . it would seem that the forms it takes. . . are such as to provide practice for adult hunting activities" (p. 108). Pellegrini (1989) has sought to test the proposition that R & T contributes to the individual's development of social competence, while I have argued (Lancy 1980) that play might simultaneously serve two distinct functions, first to maintain an optimal level of arousal—e.g., to stave off boredom; and second, perhaps to aid the individual in perfecting skills that will be critical later in life—such as hunting,[3] escaping from predators, or participating in a dominance hierarchy.[4] The point to be made here is that ethologists are as committed to grand theory as sociologists, which imposes constraints on what they choose to study as well as how they go about it.

The Dominance Hierarchy in Preschool

Ethologists have had a long-standing interest in formal, structured dominance hierarchies that arise in social groups. One of the earliest studies, characteristically, was an analysis of the pecking order among barnyard fowl (Schjeldesup-Ebbe 1922). During the early 1960s numerous studies were conducted with captive and free-living primates, which established the pervasiveness of the dominance hierarchy as well as providing descriptions of how individual members gain and lose rank (Chance & Jolly 1970). Among primates, rank is gained and displayed in several ways. One of the most common is the very straightforward "property fight"; another is "proximity"; and a third is "attention structure." This last grew out of research (Omark & Edelman 1976) showing that members of the group are more likely to glance at high-ranking than at low-ranking members.[5] A study by Abramovitch (1976) was one of the first of dominance relations among *Homo sapiens*. She and her assistants observed four preschool classes. One can't help but note the great care and precision with which she describes the physical setting of the nursery school classrooms—a hallmark of the ethological perspective.

Abramovitch and her assistants studied property fights that had winners/losers and proximity as measured by distance and attention structure, captured by "glance rate." All of these observable variables are *low-inference* behaviors.[6] They do not require that the researcher interact with the child or draw inferences about the child's mental state. Not surprisingly, agreement between observers is high. Data are then analyzed with the aid of the computer. Abramovitch's aggregated results showed, among other things, that children who consistently won property fights were glanced at (or observed) by other children more than twice as often as children who lost such fights. Proximity data showed that high-ranking children tended to place themselves in proximity to higher-ranking children and out of range of low-ranking children.

Strayer and Strayer (1976) used another of the methods recommended by Altman (1974), matrix completion. "The observer scans the immediate environs for episodes of behavior defined in the . . . inventory . . . If two episodes occur simultaneously, the one involving a child who has not been previously observed in conflict is videotaped. Toward the end of the observational period, greater attention is given to those children who have participated in the fewest number of agonistic episodes" (p. 982). Their focus was on various behaviors that corresponded to either aggression or submission. They first analyzed their data to determine whether there is, indeed, a recognizable dominance hierarchy in this group of 18 preschoolers. They looked for evidence of the ". . . linear transivity rule [, which] . . . states that, if individual A dominates B and individual B dominates C, then A should also dominate C" (p. 984). In this case 98 percent of all interactions were in the expected direction. Next they look at relationships within the data—for example, "Furthermore, the low incidence of counter attacks . . . suggests that the dominance structure of these preschool children may function to minimize intragroup aggression just as it does in other primate groups" (p. 987). Another interesting finding is that higher-ranking children initiate agonistic encounters far less frequently than lower-ranking children. ". . . frequency of initiated aggression does not determine dominance status . . . a relatively low-aggressive girl was the most dominant individual in this group" (p. 988).

The Dominance Hierarchy among Adolescents

Scholars have built on this foundation and gone on to probe developmental aspects (Melson & Dyar 1987) of the dominance hierarchy and such things as leadership style (Hold 1976). Rich Savin-Williams (1987) has conducted several noteworthy studies of adolescents within the human ethology tradition—in particular, dominance hierarchy formation in a coed summer camp where cabin residence was unisex. University of Chicago graduate assistants with experience as camp counselors were trained to observe and record behaviors via joint (with Savin-Williams) observation of volleyball games prior to the summer. For this study, the observers were able to *disguise* their note taking as score keeping during athletic contests, recording of minutes during cabin meetings, writing letters during rest periods, and so on. Hence, campers were unaware that they were the objects of a research study, as were their parents.

In view of the fact that a permanent record was being made of "undesirable" behavior—"Some, cabin bullies, physically threatened and fought . . . to assert their dominance" (p. 932)—I would guess that this study would encounter heavy sailing through the University Committee that has to pass on the ethics of any research involving "human subjects." On the other hand, it is also not clear that Savin-Williams could claim to be observing "naturally occurring behavior" if he had fully informed campers of their subject status and the purposes of the study to obtain their *prior* consent.

Weisfeld and Weisfeld (1984) took advantage of the creation of an intramural volleyball league to study dominance-hierarchy formation among upper-middle-class ninth graders. Twenty-four players, six per team, played a round robin tournament following two weeks of practice. Where the nursery school studies recorded nonverbal behaviors exclusively and Savin-Williams (1979) used a mixture of verbal and nonverbal behaviors, in this study relatively high-inference verbal behaviors are simultaneously noted on audiotape by two observers. Specifically: ". . . The identities of evaluator and recipient were recorded, along with the nature of the comment: *praise* (containing rewarding content), *criticism* (containing punishment), or *instruction* (neutral). Any verbal response to the evaluation—accepting it (*acknowledgement*) or rejecting it (*protest*)—was noted" (p. 93). They found that: "A single hierarchy seemed to emerge that was relative to volleyball ability. This hierarchy formed in the virtual absence of acts of physical aggression. The best players hit the ball frequently and instructed, praised, and criticized their teammates" (p. 96).

This mention of the absence of aggression is echoed throughout the ethology literature on the dominance hierarchy. Aggression steadily declines with age and as one rises in the hierarchy (Savin-Williams 1982). Indeed, Savin-Williams (1987) and others argue that the *reduction* of intragroup conflict (over scarce resources) is the primary function of dominance hierarchies.

Natural Experiments

Ethologists make great use of *comparative* data to determine whether a particular pattern of behavior is true only for one species or is more widely found, e.g., "Baboon infants usually do not leave their mothers' arms during the first month of life, and baboon mothers are reticent about allowing other females to touch their offspring. But the newborn langur is passed about to other females" (Poirer 1972:21).

Human ethologists and developmental psychologists also record and compare patterns of behavior in different societies, especially those that have not yet experienced the homogenizing effect of public schooling and the mass media. Their goal is to determine what aspects of human behavior or human development are universal—true for all humans, or culture-specific—true only for certain societies.[7] Eibl-Eibesfeldt (1983) for example, has spent a lifetime trying to address the following question: "Do universal patterns of mother-child interactions exist, which can be considered as a shared phylogenetic heritage of *Homo sapiens*?" (p. 179). He has made extensive film and audio recordings from unacculturated peoples around the world. Careful observation is made of such things as the amount of time the baby remains in physical contact with the mother, the time spent with mother as opposed to others, and so on. He concludes that the mother-infant bond is universal—common to all human societies.

These cross-cultural scholars also use strange devices (e.g., Lancy, Souviney, & Kada 1981; Lancy & Strathern 1981) to control for the effects of prior experience, and also to make more visible and easier to record behaviors that are often hidden from the participant observer. The late Millard Madsen developed a number of extremely ingenious game-like devices to probe the degree to which interpersonal cooperation was biological or cultural. We (Lancy & Madsen, 1981) used one such device with children in several Papua New Guinea societies. For example, we used the "coin-pull" with different groups of Melpa children. A 62 x 15-cm. board, raised 7 cm. off the table, is placed between a pair of same-sex children. Lying on the board is a rectangular block of Plexiglas with a hole in the center into which a coin is placed. Attached to both ends of the block are cords that run through eyelets at each end of the board. As the child pulls on the cord, the block moves towards his end of the board and, just before it reaches the edge, the coin will drop through a 3-cm. hole. In order for one child to draw the block to his or her end and thus drop a coin through the hole at that end, the other child must relax the grip on his or her cord. This procedure is demonstrated to them, each being given an opportunity to pull the block to his or her end and gain a coin during an initial practice phase. The task is analogous to a tug-of-war, with one difference: The Plexiglas block is actually split in half, the two halves being held together by magnets; thus, when each child pulls simultaneously, the block splits and neither wins a coin. This feature is *not* demonstrated during the practice phase. The children are told they will have 10 coins to win, and these are lined up on the table in plain view. If they take turns pulling, both children will win coins and these moves are recorded as *cooperative*; if they tug simultaneously, the block breaks, the coin is taken back and the move is recorded as *competitive*. In general we found that children from the same clan in the same village tended to cooperate with each other, while children from villages that were at war tended to compete.

Charlesworth and Dzur (1987) developed a novel device that created a reasonably authentic representation of problem-solving situations that occur in the nursery school. The goal was to document the dominance hierarchy. This was a toy, hand-operated movie viewer. It was constructed in such a way that if a child wanted to view a movie, he or she would have to persuade another child to turn the crank—the child viewing the movie couldn't reach it *and* view the movie simultaneously. Prior to the children's introduction to this apparatus, the dominance hierarchy of this particular group had been fully documented. Children were then videotaped as they used the movie viewer. High-ranking children were much more likely to gain early access to the viewer and had no difficulty in coercing others to turn on the light and turn the crank. One way they did this was by offering to help while others used the viewer. "However, children of low . . . status were strikingly ineffectual in negotiating an equal turn with their peers" (LaFreniere & Charlesworth 1987:355).

These are hybrid studies. While they use variables and experimental manipulations, they may incorporate qualitative elements. For example, great care is taken to accurately replicate the features of naturally occurring problem-solving situations in the design of these devices. Children do encounter strange things that they have to figure out, and they do need to enlist each other's cooperation in order to share resources and accomplish a goal, such as playing a game. In addition, these devices all permit the unambiguous coding of low-inference behaviors. It is quite clear, for example, when one of the children in Charlesworth's studies successfully negotiated an opportunity to view the film. Also, most of these investigators conduct relatively unconstrained observation of their eventual "subjects" before, during, and after the experiment to verify the validity of the procedures. With the Madsen procedure, pairs of children who are bent on competing try to get the jump on their opponents and pull the rope before the signal is given to begin; cooperative pairs are more cautious, they negotiate turn-taking and indicate by word or gesture that it is the other's turn to pull the block and retrieve the coin.

Ethological Research on Density

The study of group size and density will allow us to explore the relationship between two distinct traditions that share a biological perspective: human ethology and ecological psychology. An experiment by Calhoun (1962) caused an enormous stir when he documented that rats (highly social creatures) lost all social restraint when forced to live in overcrowded conditions. Positive social behaviors like grooming, nursing, and nest building were attenuated or disappeared altogether. Peter Smith and Kevin Connolly (1980) collaborated on the major study of group size and density in nursery school. Their general approach follows the R & T and dominance hierarchy studies; in particular, they draw on McGrew (1972a) and Altman (1974). They carefully document their approach and, ultimately, define and use over one hundred distinct categories of behavior. Their techniques of observation, plotting, analysis, and display of data are all worthy of attention.

They worked in several nursery schools over an extended period of time. With the cooperation of school authorities they combined smaller groups into larger groups to study the effects of group size and also altered the size of the play space available to study crowding. Among the fascinating analyses are diagrams of "sociometry" showing, in graphic terms, who plays with whom and how often. Generally, they found: ". . . the greater crowding of children relative to the equipment available did lead to greater levels of social discord and stress" (Smith & Connolly 1980:130). In addition to careful observation of the children, other "unobtrusive" measures (cf. Webb et al. 1966) may have been available, for example, ". . . popular parts of a playground should show more wear and tear than unpopular parts" (Graue & Walsh 1998:125).

Density Studies in Ecological Psychology

The remaining studies of group size and density all fall within the tradition of ecological psychology and such closely related traditions as environmental psychology (Proshansky, Ittelson, & Rivlin 1970) and human ecology (Bronfenbrenner 1979). Hutt and Hutt (1970:22–23) identify several differences between ethological and ecological research. Ethologists study behaviors at a more atomic level—facial expressions and gestures that accompany such actions as "instruction," "helping," and so on. However, ecologists do strive for precision in defining their categories and use multiple observers. Ethologists tend to study what often appear to be goalless or purposeless behaviors like play and the dominance hierarchy. In contrast, ecologists study goal-directed behavior, and they tend to make inferences about people's motives, attitudes, and intentions. Also, ethologists are more united than ecologists in their concern with ". . . four interlocking biological problems: those of causation, function, evolution, and ontogeny" (p. 24), whereas the ecologist, like the anthropologist, is more likely to let the situation dictate the problem.[8]

Roger Barker (1976) initiated the tradition of ecological psychology, and he and his colleagues carried out numerous investigations within this tradition, primarily in the 1950s and 1960s. This tradition arose at least partly as a reaction against quantitative methods in psychology. Barker describes a naturalistic study of children in which a huge data archive was assembled, based on a meticulously detailed record of a day in the life of a small-town boy. These data have been used by literally dozens of different investigators. As Barker says, "Naturalistic data have significance *per se*" (p. 226). He worked out of something called the Midwest Psychological Field Station in Oskaloosa, Kansas, which he likens to a Woods Hole or Mount Wilson—locales for marine and astronomical observatories, respectively.

In *Big School, Small School*, Barker and Gump (1964) were interested in the way size affected the life of a high school. They conducted intensive observation in over fifty high schools throughout Kansas in the years 1957–1959. Enrollment in these schools ranged from 35 to 2,300. One of their observational categories is the *setting*. Settings are emically derived and include such things as *chemistry, football,* and *medical services*. One of their more interesting findings was that the number of settings varied much less as a function of size than one might expect. Consequently, students (and one presumes faculty, as well) played many more roles in the small school in order to sustain this great variety of activities.

In this and other studies Barker and Gump (1964; Gump 1974) aim to show that enduring aspects of the school, physical as well as institutional, govern what goes on there as much or more so than the desires of the participants, social processes, and so on. They see most typical scenes in the school as having prearranged scripts—unlike ethnomethodologists, who see these same scenes as socially constructed. One of the more unusual works within this tradition is Berk and Berson's (1975) study of behavior on a school bus. A total of nineteen six- to nine-year-olds rode the bus from 20 to 50 minutes each way. Their unit of analysis is the *episode,* which ". . . is a goal-directed action on the part of an observed child that is within his own normal sphere of awareness" (p. 3). In a little over 15 hours of observation, a total of 896 episodes occurred (p. 7). The authors analyze these episodes in various ways. They also compare the children's behaviors with and without a teacher as an additional passenger, but they find that density does seem to affect social interaction—specifically that in the afternoon when the bus starts out full, there is less social interaction than in the morning.

The final study we will consider in this section also makes use of a natural experiment to probe the relationship between density in student housing and helping behavior. "Although there has been an enormous amount of money invested in building high-rise dormitories, in spite of some student dissatisfaction, little research has been devoted to investigating the effect these buildings may have on their residents. Architects and planners have appeared to be mostly concerned with the aesthetics and economics of their designs" (Bickman et al., 1973:466). The investigators compared female dorms at The University of Massachusetts at Amherst and "houses" at Smith College. The twenty-two-story dorms were taken as dense living conditions, with 500 students per building, while the houses at Smith College were two stories high and had less than 60 students. Stamped, addressed return envelopes were dropped in residence hallways when students were in class. The number of them that were subsequently picked up and mailed was taken as a low-inference, unobtrusive measure of social cohesion. In the high-density housing 63 percent of the letters, and in the low-density 100 percent, were returned. The study was replicated (with similar results) at the University of Pennsylvania where ". . . high-rises (25 stories) are emotionally depressing and socially suffocating places in which to live . . . the whole complex has been somewhat pejoratively nicknamed 'superblock'" (p. 479).

COMPARATIVE STUDIES OF SOCIALIZATION

Another major tradition of interest had its origins in the marriage—at Harvard and Yale in the 1950s—of developmental psychology and cultural anthropology. A landmark work is John Whiting and Irvin Child's *Child training and personality: A cross-cultural study,* published in 1953. Scholars were concerned with testing major theoretical propositions about human psychology, notably Freud's theory of personality development, and their *universality.* To ask questions about the relationship between child rearing (culture) and personality (psychology), Whiting and Child used a huge archive of anthropological accounts of peoples from around the world. This archive—still relied upon by scholars today—had been systematically compiled and indexed to create the *Human Relations Area Files,* better known as HRAF. Influenced by Freudian theory, the authors and their students searched through these records for evidence of things like toilet training (its early onset and severity were postulated to influence personality, e.g., the *anal compulsive*). One umbrella term for this work was the study of *socialization* —a concern for the way parents and others shape children's emerging character and interpersonal behavior, or "manners."

However, the extant anthropological record was rather impoverished when it came to accounts of children. So John and Beatrice Whiting launched one of the largest and longest-lasting investigations of children ever undertaken (Whiting 1963; Whiting & Whiting 1975; Whiting & Edwards 1988). Graduate students were sent to the four corners of the globe, armed with instructions for systematically observing children in their natural settings (Whiting et al. 1963). These instructions consisted of a sampling scheme for determining when and where to observe the target children in order to insure a representative picture. In addition, each observer made use of an elaborate list of *operationally defined* behaviors (e.g., "offers help," "seeks attention," "cooking," "herding"). These codes were developed *a priori*— unlike those used by ethologists. However, as each successive wave of researchers returned from the field, refinements were made to the coding scheme. A typical finding of this research is that, by the age or four or five, children develop a recognition that their gender is fixed. As part evidence for this thesis, they note that children tend to spend time with others of the same gender exclusively, from that age on. This result is achieved by aggregating the observations of "focal" children over many settings and many occasions (Whiting & Edwards 1988:228–230).

Obviously, this research tradition isn't particularly qualitative. Hallmarks of the tradition are the use of *predetermined*, discrete categories in observing children's behavior analyzed *quantitatively* to address questions derived, for the most part, from Western psychology; but it has certainly become more qualitative over time. Students of the Whitings—and their students—have incorporated greater and greater amounts of ethnography into their research designs, and their search for questions to pursue are nowadays more informed by cultural anthropology and sociobiology than by Freudian psychology (Göncü 1999; Harkness & Super 1996). Indeed, the distinction between enculturation, as studied by anthropologists (see chapter 2), and socialization, as studied by psychologists, has become rather blurred of late.

APPLYING OBSERVATIONAL METHODS

In recent years interest among researchers in both human ethology and ecological psychology seems to have waned. However, many of the methods and constructs developed by these pioneering scholars have been adapted by researchers working within more quantitative and applied frameworks. A typical example is Moore's (1989) ethological study of children's behavior before and after the redesign and reconstruction of a playground. Gump (1974;

1978) applied the Kansas school's methodology to an analysis of new schools with open-plan architecture (see also discussion of Kensington School in the next chapter). In essence, he found that *open-plan* did not mean "open curriculum"—teaching methods were too resistant to change. Stodolsky's (1988) comparative study of classroom activity in both math and social studies classes[9] falls very much within the ecological psychology tradition. She is seeking to discover enduring, firmly institutionalized features of math and social studies classes that are unaffected by the particular teacher and students in the classroom. Among "segments" that observers were trained to identify and check off were: "seatwork," "group work," and "cognitive level."

One of the reasons for the relative paucity of research within these traditions is that, in my view, the cost-benefit ratio is very low. I have glossed over the magnitude of these studies from a logistical point of view, but consider: the typical study utilizes multiple observers (who have to be carefully trained) to observe upwards of 100 children for as many as 100 hours, all the while dictating into a tape recorder or noting behaviors on a complex coding form (Hutt & Hutt 1970, fig. 19). In the studies that used tape, the observer's comments are transcribed and *then* transferred onto coding forms, which are in turn quantified and recoded into a computer file, which then can be analyzed. The number of variables this yields, well over 100 in some cases, can lead to an orgy of computer runs to cross-classify the variables in every conceivable configuration in the lengthy search for meaningful patterns (Hartwig & Dearing 1979).

CHOREOGRAPHING THE BEE'S DANCE

We now explore the boundary between human ethology and social psychology. Hatch's (1987) study of status and power in a kindergarten peer group lies along this boundary. His review of literature draws on classic works in both fields (e.g., Freedman 1977; Goffman 1959), and he records both nonverbal as well as verbal behavior. Hatch . . . "took a passive role . . . making every effort to avoid interaction with children and to blend into the fabric of school life" (p. 81). Unlike the anthropologist, who must develop rapport with informants, ethologists must take great pains not to disrupt the "natural" stream of behavior. He recorded children's conversations in shorthand. He made 26 visits and observed for 80 hours altogether, capturing 2,302 child-to-child interactions. Part of his report resembles much we've seen before in this chapter: "Boys averaged 8.8 dominance attempts, while girls averaged 7.6 attempts per child" (p. 89). However, Hatch more closely resembles an ethnomethodologist when he describes several reoccurring strategies that children use to enhance rank, including "self-promotion" and the "put-down."

Hence, we can see convergence in two very different traditions: studies of the dominance hierarchy from a biological perspective and studies of the social construction of stratification from a social psychological or sociological[10] perspective. Research in ethology suggests the inevitability of the dominance hierarchy, and this tradition provides a variety of techniques to document specific instances of the hierarchy and establish each member's rank.

von Frisch's (1954) study of the language of bees served as one of the foundation stones of this tradition and can serve us, metaphorically, in trying to grasp the essence of the human ethologists' and ecologists' enterprise. After foraging, honeybees return to the hive and do a *waggle* dance in a series of figure-eight rotations—however, to the uninitiated, it appears as if the bees are just "milling around." By dint of prolonged and very precise observation, von Frisch determined that: (a) the bee's dance was patterned; (b) these patterns were interpretable by other bees; (c) the patterns signaled the location of a food source that the returning bee had located; and (d) bees that had attended the dance were indeed able to locate the food source on leaving the hive.

The ethologists have the hardest job of all, in many respects, as they attempt to document patterns and behavior of which actors themselves are largely unaware, and which are *not* generally discernable to the participant observer. Hence the necessity for thorough, meticulous, and extensive sampling of discreet behaviors in order to provide a massive data archive that can be systematically searched for these illusive patterns.

These patterns are not human inventions—ethologists do not study the impact of new rules or the effect of the presence of a supervisor on the behavior of children in the playground. They study the way the playground equipment itself, its design and layout, structure the children's behavior; or they compare the behavior of girls versus boys in the same playground or the behavior of six-year-olds versus four-year-olds.

Having documented a particular pattern that has been shaped by the animal's genes and the environment in which it resides, the ethologist must speculate on the adaptive value of the pattern. Because nature is conservative, it is a safe bet that what at first appears as damaging or threatening to the organism—R & T play, the dominance hierarchy—turns out, upon close examination, to serve some very useful purposes. Just as the bee's seemingly random movements turn out to be a code that communicates vital information to the hive, the dominance hierarchy may serve to distribute scarce and/or desirable goods within the group with a minimum of discord and stress.

ENDNOTES

[1] Although I cannot cite a study in which this has been done, the technology is now available that would permit the elimination of most of these steps. An ethologist could use the same hand-held calculatorlike devices that inventory takers use in stores and supermarkets, noting the various behaviors and their duration. Periodically this recording instrument would be interfaced (either physically or via radio transmission) with a large memory computer and the data "downloaded" into prepared data files for virtually instant analysis via internal statistics programs.

[2] Interestingly, ethologists (Hutt & Hutt 1970; Tinbergen & Tinbergen 1972) have also been drawn to the study of autistics because, being nonverbal, conventional means of testing or

studying them (Lancy & Goldstein 1982) yield meaningless results. For example, Hutt et al. (1965) noted that when autistic children became distressed, they would rush to an adult to be comforted but would avert their gaze so as not to have to interact with him/her—a finding consistent with the arousal homeostatic theory (Goldstein & Lancy 1985) of autism.

[3] Peter Smith (personal communication) would add *fighting* to this list.

[4] McGrew (1992) later conducted research with young chimps at Jane Goodall's field station in Tanzania. He reports a vivid episode where 24-month-old FD "plays at" leaf-sponging, a procedure his mother uses to sop up water in cavities of trees when other sources of drinking water are not available.

[5] As we have seen in the previous chapter, attention structure has some applicability in the regular classroom context where studies have shown that "good" students are attended to by their classmates while "poor" students are not.

[6] Pellegrini (1996) has written a very up-to-date and thorough practical guide to the conduct of ethology with children.

[7] Comparative research has both extended and restricted the range of applicability of prominent theories of human behavior and development. For example, Parker (1977) has found that Piaget's model for sensorimotor development can be successfully extended to nonhuman primates such as the macaque, while Lancy (1983), using a method referred to as "experimental anthropology" (Cole et al. 1971), has shown that Piaget's model for development in later stages has a much narrower range of applicability than was first thought.

[8] Pellegrini (1991) provides a more thorough discussion of these distinctions.

[9] For a review and summary of this and similar studies, see Anderson & Burns (1990).

[10] In academe, social psychology is "shared" by psychology and sociology.

5 The Case Study

With no formally agreed-on procedure whereby students were to be dismissed . . . attempts at coordination of bus times with existing district schools resulted in uncertainties, long waits, growing parental disapproval. . . . the noise level . . . was high in all of the divisions, and the staff was unable to speak loudly enough to be heard by all of the children. Initially, in the Basic Skills Division, teachers had to do the reading instead of the students. This minimized opportunities for pupil oral reading. In the Transition Division three whistles were in evidence, and in the ISD, Liz, among others, was losing her voice and she "couldn't hear herself." (p. 156)

This painful scene was recorded by Lou Smith and Pat Keith (1971) in their *Anatomy of an Educational Innovation*. Actually, Kensington School incorporated numerous innovations, but it was the ". . . new and uniquely designed elementary school building" (p. 6) that prompted the study.

In addition to the radically designed building, other innovative elements included the provision of three clusters rather than the usual six grades; team teaching; the elimination of textbooks (staff were to design, produce, and market their own curricula); and the use of technology. The staff were not just new to the school, the majority were new to the district; many had been hired from outside the St. Louis area. The majority had MAs, three had nearly completed their doctorates, and all were liberal Democrats who had strongly student-centered views of teaching. Seven of the twenty were in their first year of teaching; nine of the twenty were male. Is this a recipe for disaster or for radical, progressive change?

As Smith and his colleagues follow the fortunes of the school over a 15-year period (Smith et al., 1987), Kensington goes through several major changes. Its initial phase ends abruptly after two years, as the superintendent and principal who had conceptualized and created the school left the district, while 18 of the original teachers were gone within four years. During that brief period, however, the school enjoyed its "moment in the sun." Featured on national television in a documentary on innovations in education, it also played host to hundreds of visitors from around the world.

Anatomy is replete with vivid and dramatic vignettes, which convey the essence of what was happening at Kensington far better than tables full of test scores and attitude survey results. It is compiled from nearly daily participant observation during the 1965–1966 school year, formal interviews with nearly every staff member, and analysis of written records and transcribed recordings of the very frequent staff meetings.

The case study differs in significant ways from the ethnography or the field study. Hence, quite a bit of the chapter gives an overview of the case study, using Linda McNeil's study of social studies instruction to illustrate these ideas. This first section concludes with a very straightforward list of the main attributes of a case study. We then proceed to review a series of case studies of innovations in education beginning with a second look at Kensington's open plan. I have broken these innovations down according to their underlying philosophies—progressive, conservative, and mandated.

Among the progressive innovations, we will examine a "lab" school in New York City, similar in many respects to Kensington. Then we consider *Thinkabout*—designed to foster critical thinking skills. The case study of *Thinkabout* is part of a larger, essentially quantitative analysis of the program. A case study of the California Mathematics *Framework* is focused primarily on change among teachers, while *Pathways* focuses on parents. We review a couple more progressive programs—those that permit students and/or teachers greater autonomy and authority—before turning to a comprehensive study of *SPECS*, an extremely conservative effort to restrict student and teacher autonomy. This study was undertaken by noted anthropologist Harry Wolcott and flirts with the border between case study and ethnography. We then follow Huberman and Miles as they compare outcomes from several case study evaluations. They offer a number of methodological inventions, including the *qualitative data display*. As we move through the chapter, the case studies become more complex, more structured and less "qualitative." This is particularly true in studies of two federally mandated programs for minority youths. Finally, we consider the trade-offs between an emphasis on *formative evaluation*—where the case study author's sole purpose is to help developers improve the program—and *generalization*—where the case study investigator seeks to generalize about some aspects of the phenomenon of interest. Along the way we garner ideas about why innovations succeed or fail and about the way case studies are conducted and reported.

THE CASE STUDY METHOD

The studies reported in previous chapters have not had a primary concern with *policy*. The issues that were addressed were important to the investigator—to his/her discipline or tradition—but they were not necessarily the sorts of issues that immediately command the attention of teachers, administrators, school board members, and so on. It is the direct policy implications of their research that sets those who do case studies apart from other qualitative researchers. Smith and his colleagues *do* ask the kinds of questions to which educational personnel, as opposed to academics, are interested in answers.

In many respects, however, I must agree with Lincoln and Guba's (1985) assertion that ". . . while the literature is replete with references to case studies and with examples of case study reports, there seems to be little agreement about what a case study is" (p. 360). "Definitions of a case study vary widely . . ." (p. 214). These views are echoed by Merriam (1988): ". . . material on case study as a research strategy can be found everywhere and nowhere" (p. xi). ". . . There is little precision in the use of the term *case study* . . . [it] has become a catch-all category" (p. xii). "Case study," like ethnography, is used as a synonym for qualitative research, even by those who write about it as a method (e.g., Merriam 1988; Yin 1984). Nevertheless, Yin (1984) does give us a "handle" to begin to grasp the unique attributes of the case study. According to him, the case study has:

> . . . at least four different applications. The most important is to *explain* the causal links in real-life interventions that are too complex for the survey or experimental strategies. A second application is to *describe* the real-life context in which an intervention has occurred. Third, an evaluation can benefit, again in a descriptive mode, from an illustrative case study—even a journalistic account—of the intervention itself. Finally, the case study strategy may be used to explore those situations in which the intervention being evaluated has no clear, single set of outcomes. (p. 25)

The case study, used alone or as part of large-scale quantitative study, is the method of choice for studying interventions or innovations—and education is replete with these. One would be hard pressed to visit any school at any point in time that was not in the process of implementing and/or trying out new curricula, technology, staffing arrangements, or student assessment procedures.

Patton (1990) is critical of conventional, quantitative evaluation efforts. "Case studies are manageable, and it is more desirable to have a few carefully done case studies with results one can trust than to aim for large, probabilistic samples with results that are dubious because of the multitude of technical, logistic, and management problems . . ." (p. 100). He says that most program evaluation is based on the false premise that educational interventions are "true experiments," when in fact uneven implementation of programs, self-interest of participants, and the difficulty of specifying (let alone measuring) "outcomes" makes it too easy and too likely to explain away or ignore negative results.

A personal experience that is consistent with Patton's skepticism re: quantitative evaluation occurred at a recent conference, where I heard a talk (Wolfe 1987) entitled "Effects of a Developmental Guidance Curriculum on the Interpersonal Cognitive Problem-Solving Skills and Social Behavior of Elementary Pupils." The author presented an exhaustive catalog of results tables covering a plethora of outcomes and, without exception, statistical analyses yielded "no effects." Then, with no transition whatsoever, the presenter concluded by saying, in effect, "But, thank goodness our program was just re-funded for another three years." The point is that advocates *and* opponents of a particular innovation can be remarkably resistant to quantitative data and statistical analysis, but the narrative account of success or failure, liberally seasoned with spicy observations and quotations, is much harder to resist. Qualitative research, relatively open ended and concerned with "how" as well as "how well," can much more honestly depict these contextual factors. Stake (1983) refers to the "responsive" quality of the case study:

> An educational evaluation is responsive evaluation if it orients more directly to program activities than to program intents, if it responds to audience requirements for information, and if the different value perspectives of the people at hand are referred to in reporting the success and failure of the program. (p. 292)

The case study does not earn blanket approval, however. Many see it as a costly alternative, further ". . . assuming that one does take the time to produce a worthy case study, the product may be deemed too lengthy, too detailed or too involved for busy policy makers and educators to read and use" (Moore 1986:33).

This suggests that the case study is subject to an *efficiency* standard that is missing in much qualitative research, e.g.,

> Highly inductive and loosely designed studies make good sense when researchers have plenty of time and are exploring exotic cultures, understudied phenomena, or very complex social realities. But when one is interested in some better-understood social phenomena within a familiar culture or subculture, a loose, highly inductive design is a waste of time. Months of fieldwork and voluminous case studies will yield a few banalities. (Miles & Huberman 1984b:27)

I do not want to imply that the case study is only used when one aims to evaluate a new program. It just so happens that innovation in education is fueled almost exclusively by grants; and granting agencies, not unreasonably, demand an accounting of what was done with these funds. Many requests for proposals (RFP) specifically require that project directors set aside at least 6 percent of the budget to hire an "outside" evaluator. Consequently, these mandated evaluations have been the stimulus for much research, including many single and multiple case study projects.

But one can do a case study, which is not an evaluation of a specific innovation. One such project that may well have an impact on policy is Linda

McNeil's (1986) study of the teaching of social studies in four high schools. In effect, she chose to evaluate average or normal patterns of instruction. She found that: "Defensive teaching was observed at each of these high schools . . . teachers . . . choose to simplify content and reduce demands on students in return for classroom order and minimal student compliance on assignments" (p. 158). McNeil probes further to discover the reason for this distressing state of affairs:

> Having reached middle age or seen their paychecks long ago outstripped by inflation, the teachers said that they no longer felt the energy and drive to do whatever was necessary to make students understand. They felt that neither the support nor the financial reward was commensurate with the out-of-class time needed to prepare learning activities adequately, or to read and comment on the student essay tests or written assignments that a real treatment of such topics would require . . . A second factor was the minimal effort students seemed willing to put forth. In two of the four schools, over half the juniors and seniors interviewed worked more than twenty hours per week in addition to going to school full-time. . . . Whatever school effort students were willing to spend, they saved for . . . math and science . . . courses, which they saw as more instrumental to job futures . . . Tired, bored and rushed to cover content, teachers and students met in a path of least resistance. (p. 176)

Following is a summarization of some of the general attributes of the case study:

1. Case study is a qualitative method and, although it ". . . does not claim any particular [techniques] for data collection or data analysis" (Merriam 1988:10), the investigator is more likely to utilize the techniques associated with other qualitative methods such as ethnography than with, say, the experimental or survey methods. Nevertheless, Smith (1986) strongly advocates *combining* qualitative and quantitative techniques.

2. However, case study does not adhere to the qualitative *paradigm*. Questions or issues are at least partly predetermined. What one studies is carefully delimited in advance. One adopts a realist rather than phenomenological stance, and one is not concerned particularly with *grounded theory*.

3. One's audience may include some subset of the academic community, but it *must* include some well-defined "client" group. This is not true, generally, for qualitative research. Further, unlike "participatory research" (see chapter 6), which does address the needs of participants, the primary audience for the case study is more likely to be those in authority—government bodies, school boards, administrators—than teachers, parents, or students.

4. As a corollary, one may meet one's "professional responsibility" as a researcher without necessarily publishing the results of the case

study. Indeed, some would argue (Patton 1990) that an oral report to one's clients may be a more effective way of presenting the results than a written report.

5. Case studies are often undertaken "under contract." Hence, the researcher's motives are primarily pecuniary rather than a quest for knowledge for its own sake. Thus the "typical" case study tends to be rather narrowly focused and atheoretical and will not be published. Therefore, the case studies reviewed in this chapter are admittedly atypical, but they are well written and address important methodological concerns. Most importantly, they are accessible.

6. Although, as I have indicated, a case study is not always construed as an evaluation, the researcher will assume an evaluative stance. She will explicitly or implicitly compare what she observes with some standard (e.g., McNeil 1986). Walker (1975), in his case study of a two-year-long project to develop an elementary school art curriculum,[1] continually contrasts what he observes with an implicit model of how curriculum development is "supposed to" occur: "If objectives were stated at all they came in the course of development work, not before it" (p. 99).

7. Likewise, the researcher is obligated to draw pointed conclusions from the case study, explicitly or implicitly making recommendations that will alter policy and/or practice. Walker's (1975) experience left him worried about the ". . . Kafkaesque image of thousands of teachers in schools . . . throughout the country . . . writing behavioral objectives . . . in response to demands from officials . . ." (p. 133).

Kensington Revisited

A number of policy issues were identified by Smith and his colleagues (Smith & Keith 1971; Smith et al. 1987) in their episodic, long-term study of Kensington School. First, a new and dynamic superintendent was able to capitalize on an opportunity—the need to build a new school to meet increasing enrollment—to implement several radical ideas that were floating around. Indeed, we will soon review another case study of a school attempting many of the same innovations at about the same time (Gross, Giacquinta, & Bernstein 1971). However, the superintendent's ideas were too advanced for what was, essentially, a lower-middle to working-class community, and soon ". . . school board members ran on a platform of firing the superintendent. . ." (Smith et al. 1987:44). While a new staff may have been an advantage in terms of their openness to innovation, their lack of experience was a hindrance, and too many strong egos (9 of 20 were male) made team teaching and democratic decision making very difficult.

From 1966 to 1976 Kensington entered a kind of golden era. Many of the innovations were retained, while a more experienced and conservative principal and staff helped to achieve a welcome increase in structure and routine. Parents and school board were reassured. ". . . intellectuality was a highlight of the school . . . the place was alive with ideas" (Smith et al. 1987:172).

A major shift occurred in Kensington's climate from the mid-1970s, precipitated by a change in the surrounding community from nearly 100 percent White suburbia to 60 percent Black "urban fringe." When Smith and his colleagues visit in 1979 after a 15-year absence:

> The unpleasant effect of barbed wire around the roof's periphery is punctuated by heavy metal grills, anti-vandal screens . . . broken glass and other litter spread over the playground . . . graffiti etched into . . . front door: "This school sucks!" . . . the office space, once open and airy, is now cluttered . . . (pp. 85–87) . . . transformation of the audiovisual nerve center to a remedial reading classroom; and, of course, the erection of walls throughout much of the interior of the building. (p. 175) . . . The change in the physical appearance of Kensington was nothing compared to . . . the radical shifts in pedagogy . . . [which] began with the fears of the staff who[se] . . . urgent need . . . to cope with the new student group drove them back to what . . . seemed to offer hope for the most control: self-contained classrooms, rigid curriculum, and tight—even coercive discipline . . . the issues of race, inner-city, and poverty, in the principal's eyes, are part of the influences that have taken the Kensington School from the most innovative school in the district to one of the most traditional in the district. (pp. 75–76) [Or, in the authors' view]: "From the culture of intellectual excitement to the culture of poverty."[2] (Smith et al. 1987:168)

In the final analysis, Smith and his colleagues believe that ". . . social change overwhelms educational innovations" (p. 282). Kensington, despite formidable odds, had managed to incorporate a progressive, child-centered Deweyian vision of elementary schooling. This case study, based on two periods of intensive participant observation by students and faculty from Washington University, with gaps filled by lengthy interviews with key informants, including many no longer with the district, is unique in its broad scope.

PROGRESSIVE INITIATIVES

In 1966–67, another study was done of a progressive innovation in Cambire, a New York City school, which occupied a nearly 100-year-old building. Cambire was similar to Kensington in several respects. It was created as part of an administrator-launched reform effort; designated as a "lab school," and incorporated what all acknowledged was a drastically different vision of the respective roles of teacher and pupil. The lab school ". . . viewed the teacher as assisting children to learn according to *their* interests throughout the day . . . children are seen as different types of candles to be lit; the task of the teacher is to light each candle. . . . The pupil is given primary responsibility of directing his own education . . . [therefore the teacher's] primary function [is] as a guide" (Gross et al. 1971:12–13). The researchers:

wanted to obtain a detailed description of the organizational dynamics
that occurred after the introduction of a major innovation into an educational organization . . . and . . . the case study method was elected
because it provided a . . . way to explore the complex . . . problem we proposed to study . . . [with] provision for the use of a variety of data-gathering methods . . . (p. 42–43)

Nonparticipant observers used a small notebook to "jot down . . . key
phrases . . . as the basis for . . . [later writing up] expanded notes" (p. 55).
Archival material was gathered, including school newsletters, teaching schedules, and reports prepared for the funding agency. Their initial impression
was that teachers were favorable to innovation in general, but they ". . . did
not have a clear understanding of the innovation [and] . . . appeared to be
receiving little help . . . from their administrators, who had asked them to
change their role performance . . ." (p. 57).

The lab school had a low pupil/teacher ratio; teachers were given a substantial salary boost to stay late two afternoons a week for staff meetings;
they also developed new curricula during the summer, and per-pupil expendi-
ture was double that in surrounding schools. Staff were specially selected as
being likely to succeed in a lab school.

However, problems were apparent from the start, and the authors make
a point of stressing the thoroughness of their interviews. They interviewed all
teachers, including student teachers, for an average of four 45-minute sessions,
although it was difficult pinning teachers down for these interview sessions.

From these interviews they constructed a "data display" to show what
commonly occurred and also what was missing: "The key idea of the innovation . . . the teacher . . . as catalyst was only touched on . . . furthermore,
these teachers could not, in spite of persistent probing, specify what it meant
to be a 'guide' or 'supporting'" (p. 125).

For a period of three weeks the investigators made random, unan-
nounced visits to observe in the classrooms. Their focus was on the behavior
of the teacher. Twelve criteria were used to determine the teacher's compliance with the new model, e.g., "permit students to choose their own activities, permit students to interact with each other. . . . These . . . criteria were
selected on the basis of an analysis of documents describing the new role
model . . ." (p. 95–96). These criteria guided their observations and the analysis of their notes. They found that overall, teachers had adopted the new
model of instruction only to a very limited degree, using it from 0 percent to
20 percent of the time. The most notable alteration was the incorporation in
many classes of "free play" time (p. 119). From the authors' conclusions it is
clear that the administrators who developed the Cambire model were quite
naive with respect to the difficulties teachers would encounter. The teachers
got little advice in general and, in particular, found the child-centered philosophy to be incompatible with a constant stream of problems: "pupil discipline . . . misuse of materials . . . lack of interest and motivation" (p. 133).

My own experience in a lab school between 1984 and 1987 confirms the impression garnered from this work (Gross et al. 1971) that the very term *lab school* is often an oxymoron. I was particularly interested in exploring the possible uses of microcomputers to create a new means of instruction. I found that the lab school staff were willing to seriously consider only those applications of the microcomputer that supported their current methods of instruction; hence, I had to create a kind of "school within a school" (actually after-school and summer-school classes) to explore various models for computer use in schools (Lancy 1987).[3]

Critical Thinking

A decade or so before the microcomputer came on the scene, there was a great deal of interest in the instructional use of television. *Thinkabout*, a series of sixty fifteen-minute programs, was developed for use in fifth- and sixth-grade classrooms to teach critical thinking skills, including: ". . . finding alternatives . . . using criteria . . . and collecting information" (Sanders & Sonnad 1982:1). It was evaluated by Jim Sanders and his assistants using a hybrid quantitative/qualitative design. The authors' goal was not to evaluate *Thinkabout* per se, but rather ". . . enlightenment, guidance in the use of *Thinkabout*, and planning for school television, in general . . . [Their research was organized around a series of questions, such as] . . . who made the decision to adopt [*Thinkabout*] into the curriculum? . . . How much change can be seen in students with respect to the series' basic goals?" (p. 3).

Testing was carried out in 241 classrooms, and 2,000 questionnaires were returned. While the survey results were highly positive, test results were mixed and the case studies raised serious questions about some of the *Thinkabout* project's underlying premises. One such finding was that ". . . students perceived it as a break from work . . . [because there were] . . . few if any assignments, tests or projects—graded or ungraded—pertaining to it" (p. 10).

One of the in-depth case studies was conducted by Hart-Landsberg (1982) in a fifth-grade class serving primarily White, middle-class children. As a trained anthropologist Hart-Landsberg was obviously given considerable autonomy, and this case study is unusually comprehensive given its complementary nature vis-à-vis the quantitative components of the study. For example, to buttress her observations of *Thinkabout* in one class, she visited several other classes during *Thinkabout* broadcasts to gauge the degree of "typicality" of the case study teacher and her class. With respect to the former: ". . . she is more interested in social development (family influences, emotions, interpersonal relations) than cognitive development (particular skills acquired, levels of achievements, academic aspirations)" (p. 17). Hart-Landsberg also seeks out other instances of critical thinking instruction taking place in this particular class. Although there were several, she finds that the teacher and class handle most of these "thought-provoking" opportunities in a shallow manner, using discussion exclusively. The issues are not used as a catalyst for further study and research.

The lack of correspondence between the published program schedule and the actual broadcast schedule thoroughly frustrated the teachers' limited attempts to foreshadow the programs and direct post-program discussions. Hence, ". . . The teacher and students did not appear to be self-consciously thinking about thinking. Rather, they seemed to try out a few isolated modes of thought without closely evaluating their effectiveness, associating them with the types of situations they fit, or comparing them" (p. 35).[4] And there was only one ". . . program which seems to have prodded the brightest minds in the class to probe deeply for ideas that were not immediately forthcoming" (p. 31).

Hence, while the quantitative data show positive attitudes towards *Thinkabout*, the case study material helps to illuminate why the test results were unspectacular. Everyone liked it but, in many cases, perhaps the majority, the program was used as a time filler, a break from "work"—students were not given an opportunity to expand on their own knowledge base or improve their ability to process information. This teacher was unable to use the program to challenge students' preconceptions. On the contrary, as in the classes McNeil (1986) observed, there was an "Avoidance of incendiary issues . . . religion, morality, power . . . money, sex, love" (p. 37).

Because of the thoroughness of Hart-Landsberg's study (it runs 172 pages; at one point she uses three pages to present a verbatim transcription of one post-program discussion), any member of one of the several sponsoring agencies should have had no difficulty "experiencing" *Thinkabout* in a classroom setting—a distinct virtue of the well-done case study.

The California Mathematics Framework

Hart-Landsberg's (1982) study, the Kensington study, and several more to be described below, approximate the holistic thoroughness of an ethnography or field study, but what faith can we place in a research project where the non-participant observer spends only three class periods observing the phenomena of interest (Wilson 1990)? That depends. A great deal, if the field of inquiry is carefully delimited; if the observation is supplemented by lengthy interviews with the teacher; if the study is one of a set of parallel case studies; and if the research team has carefully prepared their ground and drawn on published material and official documents to delineate the theoretical, and political context for this particular innovation. Such is certainly true for a study conducted by a team of faculty members from Michigan State University.

This group sought to study the impact of a new mathematics Framework adopted by the State of California in 1985 and intended to achieve profound change in the way math is taught in the schools. Textbook publishers were advised to adopt the Framework, e.g., ". . . emphasize understanding rather than rules and to include novel topics [and] . . . if they did not make major changes, their book would be struck from . . . the adoption list" (p. 350). The Framework also precipitated change in the state's student achievement test. Twenty-three second- and fifth-grade teachers in three school districts varying in size, SES, and ethnicity were studied. Background or "policy context" was established by reviewing documents, and on-site and telephone interviews were conducted with key policy makers at state, district, and building levels. The study team visited the 23 teachers twice in December 1988 and once in March 1989, two years after the Framework had first been introduced. Observations of math lessons were supplemented by several two-hour-long interviews on: ". . . what the teacher was trying to teach, why the teacher was trying to teach it, how the teacher was trying to teach the material, and what the teacher thought the students got out of the lesson" (p. 260).

Let's consider the case of second-grade teacher Carol Turner (Ball 1990): ". . . her storehouse of devices includes . . . manipulatives . . . stories . . . metaphors, and gimmicks" (p. 265). She emphasizes hands-on, active engagement, conveys enthusiasm for math, and devotes a long period each day to math instruction." While at first glance Carol appears to be in harmony with the Framework, a closer analysis reveals incongruities—for example, she does not subscribe to fundamental Framework premises: ". . . mathematics . . . is something human beings have created and continue to construct . . . is inherently beautiful and fascinating . . . a domain of inquiry . . . as making and pursuing conjectures" (p. 272). She does not view mathematics the way mathematicians and others who use math creatively view it. She does not have a "whole language" view of mathematics (cf. Edelsky 1990). Ball's interpretation of the few lessons she observes as reflecting fundamental deviation from the Framework, is strengthened by the interviews with Carol: "Carol has not actually spent any time studying the Framework or thinking about its implications for her practice . . . she stores it in a box . . ." (p. 270).

Like Carol, Mark (Wilson 1990) is ". . . an energetic and enthusiastic teacher . . . [he] . . . has a reputation in the school for 'straightening out' troubled kids." "His students score very well in statewide achievement tests" (p. 309). However, Mark was unable to understand the Framework approach as he . . . "understood mathematics to be a set of procedures that students needed to master . . . and concentrated on teaching students the methods he knew. He neither chose to help students generate their own algorithms nor explained how or why his procedures worked" (p. 312).

The other three case studies in this volume (and one presumes the 18 others that were not reported) all tell a similar tale: even with very good teachers, even with those who are in synch with many aspects of the Framework, a drastic change in policy has had seemingly little impact on practice, a familiar theme in these studies of innovation (Cohen 1989).

Enhancing Literacy Experiences at Home and School

A case study by the late David Logsdon and his colleagues (1988) suggests that parents are no quicker to change their instructional practices than are teachers. The study is also interesting because it reflects a refreshing degree of candor on the part of the researchers, who were also the program developers. Pathways was a ". . . new parent participation program [introduced] into a black, low-income, urban school . . ." (p. 24). A great deal of data were collected during the very close monitoring of the project and, gradually, the focus of their research shifted from an evaluation of the Pathways activities to a consideration of the broader social and cultural issues that were implicated. "From our rather naive stance at the beginning, we have learned a great deal about teacher and parent involvement, parent/student activities . . . and the conduct of responsive evaluation . . ." (p. 36).

A lesson that seems to need to be learned anew by each potential innovator is reflected in this comment: "It was never the teachers' project . . . they never embraced it with a level of enthusiasm that indicates commitment and ownership. Rather, the project belonged to and came from an external source: the university's faculty and staff . . ." (p. 35). Another lesson was that a majority of parents were not interested in "becoming involved" (see also Lancy & Zupsic 1994), and the highest priority for those who were was "helping children with homework."

I would like to end this section on somewhat of an optimistic note by describing a case study of an innovation that seems to have "taken hold," at least in one classroom. Carole Edelsky and her students, Kelly Draper and Karen Smith (1983), report on the classroom dynamics during the first few weeks of the school year in the latter's sixth grade class. The innovation in question is the use of *whole language* philosophy (Edelsky et al. 1991) to guide the development of a language arts curriculum. Whole language, as contrasted with "bottom-up" or molecular approaches to teaching reading, emphasizes the importance of meaning construction and the use of authentic texts, rather than dittoed "exercises." It is, in many ways, more complicated than other methods and there should be striking differences in the way the classroom is organized. The authors used ". . . the teachers' goals, as revealed in interviews, as organizers of data" (Edelsky et al. 1983:263). They ended up with eight, including "To get students to see opportunities everywhere for learning" (p. 263). Indeed, the qualities that Karen Smith seeks to infuse in her classroom bear more than a superficial resemblance to the qualities that one sees in the philosophies underlying Kensington, Cambire, and the California *Framework*.

Karen's class was selected because she was considered to be a model exponent of the whole language philosophy and because her sixth graders, poor, Hispanic, and the recipients of at least five years of a "basic skills" approach to language instruction, might be expected to experience difficulty and display "resistance" when exposed to a radically different form of instruction (see also Meeks & Lancy n.d.).

Edelsky and Draper conducted ". . . participant observation of teacher-student interaction all day, every day for the first two weeks of school and then three days per week for the next three weeks. Video and audio tape recordings, made periodically, were used to confirm and modify the focus for further observation" (p. 261). From their notes they documented the myriad strategies Smith uses to give students "freedom without license," including "privatizing reprimands" and "minimal guidance," which was effective because ". . . when students carried out their own rather than the teacher's tasks, . . . they already knew what they would do" (p. 272). These terms, while not *emic* (e.g., not Karen Smith's), nevertheless are clearly *grounded in the data*; that is, "privatizing reprimands" is a carefully phrased gloss to describe a pattern which was frequently found in the notes and videotapes.

Student interviews provide another "leg" of the triangulated inquiry and one of the more revealing findings here was that ". . . despite conducting science experiments, participating in discussions, rehearsing reading performances they would later give for first graders, and so on, they thought that . . . so far they hadn't done any 'work'" (p. 262). Finally, quantitative data were used to show that the class was "successful" in more conventional terms as well—e.g., better attendance, higher levels of academic engagement, and higher standardized test scores.

CONSERVATIVE INITIATIVES

Managing and Teaching by Objectives

Harry Wolcott's (1977) *Teachers vs. Technocrats*, a ". . . case study in educational innovation . . ." (p. 1) makes for painful reading—not because the innovation was not successful but because, although obviously doomed from the start, it continued to consume tax dollars ($1 million +) and the time and energy of a group of fine "teachers and technocrats" for years! But it also makes fascinating reading because it reveals so clearly the often ambivalent role of the evaluator. In brief, Wolcott was hired to study the *process* whereby an innovative information management system was developed and trialed in the South Lane (Cottage Grove, OR) School District. He maintains his distance and neutrality in the face of teachers who are concerned that they are being (perhaps unfairly) evaluated; developers whose jobs and/or careers may be on the line; Wolcott's faculty colleagues at Oregon; gung-ho administrators, and so on. After reading this, one is not surprised by Wolcott's confession that "Through my participation in this study I have also realized that I am far more favorably disposed towards basic research efforts that seek to learn about schools than towards developmental efforts that seek to manipulate educational processes" (p. 3).

Before proceeding to describe Wolcott's methods, an epistemological digression is in order. In the first chapter, I discussed the problem of defining the researcher's perspective—should she maintain an independent, perhaps even skeptical or antagonistic stance, or should she totally adopt the perspective of the people whose work she is studying? William Foote Whyte (1984), a great advocate of the latter position, happily reports on two doctoral students doing dissertation research in the third world, one who joined an armed resistance movement and the second who organized and led a postal workers' strike. This question takes on a special urgency when applied to the case study, because the findings can inevitably be read as reflecting on how well someone is doing their job. Hemwall (1986) identifies the conflict between protecting informants whose jobs might be threatened versus ". . . the need for the forthright answers required in an honest evaluation . . ." (p. 149).

In the case studies reviewed to this point we've seen variations on this theme. Smith and his colleagues have nothing to do with the development of the Kensington School, but they are clearly excited by and sympathetic towards all these new ideas. Wolcott makes abundantly clear his lack of sympathy for the *SPECS* project. His Introduction is subtitled: *Bias at Work: Proceed with Caution.* Gross, Giacquinta and Bernstein (1971) seem to come closest to Patton's (1990) ideal "neutrality"; one doesn't detect whether they were for or against the innovations at Cambire. Hart-Landsberg (1982) maintains a healthy skepticism; like these others she's a hired outsider. Edelsky, Draper and Smith (1983) have differentiated roles, and the systematic reporting of their data collection and analysis techniques inspires confidence. Also they stick to the "how?" question, which is a lot less sticky than "how well?" On the other hand, Logsdon, Taylor and Bloom (1988), as well as Lancy (Lancy, Forsyth, & Meeks 1987; Lancy & Hayes 1988) are developer/researchers, and their reports reveal the inherent conflict that this dual role entails. Finally, we might cite Papert's (1980) "case study" of his own educational innovation, the *LOGO* programming language, which doesn't even leave open the possibility of failure.

SPECS was developed during an "accountability" movement that swept the schools in the early 1970s, and its essence is reflected in the following: ". . . School district personnel engage in a particular kind of rational, data-based planning of the district's operating programs . . . involving . . . development of an initial plan, implementation of that plan, collection of outcome information, analysis of expected and actual outcomes, generation of alternatives, selection of a new plan, implementation of it, and so forth . . ." (Wolcott 1977:24). With very little assistance and with the program constantly undergoing revision, teachers were expected to implement the model at the classroom level by developing a set of objectives for each subject area, specifying what they would do to reach those objectives, and then carefully recording student progress towards meeting the objectives. Resistance from teachers was pronounced due to the loss of autonomy, their antipathy towards the superintendent and the developers (all of whom were seen as pursuing primarily their own career self-interests), and their belief that the *basic skills, mastery learning* philosophy imbedded in *SPECS* wasn't *needed* in their classrooms. ". . . teachers enjoyed toying with alternative labels that would accurately reflect their sentiment toward the program. One popular acronym. . . was CRAP—for Curriculum Recycling And Planning" (Wolcott 1977:82).

While Wolcott, in one sense, passes immediate judgment on *SPECS*, in another sense he is unable to reach any conclusion or lead the reader to any conclusion about the program's worth. This is because it was never really *implemented* in any sense that the developers would acknowledge: ". . . the developers had never specified exactly what constituted *SPECS* . . ." (p. 87). This failure of developers to specify the nuts and bolts of their innovative visions, coupled with the teachers' "filter," makes a final determination (*summative evaluation*) of whether an innovation "works" nearly impossible. For example, Anderson (1977) sums up the massive, multimillion-dollar evaluation of Project Follow Through, a comparison of 22 theoretically inspired models to compensate for fall-off in Head Start gains. There was no clear advantage for any program; rather: "The effectiveness of each Follow Through model depended more on local circumstances than on the nature of the model" (p. 13).

However, Wolcott is not particularly concerned that he cannot evaluate *SPECS*, because he capitalizes on the opportunity given to him as the "staff ethnographer" to look at larger, more enduring issues. In particular, he uses most of the book to discuss the different worldviews held by teachers and technocrats. In fact, he offers separate narrative accounts of the *SPECS* project from both perspectives and draws on constructs from anthropology to aid his analysis. Ultimately, ". . . *SPECS* . . . seemed simply to fade away without any dramatic final collapse" (p. 239), although it is clear that it would have faded away years earlier had it not been for the steady infusion of federal funds. One staff member commented: "This is what happens when Universities go whoring after federal dollars" (p. 110).

Aggregating Case Study Data

Some sense of the enormous number of programmatic educational innovations supported by various levels of government can be gleaned from Huberman and Miles' (1984b) comparative analysis. They conducted 12 in-depth case studies as part of a quantitative evaluation of 146 projects funded by the National Diffusion Network or Title IV-C. Sites were selected to reflect the inherent diversity in the larger sample, e.g., region of country, setting, program status (expanding, ongoing, dwindling), and program content (early childhood, reading/math, social studies), and so on. However, ". . . most of the programs we studied entailed few organizational changes; they were mostly modest, manageable, content-oriented efforts" (p. 6). During site visits the investigators used observations and interviews to ask fairly general questions, such as "What was the school like before [the innovation] entered the picture?" (p. 9). Site visits were often timed to coincide with a "decisive event . . . a district office meeting, staff planning sessions . . ." (p. 8). They reviewed documents, but in some cases ". . . the paper trail was almost nonexistent" (p. 9).

Data collection was done by hired assistants. Their observations were dictated after site visits and were then typed and coded by the "principal investigators." They started with 34 research questions. As they worked through the data, they identified 31 "core variables" (p. 13). As new data came in, there was a need to revise the code. However, the ". . . coding system stabilized fairly [early] . . . so a minimum of back recoding was required" (p. 15). All this discussion of codes, variables, the use of research assistants, structured interviews, 8–12 days observation, and so on should give us pause. Is this research qualitative? Indeed, Miles and Huberman, in *Qualitative Approaches to Evaluation in Education* (1988), acknowledge that their work fails to adhere to most canons of the qualitative paradigm. However, their report of a "power struggle" in one site suggests they were not blind to nuance. Further, there is evidence that they derive their categories *from the data*. Regardless of where we place Miles and Huberman on the qualitative-quantitative continuum, we must acknowledge the enormous contribution they have made to the repertoire of tools for data reduction and display to which the qualitative researcher has access. Annette Lareau's (1989b) field study is very evidently qualitative, but she freely acknowledges her debt to them.

Masepa School District was an example of a site where the innovation (*ECRI*: ". . . a highly regimented and task-oriented behavior modification teaching strategy" [Huberman & Miles 1984:26]) did have a fairly large impact on practice. That is, many teachers adopted the *ECRI* model. Miles and Huberman (1984b:46) developed a technique for analyzing qualitative data and creating a qualitative "data display." Some of their categories are externally imposed, such as "initial attitude toward program." Some are derived from the data ("self-improvement," "social influence"); some are low inference ("early users," "administrators"); and some high inference ("centrality"). The data display provides a kind of middle ground between narrative description (Miles and Huberman are very critical of narrative description in evaluation reports) and frequency tables.[5]

Miles and Huberman (1984b) identify 12 techniques that they use to "make sense" of qualitative data, for example: "When we identify a theme or pattern, we are isolating something (a) that happens a number of times and (b) that consistently happens in a specific way . . . [these] judgements are based on counting" (p. 215). They can then move towards quantification if this seems warranted. When they quantified their data regarding career moves (an unexpected and important theme), the analysis showed that, while there were a large number of job moves attributed to the innovation process, ". . . only 35 percent of the job-related shifts were upward ones, contrary to our early impression" (Miles & Huberman, 1984b:216). Note that they use quantitative data to check the credibility of their initial qualitative analysis of the data, in much the same way that others use qualitative material to check the validity of survey data. For example, Logsdon et al. (1988) discounted the high level of positive responses on their parent questionnaire because these were contradicted by more direct observation of the low parent participation in the Pathways project.

The principal findings of the Miles and Huberman comparative study are not aimed so much at determining which programs are good and which are bad but at a better understanding of the process itself: "As our analysis proceeded, we developed a more differentiated list of outcomes, as follows: . . . *stabilization of use* . . . [or] "settledness" of the new practice . . . *percentage of use . . . institutionalization,* the degree to which the innovation was . . . incorporated into the ordinary structures and procedures of the school . . ." (p. 188). There were some surprises as well: ". . . at least half the projects we were studying did have decisive effects on jobs changes . . . an example of a frequent, but largely unremarked, outcome of school improvement projects" (p. 188).[6]

The Evaluation of Mandated Initiatives

As Huberman and Miles (1984b) indicate, innovation may be enhanced by "external pressure." At the same time that various government entities promote various innovations on a voluntary basis, they also *mandate* change. Not surprisingly, innovations that occur as a result of these mandates are often implemented more smoothly. There is much less resistance as educators "bow to the inevitable."

Chesterfield (1986) reports on a multiple case study[7] of federally mandated bilingual Head Start programs. He does a very good job of characterizing this more ". . . 'formalized' qualitative research" (p. 147):

> . . . data collected . . . were sent weekly to the central office, where they were monitored by the supervisor/coordinator of field work . . . to provide a framework for comparing the models, a number of the qualitative data collection and data reduction procedures were standardized . . . observers' . . . job was not to define the nature of a particular social reality, but rather to focus on contextually relevant data that explained the presence or absence of outcomes or events expected by the model developers. (Chesterfield 1986:147–149)

Note the similarity in aim to the Thinkabout and Framework case studies reported above.

Although many of the large-scale studies reported in this chapter employed trained research assistants, this is one of the few reports that provides some information on how they were trained and managed.[8] Observers were further "controlled" by the use of "implementation forms" and "time and event samples" (p. 148). Descriptions of each site were written that focused on the feasibility of exporting the particular model under investigation. These lengthy descriptions were then reviewed by ". . . senior staff [who] distilled them into . . . categories, each containing a list of specific factors which the individual researchers had identified as facilitating or impeding implementation . . ." (p. 153).

Chesterfield (1986) presents only a sampling of the findings, e.g., ". . . a single half-day session was the most effective type of daily schedule . . ." (p. 153). He also indicates some of the ways that observational data were used to aid in interpreting or qualifying the test results. For example, "Spanish preferred" children had a very different pattern of language development over the year depending on whether they started the year "knowing some English."

Vanguard, the gifted and talented program in the Houston Public Schools, became a critical agent in the federally mandated desegregation effort. In particular, specific schools were designated as Vanguard or "magnet" schools. Thus, racial segregation was replaced by segregation based on academic talent. Ferrell and Compton (1986) describe their case study of Vanguard during the 1981–82 school year. They made three site visits for observation and also conducted open-ended interviews with key personnel, including 23 teachers, 9 counselors and 10 principals. Students were assessed in focus-group interviews; parents were surveyed by mail. One very interesting issue they address is that: "Despite the fact that one of the purposes of magnet schools is to integrate the district at both student and staff levels, questions related to whether or not prejudicial attitudes existed and the extent to which integration was taking place were deleted by administration" (p. 175). Others report similar problems, suggesting the level of antipathy towards evaluative research for which one should be prepared.

Overall their results reflected positively on the Vanguard program, academic achievement was high and, more importantly, there was little or no segregation or interracial conflict observed or mentioned in the interviews. "Vanguard students . . . stuck together. They were a very close multi-racial group" (p. 187). However, some problems were identified. Since the court order specified that any "magnet" program had to have a racial composition of 44 percent Black, 30 percent Hispanic, 23 percent White, and 3 percent Asian, many White applicants with higher scores were turned down than Black and Hispanic students who were admitted. The quality of teachers was uneven and wealthier parents, in particular (see also Lareau 1989b), were likely to be dissatisfied with the quality of teaching. Another problem was that the curriculum was not terribly distinctive; however, they did note a greater ". . . emphasis on the development of research skills by students" (p. 184).

Finally, Ferrell and Compton (1986) make a number of recommendations, including ". . . the development of a district-wide job description for Vanguard teachers . . . [also to] look for better ways to identify gifted minority children" (p. 190). These recommendations raise an important issue that we have just barely addressed. Despite what I said about the problem-solving nature of the case study in the introduction, one may not actually encounter any recommendations in the published report of the case study. First, this may happen because the authors may be concerned primarily with process rather than outcome (e.g., Wolcott 1977). Second, recommendations may well have been included in the unpublished report to one's clients but in published work addressed to other academics; the emphasis may be on aspects of methodology or grand theory (Smith & Keith 1971). Third, the report may indeed be aimed at a *summative* as opposed to *formative* evaluation (Scriven 1967). The former assumes that the innovation is "finished"—what we want to know is whether it worked (e.g., Robbins 1986), not how to improve it; while the latter assumes that there are still opportunities to modify the program, thereby rendering "recommendations" essential. The last case study to be reported in this chapter was designed from the start to serve the purpose of formative evaluation.

Mainstreaming is one of the legacies of PL94-142, described in the socio-logical perspectives chapter. Hemwall (1984) conducted a study designed to provide ". . . an understanding of *everyday* mainstreaming experiences" (p. 134, italics added) for a group of seven hearing-impaired students in a sec-ondary school. Aside from the clear emphasis on formative evaluation, her report is unusual in the thoroughness of the historical context she creates. She reviews attempts as far back as the 1820s to integrate deaf students into regu-lar classrooms. The study was conducted during the 1979–1980 school year. It was the third year of the program and it was not running smoothly, despite the fact that it was only a "part-time placement . . . and . . . [provided a] full range of supportive services including tutoring and sign interpreters in the classroom" (p. 136). The staff had mixed feelings about Hemwall, wanting her help but concerned that they would come out looking bad ". . . even though they had been assured that no direct evaluation of their teaching was being done" (p. 148). She played a *participant-observer* role (she was a tutor), which probably helped to ease these concerns.

Among the problems Hemwall was able to identify was that the hear-ing-impaired students made little attempt to "attend" to class proceedings as they became dependent on their note-taker/tutor/interpreter to teach them after class whatever was covered during class. Teachers reinforced this ten-dency by addressing remarks to the interpreter rather than to the students. The teacher also, unwittingly, gave them license to "tune out" by not holding them to the same discipline standards as the other students.

Hemwall (1986) made a number of formal recommendations—for example, the program should strive to promote independence on the part of students; and teachers should require much more inservice training to assist them in working with the hearing-impaired. However, she claims that ". . . the nature of [qualitative] data is such that it allowed the staff . . . to be actively in-volved. . . . They awaited the latest . . . tidbits . . . with great anticipation . . ." (p. 150). This contrasts with the enormous frustration that teachers involved in the *SPECS* project felt at not getting feedback from the researchers, which moved Wolcott (1977) to write: "'When are the developers allowed to learn what the researchers find out?' To a developer, the satisfactory answer is, 'as soon as possible.' To a researcher, the satisfactory answer is, 'As soon as the project's completed and the information itself will no longer affect the course of events'" (p. 89). But note that in the *SPECS* case the researchers were charged with the task of summative evaluation, even though it is very clear that *SPECS* was not by any means a finished product.

Indeed, the "in process" nature ("expanding," "ongoing," "dwindling") of so many innovations precludes *summative evaluation* in many cases. Even when summative data are called for and are available, their implications may be ignored (e.g., Wolfe 1987). Alkin, Daillak and White (1979) were interested in the question of just how evaluations (including both qualitative and quanti-tative studies) are used. They conducted case studies of five innovative projects in California that had a built-in evaluation component. In one case study the client felt hampered by the evaluation; the need to keep detailed records took time away from other things. Also, it was difficult to specify and measure "outcomes" as required by the terms of the grant. In this and other projects the teachers and administrators were unwilling to accept "standardized test scores" (which, presumably, didn't change) as evidence of the project's success or failure.[9] Another issue is that ". . . evaluators must be able to talk in the language of school people. Statistics frighten many people . . ." (p. 123). Indeed, many of the school personnel felt that the ". . . evaluator should be totally involved in the full range of activities" (p. 105). Overall, they found that where evaluation results were formative in nature, couched in the form of useable recommendations, they had an impact. If they were presented primarily after the fact as summative judgments, they tended to have less impact.

WHAT IS THE CASE FOR GENERALIZATION?

As we have seen, the norm in qualitative research is long-term immersion in the field, which gives credence to the researcher's claim to speak for all similar groups or situations: "If the truth be known, ethnographers, like the rest of us, make whopping generalizations from rather modest observations of a few cases. Their forte lies in knowing those cases exceedingly well and in recognizing a critical distinction between generalizing and over-generalizing" (Wolcott 1987:50). However, the examples presented in this chapter make clear that this criterion is rarely met in the case study. Instead Stake (1978) offers a different view of generalization as applied to the case study: ". . . case studies . . . may be . . . in harmony with the reader's experience and thus . . . a natural basis for generalization" (p. 5). Put differently, ". . . generalizability is ultimately related to what the reader is trying to learn from the case study" (Kennedy 1979:672). This is comparable to the law where the applicability of a particular precedent case must be argued in each subsequent case. The reader must decide whether the findings apply.

I referred earlier to Linda McNeil's (1986) study of "defensive teaching." In her 234-page book, McNeil's entire methods section takes up only a single 70-word paragraph. This brief statement alone hardly inspires confidence in McNeil's very broad generalization of her findings. However, I was prepared to treat them as credible because they so faithfully mirror my own observations and are consistent with findings in other case studies of instruction in high school.

What, then, can be said about *innovation* in education? I reproduce below two assessments written in 1971, the first in the United States and the second in the United Kingdom: ". . . negligible educational effects resulting from the numerous innovations that have been introduced into . . . schools" (Gross et al. 1971:4).

> For nearly two decades now, we have seen large amounts of capital invested in the production of a variety of new curricula. Unfortunately,

evidence is beginning to accumulate that much of this effort has had relatively little impact on the daily routine of the average classroom . . . [the writer goes on to identify the critical event in the process of extinction] . . . grant expires and . . . outside consultant or team leaves the scene. (Herron, cited in Stenhouse 1975:209)

Nevertheless, hope springs eternal and "programs" (e.g., as opposed to just spending lots more money than we do presently on salaries, materials, and physical plant; or drastically raising teaching certification standards) will continue to thrive. This means that studies of some sort in the form of quantitative evaluation or more naturalistic case studies will be drawn along in their wake. I would hope, therefore, that we can continue to improve these studies and that we seek to find a larger audience for the final report so that the public knowledge base (e.g., *ERIC*) will continue to grow—because, to agree with Stake (1978; 1995), most project directors will make more reasoned decisions if they have access to a rich collection of reports bearing on similar situations.

ENDNOTES

[1] For a more recent analysis of elementary arts curricula based on the perspective referred to as "educational criticism" see Barone (1987) and the critique of Barone's analysis by Rist (1987).

[2] The original culture of poverty theory comes from Lewis (1966) and has been critiqued by Valentine (1968). Much the same concept is now referred to as "the permanent underclass."

[3] We used interactive fiction to stimulate interest in reading (Lancy & Hayes 1988); simulation games to teach social studies (Forsyth & Lancy 1987, 1989; Lancy 1990); word processing in a composition class (Lancy, Forsyth, & Meeks 1987); and electronic construction sets to teach reasoning (Lancy 1991).

[4] More recently, Alan Davis (1996) has studied a classroom (fourth and fifth grades combined) whose teacher seemed to be following the whole language model with excellent results. Her urban minority students were very enthusiastic about school, and their test scores were well above expectations.

[5] A variety of computer programs which can be used to facilitate qualitative data analysis are described in Pfaffenberger (1988) and Tesch (1990); however, ". . . such programs are substitutes for scissors, typewriters, folders, index cards, and so on. They do not analyze or interpret data" (Merriam 1988:158).

[6] Stenhouse (1975), in an earlier comment, is critical of the involvement of teachers in curriculum development projects: "First, teachers working on projects give too much weight to their own past experiences, which is not as generalizable as they often assume. Second, teachers commonly change radically and rapidly on taking up an appointment with a project; they become curriculum developers!" (p. 221).

[7] Another example of such "formalized" qualitative research is the "team ethnography" described by Woods et al. (2000).

[8] But there is no information on how they were selected, and as Yin (1984) notes: "The problem is that we have little way of screening or testing for an investigator's ability to do good case studies" (p. 22).

[9] From my experience, the problem is not test scores per se but that inappropriate comparative data are provided. I believe "building level" personnel don't find "national norms" an appropriate reference point. Rather, comparison with the students' own previous score (e.g., "gain score") would be helpful, as would comparison data drawn from a similar population—for example, if you are teaching a second-grade class that is predominately Black and on ADC, you want to see reading scores for other students who fit this same developmental profile.

6

Personal Accounts

I decided to teach school and help with the family finance, but it was in the days before free public schools and I had no building in which to work. Brother Charles A. Terry loaned several planks and blocks with which to improvise seats. Sister Whitmore loaned me an old kitchen table of small size for a desk. I mustered up another degree of courage to ask the loan of a blackboard from the school. Their refusal abashed me and I felt belittled for having been turned down. Auntie came to my relief. She took the large bread board and painted it. This great board, four feet by two and one-half, I carried to Brother Kelsey that very night under cover of darkness, and for five cents, he gave me a good coating of blacking. A piece of white chalk from my husband's tool box, and I was equipped. Now for my trial class. (Kinkead 1997:98)

This is an excerpt from the unpublished reminiscences of Martha Cragan Cox that describes her initial attempts to establish a school in the frontier town of St. George, Utah in 1869. Written when Martha was 77, these reminiscences were meant for the edification and enjoyment of her many progeny. They reflect the enormous hardships faced by early public school teachers, who were "pioneers" in every sense of the word.

Cox's autobiography is part of a collection of autobiographical writings (including diaries, confessionals, and cradle-to-grave histories) assembled by Joyce Kinkead (1997). Kinkead had two broad aims in this task: first, to bring this obscure material to light and thereby illuminate important chapters in the history of teaching and the history of the western United States, and second, to redress a limited and one-sided view of the early Western "schoolmarm." Unlike most of the Western frontier where schoolteachers were unmarried, in Mormon Utah they not only married, many were, like Martha, the second, third, or even fourth wives in a polygamous arrangement. Martha's account is

127

filled with her struggles to support her own eight children as well as those of her co-wives with little help from her mostly absentee husband.

Kinkead provides the reader with lightly edited autobiographies so that the unique, *idiographic* aspects of these women's lives come through. However, by aggregating across 24 such personal accounts and by drawing on already published material, she also is able to search for and find *nomothetic* or general patterns that hold true for the group as a whole.

WHAT ARE PERSONAL ACCOUNTS?

This chapter differs from the others in an important respect. In prior chapters, I started with fairly well-established traditions and could write a largely descriptive account of what one finds when one samples the literature in a particular tradition—but *personal accounts* is not a term found in the literature.[1] Rather, I have pulled together and analyzed a great variety of material, which I see as naturally coalescing into a coherent body of scholarship in order to "invent" a personal accounts tradition.[2] I see this area as growing in importance, as we find that humans use story or narrative to organize their understanding and memory of events (Bruner 1986; Polkinghorne 1988) in general, and that our best access to teachers'[3] and students' understandings of the meaning of classroom experience may be through life history narratives rather than through structured classroom observations and interviews (Connelly & Clandinin 1990).

Personal accounts, as the name suggests, are different from other kinds of reports in the social science literature because they focus on whole lives, or "people in the round." The person is examined not just as a convenient exemplar of a category in which we are interested (e.g., *secondary social studies teacher*) but to get at his or her very personal life story, views, and accomplishments. However, the way in which these personal accounts are gathered, presented and analyzed varies enormously (Denzin 1989), and table 6-1 charts some of the more evident dimensions.

Before discussing the table, I want to stress again that there is much ambivalence about where in the overall scheme of things personal accounts belong. Madelein Grumet, who has drawn on life histories in her feminist analysis of teaching (1988), says, ". . . before I began to think of narratives as forms for educational research and criticism, I thought of them as literature" (p. 67). However, how can we treat life history material as research data when ". . . every telling is a potential prevarication . . . our stories are the masks through which we can be seen. . ." (p. 69). In short, I have done my best to present a tidy picture, but you should be aware the road ahead is a rough one.

As you can see in this table, personal accounts can be self-generated, or they can be solicited by a scholar—a "professional stranger." Clearly the purpose will differ. The autobiographer is not bound by the canons of scholarship to address a larger issue or question, for example. The Cox auto-

Table 6-1
Personal Accounts

	Life History	Case Study
Self-generated	Autobiography: memoir, chronicle, diary, reminiscence (Gardner, 1994; Robinson 1978; Walter 1981)	Teacher as researcher (Ray 1987)
Joint effort of subject and scholar	Compiled autobiography (Reilly 1990) Collection of autobiographies (Kinkead 1997; Schoen 1991)	Teacher-researcher collaboration (Clandinin 1986)
Generated by anthropologists, historians, psychologists, journalists	Biography (Strane 1990) Multiple biography (Clifford 1989) Collective Biography (Tyack & Hansot 1982)	Case study (Wolcott 1973) Multiple case study (Fordham 1996; Spencer 1986) Collective case study (Hargreaves 1984)

biography that opened the chapter actually lies in a fuzzy area between the two as, while the original material was self-generated, it is now in the hands of a scholar whose methods and purposes are quite different from Martha Cragan Cox and her fellow Mormon schoolteachers.

The autobiography itself can take on a variety of forms: diary, memoir, confessional. There seems to be a noticeable split between works that describe the author's life during a highly circumscribed period (e.g., *Where's My Apple? Diary of a First Year Teacher*, Walter 1981; Cooper & Heck 1995), which I refer to as a *chronicle*, and works that cover the entire life span (e.g., *Sarah Jane Foster: Teacher of the Freedman, A Diary and Letters*, Reilly 1990). The autobiography is a venerable literary form. What is considered the first "modern" autobiography was written in 1576 by a music tutor (Osborne 1961). For at least two hundred years, a hallmark of the educated person in Western society has been the keeping of a personal record, a journal, a diary, and/or the crafting of a reflective account later in life.

The existence of these materials is a boon to biographers and historians (Rury 1991). What determines whether or not one's (auto)biography is *published*? It seems this occurs for one of three reasons. Jesse Stuart's (1970) *To Teach to Love* makes very good reading, but would it have been published if he hadn't gone on from teaching to become a best-selling novelist? In other words, it helps to be famous. Alas, there were few famous teachers. Second, the individual in question may have been caught up in an important historical event or movement, as were the pioneering teachers whose accounts are reviewed in the next section. But teachers are not generals or political leaders, so again the published literature is not voluminous. Third, we often wish to ". . . record the direct testimony of those rare individuals who are able to provide us with a vivid picture of life in realms otherwise closed to us outsiders" (Langness & Frank 1981:5). Many of the portraits of Native Americans were published for this reason (e.g., "Ishi"—Kroeber 1961), as were oral histories of urban types (e.g., Stanley the "Jackroller"—Shaw [1930] 1966) collected by the Chicago School of Sociology. Dianne Manning's (1990) oral histories of teachers from rural Texas are an example from the genre of education.

I find that another important dimension is the *number* of accounts with which scholars are working. Single accounts focus on the subject and his/her perspective. Multiple accounts open up valuable opportunities for comparison and contrast and for addressing nomothetic problems; however, there is the danger that we will lose sight of the individual. The coherence of a single life is sacrificed for topical coherence. Indeed, this is the explicit methodology of the *collective* biography (e.g., Tyack and Hansot's [1982] history of the superintendency). *Biography* provides distance between the writer and the subject. At one time the subject must have been an important figure to qualify for biographical treatment, but beginning in the 1970s there has been a movement to spotlight the ordinary person—hence the explosion of work on teachers, prostitutes, women prisoners, frontier nuns—in fact, women in general.

Turning to the right side of table 6-1 we encounter the *case study*. In the case study, the focus shifts more obviously from the individual (Ed Bell) to the role (elementary school principal), although life historical details continue to be crucial to analysis and explanation. While we expect the subject of (auto)biography to be proudly identified, the subject of a case study is inevitably anonymous. One of the reasons for this is that the case study is (as we saw in the previous chapter) directly linked to the improvement of practice. Hence, judgments will be drawn; subjects may be identified as "typical" (Wolcott 1973), as "experienced" (Spencer 1986), or as "failures" (Knowles & Hoefler 1989).

The most evident difference between works I would place in the case-study as opposed to the life-history column is that the life-history material constitutes only a portion of the data collected on the individual or individuals. Hence, there are opportunities to triangulate among the various strands of data and to use insights gleaned from one's observations of the subject to guide one's elicitation of narrative material. Signithia Fordham's (1996) critical study of African-American high school students is a stellar example. While focusing on high versus low achievers and males versus females, she augments her portraits with extensive interviews with parents and teachers. In fact, by probing[4] students' personal accounts of schooling, she can offer a corrective to the prevailing wisdom: low-achieving African-American students are not ". . . helpless victims of the forces of society and the economic structure. They see clearly what their choices are" (p. 367).

Finally, those who do use case studies can choose to study a single individual (Knowles 1990) or a number of individuals whose individuality is retained (Spencer 1986); one can do a collective case study in which the subjects are blended together into a single composite portrait (Hargreaves 1984). Having said all that, let's have some stories—let's get down to cases.

Initially we will look at autobiography and biography, focusing in particular on women teachers who were "pioneers." Then we consider a unique collection of personal chronicles of men who taught in elementary schools serving poor Black children. A theme that runs through much of this literature is *culture shock*.

The next several sections review case studies; first we look at beginning teachers and then consider the lives of more experienced teachers. We contrast single, multiple and collective case study research. Space does not permit an exploration of the "Teacher as Researcher" case study (see Burnaford et al. 1996; Lancy 1993:200–202). Finally, a section entitled Action and Knowledge in Education considers the tendency for educators (including our primary subject in this section, an elementary school principal) to rely primarily on their own personal experience in making decisions. Also in this section we take up the issue of teacher-researcher collaboration.

THE TEACHER AS A PIONEER

> Arrived—went about gathering scholars; have forty. Did well enough till it rained; since then have walked three miles a day, ankle-deep in thick, black mud, that pulls off my shoes . . . school . . . the rains sweep clean across it, through the places where the windows should be. I have to huddle the children first in one corner and then in another, to keep them from drowning or swamping. (Hoffman 1981:112–113)

This anonymous letter home from a Northern woman teaching newly freed slaves is taken from an anthology of teachers' autobiographical material. This excerpt reflects the hardship and dedication such service demanded, as well as the burden of trying to live in an angry and deeply racist community. In the latter half of the nineteenth century, White, middle-class, unmarried women turned out in droves to teach in isolated rural areas—on the Western frontier, in schools for Blacks in the reconstructed South, and on reservations. Hoffman draws on the personal accounts of these teachers to uncover a significant chapter in the history of women in the United States. Indeed, it has been the rise of feminist scholarship (see also Acker 1989; Grumet 1988) as much or more than an interest in the history of teaching that has provided the impetus for this new area of inquiry in education. Teaching was nearly the only way a woman could leave the confines of her own home. Once out in the world these women wrote about their experiences, what they saw, and the people—especially students—who touched their lives. The autobiography of Sarah Jane Foster, another Northern woman who taught in a Southern freedom school, was constructed (Reilly 1990) from her voluminous writings including two diaries, 23 letters, and assorted short stories, poems, and essays.

This is not to say that these materials are just there for the asking, as Strane (1990) cautions us. "Researching a minor historical figure like Prudence Crandall requires a lot of detective work" (vii). Strane chose to study Crandall because, however minor, she was a woman who did play a dramatic role in the abolitionist movement. She attended the Brown Seminary in Providence, where she came under the influence of its abolitionist director. Returning to her home in Canterbury, Connecticut in 1831, she opened a female seminary. An ad was run to attract students, and it had the desired effect.

However, a young woman of mixed race asked to be admitted to the seminary in order to get "a little more learning" so she could teach "colored children" (p. 25) Although public elementary schools in Connecticut admitted Blacks at that time, secondary schools—called seminaries or colleges—were segregated and private. Prudence, strongly influenced by the very active abolitionist press of the time period, agreed. Crandall was supported by William Lloyd Garrison and other abolitionists, and her school became a cause celebré, prompting the enactment of racially motivated statutes in the Connecticut legislature. Finally, on September 9, 1834, a band of men attacked the school and tore it to shreds, terrorizing the students in the process. Prudence was forced to close the school.

The term pioneer takes on a broad definition when applied to women in education. Marion Talbot was one of the earliest female faculty members at a major U.S. university. Her biography (Fitzpatrick 1989) appears as one of seven of early female academics in a collection titled *Lone Voyagers* (Clifford 1989; see also Gerlach & Monseau 1991). She had studied at MIT and was a proponent of legitimizing the study of the household and family as an academic discipline. She was offered the position of assistant professor of Sanitary Science at the University of Chicago by the first president, William Rainey Harper. Her reply (dated August 11, 1892) shows just how much moxie these pioneers had, in stark contrast to the Victorian-era stereotype of the genteel and modest "schoolmarm": among several requests, few of which were granted, she proposes the creation of an entire *department*.

Another source for biographical material is the *oral history.* Manning (1990) uses this approach. She chose the Hill Country area of Texas as it was one of the last areas in the United States to be electrified; one-room schools were the norm until the 1950s. She found her subjects through the Hill Country Retired Teachers Association. Over 15 months, she interviewed 20 teachers at least twice for 3 hours or more. Manning finds some common themes, including the prohibition against marriage. ". . . [O]f equal importance was church life, and the young female teacher who failed to meet community religious standards lost her contract" (p. xvii). Nevertheless, she finds that all of these teachers seemed to have ". . . the ability to extract positive elements from almost every situation and emphasize them over negative aspects" (p. 81). However, the value of these accounts lies in their vivid idiosyncratic detail. Gladys Peterson Meyers started teaching at age 17 in a one-teacher school in Knoxville, Kimble County, Texas. ". . . Gladys knew as early as third grade that she wanted to be a teacher. She recalled loving the smell of Crayolas and wanting to teach so that she could always be around them" (p. 65). Manning (1990) sums up the stance taken by the biographer vis-à-vis her subjects: "Doing oral history is a lot of work, but the hard part is seeing to it that the trust these contributors have placed in me is not tarnished, even inadvertently" (p. xxi).

As difficult a time as Gladys Meyers had, Dorothy Redus Robinson's (1978) autobiography makes clear that a Black teacher in rural Texas teaching at an all-Black school had an even tougher time. Her account is a litany of privation brought on by penurious salary, non-existent supplies budget, and needy relatives, but as her minister says in the forward: "She tells her story without bitterness, without blame. She simply tells it like it happened" (p. x).

Neither the Meyers nor the Robinson autobiography follows what we would recognize as conventional chronology. In a single page Meyers takes the reader from 1932 to the present and then back to 1925. This is just one aspect of women's autobiographies which distinguish them from men's, according to Jelinek (1980). Male autobiographers tend to focus on their achievements and their relationship to important events. The narrative is linear and focused—on a particular time period, a theme, or a personality characteristic. There are relatively few personal details. By contrast, female autobiographers (see, e.g., Christman, et al. 1995) are very personal and focus on family (children, spouses). They include the day-to-day details of domestic life rather than affairs of state. The narrative is distinctive, with flashbacks and digressions. It would seem that women are more likely to write "confessions"—revelations of feelings, beliefs, and spirituality—while men are more likely to write "memoirs"—straightforward chronologies of the main events in their lives (Cox 1971).

These differences in narrative style are just now beginning to attract scholarly attention and are, in any event, just one facet of life history to which the biographer must attend. Langness and Frank (1981) have prepared a good introduction to the methodology of biography from an anthropological[5] point of view; their work can be supplemented by Watson and Watson-Franke's (1985) work, which incorporates a feminist perspective. Denzin's (1989) brief overview is particularly useful with respect to epistemological issues, especially the relationship between subject, biographer, and reader. "When a writer writes a biography, he or she writes him- or herself into the life of the subject written about. . . . When the reader reads a biographical text, that text is read through the life of the reader" (p. 26). But the most practical and direct guide to doing biography was written by Lomask (1986), himself the author of numerous biographies. Among his pithy comments: ". . . the biographer . . . [while] gathering his material . . . uses the quasi-scientific methods of the historical researcher; writing his book, he uses the techniques of the fiction writer. . . . A biography is not a compilation of facts. It is a portrait in words of a man or woman in conflict with himself or with the world around him, or with both" (pp. 1–2). The most important step is ". . . to pick the subject that is right for you" (p. 5). His book is particularly helpful with the research and documentation aspects of doing biography (e.g., citations, notes).

CULTURE SHOCK:
CROSSING CLASS AND ETHNIC BOUNDARIES

The modern equivalent of teachers being sent out to the frontier to teach school and save souls is the pilgrimage of White middle-class North American teachers into schools in the urban ghetto. For several years I taught a freshman orientation class in a department of elementary education. My model student was 17, blonde and blue eyed, the third in a family of seven, who had grown up on a dairy farm in Fernley and had never been out of the state—Utah. Demographics dictated that she would be unlikely to find employment in any environment remotely similar to the one in which she went to school, but would in all likelihood be recruited by any one of several large urban school districts in the West—Salt Lake City, Las Vegas, and Los Angeles, among others. Since I knew from graduates who took my masters-level classes in the Salt Lake area that they had felt utterly unprepared for the urban teaching experience, I began to gather a collection of chronicles for them to read, written by teachers in urban schools and other settings dramatically different from that of rural Utah.[6]

These works represent, in my view, an untapped resource for inquiry into the phenomenon of culture shock (among many other potential themes) in the lives of teachers. Peter McClaren's (1980) *Cries from the Corridor* is, for me, the most compelling from a subgroup of this genre. These are works written by well-educated, middle-class White males who, fueled by what McClaren freely acknowledges as "sixties idealism" (p. xiii), decide to teach on the "Frontiers of Despair." Here is his description of his first classroom:

> The inside of the portable classroom was cold and lifeless and looked more like a funeral parlour than a classroom. An old-fashioned roller blind filtered the winter sun, shining a dead green light over the empty desk. . . . Desks were hacked and gouged, while the wobbly chairs were often equipped with only three legs. The green blackboard was in such poor condition that you almost had to chisel letters into it. (pp. xvi–xvii)

The book consists of intermittent journal entries written during the three years McClaren taught in an ethnically mixed, lower-class neighborhood of Toronto. He describes the dissonance between his idealism and the reality of school. Another theme common in teachers' narratives is his inability to provoke "shop talk" with other teachers.

> ". . . what kind of techniques do *you* use with the kids? Maybe we can exchange ideas."
> She cleared her throat, looking down at her lunch, smiling. "There *is* one thing that I find helps me make it through the day," she said softly.
> "Yes?"
> "I never talk about the kids during lunch. That's *my* secret for success!" (p. 27)

Like so many teachers (e.g., Devine 1996), McClaren also suffers from the "discipline" crisis. "I found it hard to act 'the heavy.' The kids sensed my authoritarian image was merely a tactic and called my bluff. When a class enjoys wearing down the patience of its teacher, all it needs is a hint the teacher is out of control. Then it moves in for the kill" (p. 17). The reader notices the conspicuous absence of anything resembling "education" going on in the classroom, and McClaren lamely avers: "Although little learning in the strict academic sense seemed to have taken place, the kids did pick up some skills" (p. 61). He becomes discouraged by the lack of parental support for the children's education and gradually becomes disillusioned: ". . . I started blaming the entire universe for the problems I was encountering at school: parents, the school system, the government, Western culture in general. I'm becoming quite a cynic . . ." (p. 46). At the end of his third year, he can't take it any more. "The thought of teaching for another year made me feel that I was trapped in a dungeon, losing all count of time. The warden might be a nice guy and the food not bad, but I was suffocating—I had to get out. I'd put in my time" (p. 181).

Pat Conroy (1972/1987), the noted novelist, fictionalized the year (1969–1970) he spent teaching a sixth/seventh grade class in the only school on an extremely isolated (no electricity, phones, or running water) island in Tidewater, South Carolina. All of the students were Black, and they presented formidable obstacles to his zeal. Their reading and writing skills were at minimal levels—some didn't know the alphabet, couldn't write their names. "Each question I asked opened a new lesion of ignorance or misinformation" (p. 33). The language problem was enormous—the kids spoke a distinct dialect that he couldn't understand, while they couldn't understand Standard English. Nevertheless, like all of the teachers in this section, Conroy set very high expectations for himself and his students: "When I brought Leonard Bernstein's Children's Concert to the school, Leonard was a mild if not overwhelming success." (p. 49). However, unlike McClaren, who has a sympathetic and dedicated principal, Mrs. Brown, herself Black, terrorizes the children and undermines Conroy's attempts to make schooling interesting and meaningful. Nor are the school district authorities any more supportive. Their racism appalled him, and after 18 months of running battles he is fired. As an author, however, he can take some parting shots; he writes that his adversaries:

> . . . were not evil men. They were just predictably mediocre. Their dreams and aspirations had the grandeur, scope, and breadth of postage stamps. They had rule books and Bibles and golf clubs and nice homes on rivers . . . They quoted the Bible liberally and authoritatively and felt the presence of the Savior in their lives. They did not feel the need for redemption, because they had already been redeemed. The only thing they could not control was their fear. (p. 255)

Conroy's book makes compelling reading (it was made into a motion picture with the title *Conrack*); the tension between the author and the authorities steadily builds to a climax. But it is also, oddly, very personal. We learn a lot about his friends, his courtship, and marriage; it is clearly more autobiography than novel.

Herb Kohl (1967) graduated from Harvard with a degree in philosophy, and after a year's training at Teachers College in 1962 he took on a sixth-grade class in Harlem. Although he opens with a confession ("It was a shock to see thirty-six black faces before me.") (p. 13), the book is written with a level of confidence that he couldn't have felt that first year. Pascal (1960), in *Design and Truth in Autobiography*, says:

> Autobiographies are suspect to historians not so much because of particular incorrect facts as because of the perspective of the writer, who must see the past from his present standpoint, in the light of all his experiences and knowledge since the facts recorded took place. These later experiences will sift the past and determine what was important and worth talking about from what merely seemed important then, will therefore give the author his coherent theme. (p. 69)[7]

By the time Kohl wrote *36 Children*, he was well on his way to becoming one of the most influential educators in America[8] and was already addressing future teachers.[9] We learn relatively little about Kohl (although, like Conroy, we learn of his courtship and marriage), little about the school system; the focus is on the 36 children. He even shares with us many of their stories and artwork. It is a hopeful book. We marvel at what he accomplishes with these children, but after two years he takes off for Europe.

Another Harvard graduate (and Rhodes scholar), Kohl's friend and contemporary, Jonathan Kozol's ghetto teaching career is even shorter. His audience and his message are subtly different from Kohl's. His message is not that ghetto children (in this case the Roxbury section of Boston) can be reached with the right approach, although he uses by-now familiar tactics. "We had been spending the month reading and talking about Paris and about France" (pp. 194–195). Rather, this book is an exposé in the veritable tradition of muckraking journalism. He wants the public to know how bad the segregated schools of Boston are (this was in 1964–1965) and is not afraid to use hyperbole to make his point, starting with his title (1967/1985), *Death at an Early Age: The Destruction of the Hearts and Minds of Negro Children in the Boston Public Schools*. He provides both vivid description—focusing on Stephen, a particularly pathetic child in his class—and official statistics to highlight the imbalance in school spending between Black and White areas, the revolving door of substitute teachers in his school (permanent teachers appear to be ". . . senile, physically degenerate, mentally unstable . . ." [p. 155]), and the grim physical conditions. He, too, is fired for reading an unsanctioned work—Langston Hughes' "Ballad of the Landlord"—to his class. *Death at an Early Age* no doubt sped the eventual integration of Boston schools; however, Kozol, writing the epilogue in the 1985 edition of his book, sees this as ". . . a pyrrhic victory . . . today . . . poor Whites, poor Blacks, and poor Hispanics now become illiterate together" (p. 234).

WHY STUDY PERSONAL ACCOUNTS?

I can but give the flavor of this body of work here, but I would like to pause to address two issues: Why would one want to review such a body of literature in the first place and, second, how should one go about conducting an analysis and synthesis? I have already suggested an answer to the first question: given demographic trends, future teachers will teach children whose family life is radically different from their own, and the nature of the school and classroom environment in which they teach will be quite different in important ways from what they have experienced. We need all the information we can get on how beginning teachers react when they first cross these boundaries.[10] A program which has received much attention, Teach for America, gives added urgency to this quest as 500 bright, well-educated, middle-class graduates with academic majors from elite colleges are being trained to teach during an eight-week summer session and placed in ghetto schools or those serving the rural poor. If this program is less successful than its organizers hope, one reason may be the failure to learn from the ample precedent available in these chronicles.

The second question is more difficult to answer. James Herndon's (1968) *The Way it Spozed to Be* is broadly parallel to the works we have just been reviewing but, unlike the others, he does indicate an intended audience.

> In this book I'm trying to tell about my year teaching—learning to teach—in a public school, a year spent in a particular school, at a particular time, and with particular students. The particulars are my anecdote. It is certainly the anecdote that counts. Not the moral, the point, or the interpretation. If just the particulars can be kept clear, then there will be a kind of thing made, something to see . . . the interpretations may then be numerous as readers. (p. 6)

This suggests that there is no single interpretation, that each reader must *deconstruct* (Derrida 1981) the text for her/himself. The issue of interpretation—by whom, for what purpose—is clearly central in the literature of personal accounts (Polkinghorne 1995). McClaren (1989), after leaving teaching and going through a doctoral program, had doubts about how his journal was being interpreted: "I ran the risk of allowing readers to reinforce their stereotypes of what schooling was like in the 'blackboard jungle'" (p. ix). Hence, he turns his (auto)*biography* into a *case study* by incorporating it into an overview of Marxist/critical theory as applied to North American education. Now, instead of the "interpretations being as numerous as readers," McClaren tells us how his journal *should* be interpreted. By contrast, Barone (1995) argues that "Narrative accounts unaccompanied by scholarly analysis are viewed as incapable of advancing knowledge about educational matters" (p. 63). Convery (1999) is also critical of taking teachers' "stories" at face value.

As I have suggested, there are two further alternatives for analyzing and interpreting these works. Operating as a qualitative researcher, one can conduct a *content analysis* searching for themes in these personal accounts. For example, it is easy to see a common tendency in McClaren, Kohl, Kozol, Conroy, and Herndon to want to throw out the existing boring, plebeian curriculum and replace it with elements of high culture—Miro and Klee, Greek mythology, classical music. Another pervasive theme is the violence that pollutes the schools, the streets, the homes. We can also treat these accounts as a kind of dendrochronology by comparing similar narratives by similar authors at different points in time (e.g., Kohl 1967 vs. Meier 1997).

But these chronicles are first and foremost works of literature—they were not written to serve as data to advance the cause of science. Hence, one can quite appropriately draw on the field of literary criticism for inspiration in conducting one's analysis and interpretation, as I have done in noting differences in literary quality (McClaren: journal, confessional in tone; Kozol: exposé, persuasive in tone). "Students of biographical method must learn how to use the strategies and techniques of literary interpretation and criticism" (Denzin 1989:25). Until personal accounts acquire the institutionalized trappings of a unique tradition (Kuhn 1970), we must perforce read them through the lenses of one or another of the more established traditions.

More on Culture Shock

To return to culture shock, I want to briefly review several other works that are more diverse in character and which show that the phenomenon is by no means limited to White males teaching in the urban ghetto. For example, Valerie, one of Spencer's (1986) subjects, is herself Black and grew up near the poor Black neighborhood in which she found herself teaching, but she, too, experiences extreme dissonance. "Despite Valerie's own poor background, she always blamed parents for children's problems and had little sympathy for the poor" (p. 136). "She hates her job and describes the school grounds as looking like a war zone in World War II" (p. 136). Valerie wants so much to abandon her class origins. On the other hand, Ryan and Sackrey (1984) sum up their collection of 24 life histories of men and women from working-class backgrounds who have become academics and thereby join the elite: "What is clear, though, is the sense of not belonging, and more often than not, feeling one degree or another of contempt for those who do 'belong'" (p. 312). However, they also caution that ". . . we make no pretense here that we have, in any scientific sense, a representative or random sample of academics who hail from working-class backgrounds. Our respondents are predominantly social scientists, and a few are from the humanities" (p. 7). Although there is no longer a "frontier" in its traditional sense, many teachers still feel that they are pioneers in spirit.

One of the most poignant stories of conflict during the transition across class boundaries is Richard Rodriguez's (1982) account of his education. He strove to be successful in the middle-class Anglo world of the public school—and he was, spectacularly so, but he earned the derisive ¡pocho! (an "Americanized" Mexican) from his Mexican-American classmates for his pains.

Fordham's (1995) "high-achieving" subjects similarly struggle to hide their success to avoid being labeled "brainiac," "boot-black Black," or being accused of "acting white." They also "lease" rather than attempt to gain "ownership" of Standard English, using it only when required by their teachers—otherwise, they use Black English (Fordham 1999).[11]

It is not difficult to find depictions of class and ethnic conflict in the literature of personal accounts in education; however, I will review only one final work in this section. Estelle Fuchs' (1969) study of first-year teachers in New York schools, while focused squarely on culture shock, provides a convenient transition as we move from life history to case study. From 1963 to 1967, she followed the initial careers of 14 beginning teachers, meeting with them on consecutive Saturdays for lengthy, taped interview sessions. It is somewhat difficult to decipher Fuchs' intent; indeed, it was in wrestling with this work that table 6-1 was initially sketched out. One's initial sense is that the work is biographical, that we will be treated to 14 portraits or character studies. Although Fuchs uses much verbatim material from her interviewees, these are extracted in a checkerboard fashion so that one never really gets to know any single one of them. Next, one is attentive to the possibility that Fuchs has undertaken a systematic study, as we are treated to several generalizations. For example, all experience an initial honeymoon or euphoria phase, which does not survive the first day in most cases as the next phase, "culture shock," reflecting their inability to cope, leads to a ". . . state of near collapse" (p. 21). But in other respects Fuchs deviates so widely from established canons of science—the only sampling detail provided is the size—that this cannot be her motive. Eventually one learns that she is using these narratives in a purely *illustrative* manner (as McClaren [1989] does with his journal; see also Britzman 1991; Bullough 1989; Connelly & Clandinin 1988). She wishes to show how concepts borrowed from cultural anthropology can be applied to the problems of preparing teachers for the inner-city schools, so she uses anecdotes as points of entry for a series of mini-lectures. First, the teacher's narrative:

> I went on a trip this week with my children . . . I think the thing that impressed my children most was the escalator. None of them or practically none of them had ever seen an escalator before. . . . Many of the children were frightened to get on the escalator. I think that this experience helped me to understand that these children are from a very deprived background . . . . It helped me to realize that I was assuming too much about these children. (pp. 38–39)

Then Fuchs' analysis:

> This teacher's misconception really is a very common one. It connotes the notion that if you do not share knowledge of "my culture," more of specific *details* of "my culture," that you are devoid of culture—for the word "deprived" has come to carry with it the belief that the "deprived" lack ability and are crippled by deficits that have prevented them from learning or achieving. (p. 42)

In the remainder of the chapter, we will limit our focus to contemporary accounts and issues that preoccupy those who would understand and improve *today's* schools.

THE BEGINNING TEACHER

One of the very interesting paradoxes that the study of personal accounts has uncovered is that there appear to be detectable "stages" in the teachers' narratives (Newman 1980; Sikes 1985) and, at the same time, "The teaching profession, as it is traditionally construed, is 'flat.' It deals inadequately with the developmental processes of adulthood, with aging, with the passage of time in a person's life. There is no sense of movement, no distinction between apprentice, journeyman, and master craftsman" (Raphael 1985:97). Newman (1980) and Sikes (1985) sought evidence of stages in the 10 and 48 life histories they respectively collected from mid- to late-career teachers. Neither analysis is compelling with respect to the thesis that all teachers go through roughly the same stages. The earliest stages seem not clearly demarcated, perhaps because these older teachers may have had some trouble remembering the details.

Measor (1985) has had commendable success in understanding the transition in teachers' careers by having her subjects organize their narratives around ". . . 'critical incidents' which are key events in the individual's life, and around which pivotal decisions revolve" (p. 61). Evidently, the commonly observed theme that discipline is a problem during the initial phase of teaching is highlighted in these critical incidents, and there is often an incident that leads to resolution—the individual either exits from teaching or no longer has serious problems.

Bullough's (1989) case study of "Kerrie's" first year of teaching seems to serve two ends. It is, first, a straightforward attempt to understand the nature of the beginning stage of teaching and, second, a research report. Kerrie, too, has trouble with "discipline." She wants a "fun, warm, snuggly" class but feels she must be a "bitch . . . a policewoman" (p. 28). "Kerrie had very little time to pause to consider the implications of her actions. Instead she, perhaps like most beginning teachers, fell back on long-established patterns of belief and action . . ." (p. 43). Bullough, however, follows her into her second year, where she seems to right herself and move out of the "survival" stage (Ryan 1986). *First Year Teacher* is also an attempt to convey to a beginning teacher what to expect. Much like Fuchs (1969), the case study is wrapped around with didactic material, including questions and activities at the end of each chapter and an appendix entitled "Advice on Selecting a School and Surviving the Year." This work is also our first example of the *Teacher-as-Researcher* case study as Bullough, a Professor of Education, reflects on the implications of the case study for his own professional practice: "I reconsidered much of what I did in the past and have made some changes in content among other things" (p. 146–147). Finally, note that, while we certainly obtain a more rounded portrait of Kerrie than we do of Fuchs' beginning teachers, Bullough makes clear that he has been quite careful to select aspects of her narrative that he sees as being typical of the beginning teacher. We do not see the attributes that make her unique. She is ". . . an object rather than a subject of study . . ." (Hoffman 1981:xvi).

With Lisa, prepared in the same program as Kerrie, we are shown unique aspects of her personal history, and the researcher (Knowles 1990) relates this history to Lisa's initial experience as a teacher. Gary Knowles (see also Ball & Goodson 1985; Beynon 1985; Goodson 1989; Pinar 1980) argues that we can only understand the beginning teacher's situation if we are in possession of his/her life history. Lisa carried ideals that were incompatible with what she actually found in the urban, lower-middle-class high school where she is first employed.

> I am feeling like there's no hope for the public school system. I don't feel like it's worth a teacher's time to get out day after day and have to face students who don't want to be here, don't want to do the work [and] are not interested in what you are doing. (p. 706)

Lisa, the eldest of seven children, a youth group leader and teacher for many years in the Mormon Church, evidently expected her public school students to behave like her siblings and church-school students. When they don't, she is bitter.

> Lisa believes that "teachers are not considered professionals." She explained that teachers have "lost the status of being professional" in part by unionism. At the beginning of the school year during a teacher orientation session she was "bombarded by union members . . . and . . . felt like a factory worker." (p. 710)

Interestingly, unlike Kerrie, who does begin to feel success and maintains a good working relationship with the researcher until the end of the case study, Lisa does not and she gradually and painfully withdraws from the case study (Knowles, personal communication).

Another of Knowles' subjects (Knowles & Hoefler 1989) is even less successful than Lisa. Angela encounters much the same problems as Lisa for much the same reasons: "Angela considered herself 'radical,' she had read the works of educational reformers such as Holt and Illich, and she disagreed with the general social organization of schools" (p. 16).

> I found out really quickly that teaching wasn't what I'd thought it would be. Instead of being able to enjoy presenting an interesting lesson, I was undermined by administrative details, disruptive students, and a general unwillingness on the part of students to take the class seriously. (p. 18)

She is unable to control the class, and the breakdown in discipline is increasingly evident to everyone. She does not "survive" the survival stage and drops out after seven weeks. But, unlike Lisa, she continues her association with

Knowles. With her help (Knowles & Hoefler 1989), he gains further insights into the role of life history factors in one's initial orientation to teaching.

These accounts of beginning teachers do make painful reading, but one hopes we can learn from them enough to fuel and guide the reform of teacher education.[12] This is Britzman's (1991) avowed intention in conducting a pair of case studies of student teachers. However, like several other authors we have reviewed, she seems more intent on using her cases in an illustrative manner, in this case of her *critical theory* of education, than on taking a *grounded theory* approach to follow the cases to what seem like the most evident conclusions. Jamie is a graduate in English completing a fifth-year teacher-training program. A number of unexpected events occur; hence, ". . . Jamie's student teaching experience . . . was far from normal" (p. 63). Also, Britzman is denied permission to observe while Jamie is teaching. Despite these problems, Britzman evidently believes the interview material is sufficient for her purpose. Jamie starts out by trying to conduct a class analogous to some of the "wonderful seminars" she took as a senior ("Culture Through Literature" and "Marxism, Feminism and Black Nationalism" [p. 71]), and her students respond with silence. When she tried having them role-play, ". . . the role-playing activity did not work; students became silly and giggled" (p. 78). She then swings to the opposite extreme with no more success:

> We started to do notes, and I found out they don't know how to take notes. They feel everything is important and I had to slow down everything. One person started to say to the class, "Not everything's important." And they all told him to shut up, just because he knows how to take notes and they don't.
>
> I felt at a loss as to how to deal with that. How to say, well, this is important and this isn't important. But important to whom? To me? To them? To the quiz? An important fact? A lot of it was just trivia. But when I started to speed up, it was like, "Wait! Wait! We got to get this all down." (p. 95)

My reaction to this case study is very visceral—Jamie's teacher preparation program has sent her down some class-five rapids without a paddle. But this is Britzman's analysis of the note-taking lesson:

> As Jamie attempted to transfer her authority onto the curriculum, and give the canon the floor, she still found herself in the uncomfortable position of justifying the curriculum's power and relevance. Her story's language speaks of disengagement: Jamie depicted herself as being trapped in a predetermined curriculum whose implementation, as she read the situation, obligated her to "police" student learning. As the press for social control became coupled with pedagogy, the curriculum became an oppressive effect of institutional authority. (p. 95)

Jack, her second subject, is observed and interviewed during his student teaching in secondary social studies classes. Jack's experience is similar to Jamie's; he, too, tries a seminar approach and then abandons it to teach note taking and outlining—with predictable results. Despite the fact that Jack has left his teacher preparation program with few clear plans for organizing his classes, he refuses to place himself in a protegé relationship with the two cooperating teachers he is assigned. The one seems too conservative and traditional; the other, while ". . . she used games, projects and styles of discussion that engaged her students" (p. 138), did not address critical social and political issues in her classes. Jack's self-immolatory behavior is immediately clarified when we hear, via Britzman's interview, from "Joe Probe," his social studies methods instructor. Joe emphasizes the need for the pre-service teacher to develop critical attitudes; they should then develop their own pedagogy. He is opposed to teaching "methods" in the methods course. He tries ". . . to instill an impatience or adversarial attitude toward existing arrangements . . . I'm not interested in training technicians or skilled transmitters, or masters of the latest technology in education. They'll adapt to that naturally" (p. 209). However, he also says: "But I would never teach in the public schools right now. I couldn't teach. I'd have a heart attack the second day, I think" (p. 209).

Although I came away from Britzman's case studies with very different conclusions than she did, I do not see this as problematic. Indeed, I think one of the things that make personal accounts so central to the qualitative research enterprise is their susceptibility to reanalysis, by scholars with differing purposes, ideologies, and theoretical constructs, or from different historical epochs.

We don't really have this opportunity with the last study to be described in this section, a report of fifty life histories, focused on the process of "becoming a coach." Sage (1989) makes clear that he has an enormous amount of interview and observational material on his teacher/coaches, but unlike Britzman (1991), who has the luxury of a 250-page book in which to report her two cases (reporting the case material, however, takes up less than 10% of the book), Sage must make do with eleven journal pages. Hence, he offers a collective portrait: like beginning teachers, aspirant coaches also suffer "reality shock," but its nature is different. "One of the most prevalent . . . reality shocks . . . for neophyte coaches is the extent to which an ethos of hard work and long hours underlie the culture of coaching" (p. 89). "There was the bookkeeping and the maintenance, getting the busses running, keeping discipline—things that I had never thought of before. . . . The amount of hours that we put into coaching [was] a surprise" (p. 89). Also, unlike beginning teachers, apprenticeship seems to be far more central in the experience of beginning coaches.

THOSE THAT SURVIVE: EXPERIENCED AND MID-CAREER TEACHERS

Some themes characteristic of the beginning stage—culture shock, discipline—wane, as teachers lose the sense that they are pioneers. Others—the search for an effective pedagogy and the isolation from peers—persist into later stages. We now consider some of these additional themes. Nias (1985) conducted a collective case study of 99 elementary school teachers that had done a graduate program with her. She began her research by observing in their classrooms and then conducted semi-structured interviews. "Respondents were encouraged to give long, and if necessary, discursive replies. . . . the shortest of the interviews took one and a half hours, the longest five hours. Most took about three hours" (p. 108). In the interview she directed the teachers' attention to the general area of "reference group"—that is, she wanted to know whom they relied upon for feedback and support in their work. In addition to the transcribed interviews, she had 22 keep a diary for one term, which she ". . . used to triangulate individual accounts of perspective and practice" (p. 109). She found that "The most frequently invoked reference group of these teachers was pupils" (p. 109). Many specifically eschew other teachers as a reference group either for teaching or for personal interests: "I love the children and the work, but I have no contact with any adults with whom I have any ideas in common. I feel intellectually starved" (p. 112).

Even when teachers identify with other teachers, this was not necessarily a positive outcome: "We make each other lazy; it's difficult to work hard if no one [else] does. The norm here is about putting teachers' interests first" (p. 113). A major mitigating factor against the creation of strong, professionally committed reference groups of teachers within schools (see also Little 1990) appears to be an aversion to "talking shop." "It's been hard to get teachers in this school to talk about their philosophy; I always wanted to talk and they wouldn't" (p. 115). What teachers *do* talk about in the "staff room" (Hammersley 1984) does *not* reflect favorably on the profession.

Home versus School

Another factor here may be that mid-career teachers' lives outside of work are often stressful and demanding. Following are excerpts from Dee Ann Spencer's (1986) thesis in a study that combines aspects of the multiple and collective case study. Spencer very carefully selected her sample of eight female teachers in order to insure a reasonably representative group.

The core of the book consists of one chapter devoted to each of eight teachers, sectioned into (1) typical day, (2) personal history (growing up, education, work, personal relationships), (3) school life (cultural setting, school administration, school facility, teacher morale, students, classes, leaving school), and (4) home life (household duties, financial conditions, leisure activities, health). As these portraits show, teachers are unable to prevent the interpenetration of home and school. For example, Sylvia sometimes felt she was sacrificing her home life for her job.

> I get jealous, envious, or frustrated when I compare myself with teachers who don't take schoolwork home. . . . Are they superefficient or do they not give as much work. . . ? I know that everybody is different and that I shouldn't compare myself to others, but how do I keep from doing it? . . .

> Maybe I'm defensive because there have been several teachers in this school who are adamant about not taking work home and who look with disdain at those of us who do. (p. 80)

At the same time, according to Spencer (1986):

> When personal problems were particularly stressful, Chris' enthusiasm in the classroom was low and she lacked motivation to interact with students or help them learn. Her affect was flat and her facial expression and bodily posture exhibited exhaustion and depression. (p. 50)

Only one of the eight seems to enjoy a completely successful relationship with a significant other. One surprising (for me) finding was the fact that all but one of the teachers had a very poor diet. ". . . she ate no breakfast, ate either a school lunch or something from a fast-food restaurant, and overate in the evenings. She had a very small body frame and was about 15 pounds overweight. She worried about her weight but exercised only occasionally when she had the time or motivation" (p. 142). This lifestyle also probably contributes to the high incidence of chronic illness recorded in the diaries.

In addition to the eight teachers studied in depth, Spencer conducted interviews with 42 other teachers (1.5 to 5 hours in their home) from six states and four regions of the country. This allows her to move from the idiographic details of her small sample to a more nomothetic characterization of "contemporary women teachers." We see confirmation that the teacher's working day can vary widely: ". . . of the 50 teachers in the study . . . 28.6% took no work home at all . . . 30.6% took work home periodically, 8.2% did less than one hour of work at home daily, 22.4% worked one to two hours and 10.2% worked over two hours daily" (1986, p.186). Other nearly universal stressors are persistent financial problems, autocratic administrators, and students who are rude and turned off. Spencer is able to balance the data from her small, thoroughly studied sample and her much larger, less well-studied sample. By giving free reign to their thoughts in the diaries, some of her eight teachers are likely to mention themes that the investigator might never have thought of during the career-history interviews. On the other hand, she can compare the characteristics for the eight with the "statistically averaged" 42 and better judge their typicality. Her very thorough treatment of methodology in the appendix also recommends Spencer's (1986) work as a model for anyone who contemplates using a personal accounts methodology.

The Stories of Successful Teachers

By now some among you may be questioning whether my sampling is biased since teaching appears, in these pages, to be such a negative experience. In fact one of Spencer's subjects, Marie, led a happy, stress-free life: her husband had a good income and her home life was comfortable. She had entered a teaching career as an insurance policy against something happening to her husband and because it fit best with having a family. Further: "Marie's case shows the positive effects of a good teaching situation. The gifted children in her classes were highly motivated, her classes were quite small, she taught in a good facility, and she was freer from administrative control than other teachers" (p. 53). But to find numerous examples of teachers who feel good about their careers, we need to look back, briefly, at the life-history side of table 6.1. Ken Macrorie's (1974) autobiography is upbeat because he can share with the reader the aftermath of the ". . . day in 1964 . . . [he] turned [his] teaching around" (p. 5). As an English teacher he decided to take risks, to expose his vulnerability to students, and to encourage them to do the same. Twenty years later, Macrorie (1984) published a collection of twenty first-person accounts that he had collected over the years from "outstanding" teachers. Not surprisingly, these accounts all pivot on turning points (see Denzin 1989), signaling a stage shift (Newman 1980; Sikes 1985) in the teacher's career. These turning points revolve around the teacher breaking free from conventional pedagogy. Raphael (1985) published a similar collection of 14 life histories. In these situations we see teachers who learn from their colleagues, are nurtured by their principals, and are liked by their students. Herb Kohl's praise on the cover of Raphael's book expresses sentiments many of its readers will share: "The book lends dignity and depth to the lives of working teachers." Ayers' (1989) collection includes the stories of six *successful* preschool teachers, and I found his listing of the guiding questions he used in interviewing his subjects (pp. 9–10) extremely useful.

However, a note of skepticism is in order. Ayers', Raphael's, and Macrorie's teachers were not selected in any systematic way. It is not clear that these individuals were carefully chosen to reflect the best of their profession. On the other hand, enough details are provided to suggest that they are probably not typical either. So, contrary to the editors' claims, I don't think these books can serve to ". . . elucidate the *common* occupational hazards of the educational profession" (Raphael 1985:14, emphasis added).

Of course, none of these scholars claim to be gathering data in the traditional sense; these are not *case studies*. However, I find that the typicality-generalizability problem also extends to works prepared by university researchers in the field of education. For example, in one of the chapters in Witherell and Noddings' (1991) collection, the author (Makler 1991) describes an interesting writing assignment she developed for her high school social studies classes which allowed students to ". . . seek meaning in the history we were studying . . ." (p. 30): they write a fictionalized autobiography consistent with the time period they are studying. She also has them do research on their family origins. "I was surprised by the power of this curriculum, by the level of interest it generated among students and their families, by the change it provoked in my classroom" (p. 31). This remark cannot be interpreted without the contextualizing details that indicate the nature of the students, her school and the community. These are not provided; neither does the author nor the editors juxtapose this description with the normative and very different portrait of high school social studies instruction offered by Linda McNeil

(1986). In short, I am left with a nagging sense that most of the "uplifting stories" all come from elite schools (e.g., Paley 1992) and/or classrooms of gifted students.

This sense was exacerbated recently following my reading of Tracy Kidder's (1989) bestseller *Among School Children*, a year in the life of a fifth-grade teacher in an ethnically mixed working-class community. I found it to be interesting reading on at least two levels. First, I was struck by the similarities and differences between his method—investigative journalism—and the methods identified with qualitative research. The level of detail and spontaneity in the description; the provision of a rich contextual background in which to set Chris Zajac and her class; the detached, neutral, and nonjudgmental stance of the observer all suggest the work of a qualitative researcher. However, Kidder provides no details of how he came to select Zajac; there is no "methodology" whatsoever. His prose reflects artistic license not permitted to scholars ("Pedro just didn't know how hard his life was, but he'd be a teenager soon, and then he would, and the comfort dispensed by drug dealers would be waiting for him . . ." [p. 84]) (see also Freedman 1990; Sachar 1991 for similar, recent works).

But the work is more interesting for the absolutely schizophrenic reaction it provokes in the media—both laudatory (Theroux 1989) and scathing (Ohanian 1989) reviews. Chris Zajac struck me as a good teacher, dedicated to making the most of a difficult situation. Indeed, it is one of the few contemporary "uplifting" stories from a *non-elite* school. However, this pragmatic perspective is juxtaposed with an idealist or romantic perspective that seems to say that any teacher is bad who is unable to reach and assist every single child in her classroom. This distinction is important to bear in mind as one reads the personal accounts literature—indeed, I began to feel a little schizophrenic myself (see also Hargreaves 1984) by the thirtieth or fortieth account.

ACTION AND KNOWLEDGE IN EDUCATION

Here we will take up another common theme in the personal accounts literature, the *origins* of the teacher's (and principal's) knowledge. A quotation from one of Raphael's (1985) colleagues pretty well sums it up: "I started teaching not from something I had learned in a book; I started to develop my own style. I started looking inside *myself*" (p. 62). One's collection of classroom lore, consequently, is more critical in guiding teachers' action than previous education, in-service training, professional organization, or one's colleagues.

Hargreaves' (1984) collective case study is a thorough inquiry into this phenomenon by documenting an event in the life of the teaching staff of Riverdale, a newly established middle school. He records twenty meetings held over the summer in which the mostly young staff are to develop the curriculum for the school. In this they are encouraged by well-trained and democratically leaning administrators. One- to two-hour interviews are also conducted with each member of the staff, and Hargreaves finds some discrepancies between the private and public personae of his subjects.

> At Riverdale meetings, when teachers accounted for their practice, they drew overwhelmingly not on the logic and principles of formal education theory but on their own experience. . . . of all the different kinds of experience that Riverdale teachers might have cited, it was their experience with pupils in the classroom that seemed to count most and that provided their most common source of justifications. . . . the specific examples that teachers cited were often populated by some of the school's more popular characters, sometimes to provide support for a proposal (if pupil X can do this, then anyone can) and sometimes to pour cold water on it (you couldn't do it with pupils like X). But in either case they played a crucial role in staff discussion. (p. 246)

First-year teachers had less experience to refer to, so they drew on—apologetically, according to Hargreaves—their college training. But even here they cited their practical experiences more often than formal classes. Ultimately, the staff is unable to complete the curriculum development task—they don't seem to be making much progress and the fall term is upon them. The head took the task on himself, thus leaving everyone demoralized. Hargreaves suggests that teachers' exclusive reliance on their past experience to mediate any change in their practice provides a powerful barrier to innovation (see also Datnow 1997).

It's not only teachers who rely on personal experience; so do their administrators. Harry Wolcott's (1973) meticulously researched principal, "Ed Bell," did not feel ". . . that his formal course work in administration was . . . related to his actual work as a school principal" (p. 200). Upon reading a draft of the case study, Ed admitted distress because he felt that at times he personally and the principalship in general appeared rather inept. He particularly pointed out that many of the things which principals do—like chasing dogs off the school grounds or tracing a missing sandwich—are done not because principals want to do them but because other people expect it. The limitations of the principal's role is linked to the restraints imposed by constantly having to meet the expectations of a multitude of others. "The demands of a position in which 'every problem is important' mitigate the opportunity for constructive accomplishment" (p. 318). Perhaps this is why there is little connection between Ed's formal training and his actual role?

Wolcott (1973) begins by stating his purpose ". . . to a literature that has dealt almost exclusively with the behavior of school administrators as it *ought to be* or as it is interpreted and reported by the person performing it. The present study adds another dimension: what an administrator actually does as observed by someone else" (p. xii). Then he describes his methods, paying particular attention to the laborious process of selecting a principal for study[13]—for example, "I did not want a subject whose success as a degree candidate might in any way be complicated by our research relationship" (p. 2). He raises the issue of the grass-roots versus the top-down approach. He did not want central administration to "... assign some fair-haired principal to be my cooperating subject ..." (p. 3). On the other hand, he ran the risk of, after having laboriously searched for and found Ed Bell, being shot down by the central administration because he hadn't gone through proper channels.[14] To everyone, Harry became "the shadow."

The amount of data that Wolcott amasses on Ed Bell and his principalship is awesome and allows him to do several things that aren't always found in a typical case study. First, it allows him to spice his "scientific account" with authenticating life history details, such as Ed's tribulations with his Ford Falcon. Second, it allows him the luxury of viewing Ed's role from several different perspectives. For example, he examines the principalship as both an annual cycle of activity (chapter 7) and as a daily cycle of activity (chapter 6). Third, his notes are so complete that he can actually quantify certain recurrent patterns in order to achieve a statistical profile of the principalship (chapter 5); for example, Ed had 7–10 phone calls daily and spent just over 10% of each day on the phone.

Throughout the study, Wolcott (1973) continues to check on the typicality of his case. For example, from his interviews with Ed's mother, he began to appreciate the importance of the church in Ed's life history. Ed's embodiment of the protestant ethic is quite evident in his fulfillment of his role.[15] Wolcott also measures Ed's typicality by comparing him to the many other principals he meets and interviews when he accompanies Ed to principals' meetings and conferences. It is also possible, having read about many principals in the personal accounts literature,[16] for one to comment on Wolcott's selection. In my view Ed is typical of those considered to be "good" principals as opposed to, say,

> Julie's first principal, who dressed in a leisure suit with a brass belt buckle that said "Jesus Saves," spent little time in the school because he planned early in the year to move on to another job. When in school, he avoided teachers, disciplined students, or lifted weights in his office. The second principal also lasted only a year and was seen as weak and ineffective by the teachers. . . . (Spencer 1986:115)

RESEARCHER AND SUBJECT

Finally, I want to draw on Wolcott to introduce an important methodological issue, namely, his relationship with Ed.[17] Wolcott (1973) goes to considerable lengths to protect Ed's anonymity. He also seeks to shield Ed by not providing *evaluative* feedback. In addition, he "... was conscious that 'friendship' could present another nagging problem: How does one develop a close working relationship with his subject without the degree of involvement that has ultimately left some anthropologists unable to continue to write analytically about a people whom they have studied for years?" (p. 6). Lastly, Wolcott had to be careful not to become so closely identified with the principal that the staff would feel they could not speak to him without everything they said finding its way straight back to Ed. However, he willingly shares his findings with Ed and solicits his input.

Ed and Harry respect each other and are able to acknowledge that each will have a slightly different perspective on the same events because, while they may share in an overall goal of improving education, their self-assigned roles in this enterprise are quite different. Following are reviews of three more studies whose authors seek to blur the distinction between teacher and researcher by conducting *collaborative* research where ". . . the knowledge claims depended upon the shared meaning created by researcher and teacher participants" (Clandinin 1986:13).

One of the first such projects was undertaken by Elbaz (1983) in 1976 as her dissertation. The problem she wishes to address, again, is the teacher's apparent aversion to the use of professional knowledge: ". . . teachers are not commonly seen to possess a body of knowledge and expertise appropriate to their work, and this tends to diminish their status in the eyes of laymen" (p. 11). Elbaz obviously is very critical of the existing research literature on teaching practice and argues that, in lieu of professional knowledge, teachers develop and use "practical knowledge" (what Schubert [1991] refers to as "lore") that functions like the professional knowledge of doctors and lawyers.

Contrast Elbaz's selection strategy with Wolcott's. She chose Sarah because she ". . . was a friend whose work I found interesting, and this made it probable that we would establish a rapport easily and early on in the interviews" (p. 24).[18] Over 18 months she conducted five informal interviews with Sarah, each about two hours long, and two periods of classroom observation, then analyzed her material. ". . . when the analytic portion of the study was complete I gave it to Sarah, and we held a final talk which was taped but not transcribed" (p. 24). She doesn't really reveal what Sarah's reaction was; however, she suggests that it wasn't entirely positive: ". . . I undertook to disclose any purposes and interpretations to the teacher and to solicit her own purposes and interpretations. This proved to be much more difficult than I had anticipated . . ." (p. 25). At the end of the book Elbaz makes a brave admission that researcher-teacher collaboration isn't a walk in the park.

I think that the major reason for her discouragement is that Sarah was, in a sense, uncooperative. Given Elbaz' preamble, we expect to see a "Super Teacher," someone who can handle any classroom contingency. On the contrary, Sarah does not appear to be an effective teacher and it is not hard to account for this, ironically, by her evident lack of professional knowledge. After ten years of experience, Sarah finds herself teaching predominantly "academically oriented" high school students in a suburban, middle-class neighborhood. Despite getting this very desirable class, she seems unable to find ways to help students relate to English literature.[19] We are, therefore, also not surprised to learn ". . . she had done no in-service work in English literature, partly because she had felt no need for it, and partly because the trend . . . had been to focus on broad professional development concerns such as personal growth, values clarification, and group dynamics, rather than on specific content areas" (p. 34).

Dorothy Clandinin (1986) draws heavily on Elbaz' approach in her pair of case studies of Aileen and Stephanie and suffers comparable problems, in my view. Clandinin becomes very involved with her subjects, and she reproduces letters she writes to them in which she reflects on her ongoing analysis. She also shares with the reader excerpts from her journal—excessively, in my view. Aileen and Stephanie[20] are primary teachers; their selection, like Sarah's, had been dictated by convenience and access rather than typicality. We are left to wonder also about the typicality of their teaching situation. Clandinin tells us almost nothing about the students, the schools, the community. We are forced to play detective and infer from statements like the following that Aileen, at least, is teaching in a middle- to upper-middle-class kindergarten: ". . . she asked the children to name their favorite nutritious snack and then to classify the snack as fruit or vegetable" (p. 61). We learn a great deal about these teachers' beliefs and philosophy, but we rarely see it implemented (compare Grossman 1991). Equally distressing, we learn almost nothing about their backgrounds and their lives outside of school, especially considering the following indictment from Clandinin of others' work: ". . . research studies may assume that teachers' thoughts and ideas have a history, but the studies do not take that history into account" (Connelly & Clandinin 1988:19).

Perhaps my greatest disappointment with this and similar reports is the failure to present the teachers' perspective[21] on the research enterprise—this *would* constitute a methodological breakthrough. That is, Clandinin regularly solicits feedback from the teachers to her preliminary analyses and theoretical constructs, but she never shares with her readers what these reactions are. We never hear what they have to say. Nowhere in these two books do I hear Sarah, Aileen, or Stephanie addressing me; they address only the researcher. Consider, by way of contrast, the narratives in the Raphael (1985) collection. Frances Marinera is not addressing Raphael here, she's addressing the *world*: "What I see happening in education is that these outside expectations are getting to be more numerous. I see teachers doing these bureaucratic chores, and they hate it" (p. 66).

The final note of caution regarding teacher-researcher collaboration is provided by a soul-searching report (Munro 1991). Petra Munro, a doctoral student of Harry Wolcott at Oregon, notes that her ". . . first attempt at establishing a collaborative relationship was flatly rejected" (p. 7). Eventually, she secures the cooperation of two teachers, one of whom is retired; both, however, refuse to keep a journal or write about how they experience the research process. While Munro saw the meetings and interview sessions as "enjoyable talk," they saw it as work (contrast with Ayers' [1989] subjects). They were willing to tell their stories, to facilitate interviews with principals and other teachers, to provide personal memorabilia, to let her poke and probe, but they resisted collaboration.

"In establishing a collaborative relationship, I believed I should also share my story. I engaged in life history because of its reciprocal nature concerning mutual storytelling" (p. 8). However, her informants were ". . . not interested in hearing the researcher's story" (p. 8). Munro is also concerned about the following paradox: if "new" narrative inquiry requires mutual openness and revelation, won't the researcher's openness about her values and expectations "bias" the responses of her informants? In this case, Munro is an avowed feminist. She isn't sure she should reveal this to her teacher informants, or, as she calls them, "life historians." Another problem emerges as she picks up a theme in which *she* is interested—a teacher's "allies"— and deflects her informant from another theme—her "travels"—in which she is not interested, but about which the informant clearly is interested in discussing. "I questioned whether it was truly the life historian's understanding of her experience I was seeking, or if I was structuring the interview so that the subject told the story that conformed to my outlook" (p. 12).

PROMISES AND LIMITATIONS

One of the most noticeable trends in the literature has been the incorporation of personal accounts[22] in the data-collection arsenal of the qualitative researcher—whether he or she is engaged in a field study of a school (Devine 1996) or case studies—of a training program (Hull 1993) and an intervention program to prevent school failure (Romo & Falbo 1996). I see the study of personal accounts as having enormous potential. Rather cursorily I have reviewed several works (e.g., Conroy and the others) that can be profitably studied as a group, their collective wisdom about cross-cultural teaching, the role of values, institutionalized racism, and so on being much greater than the sum of the individual chronicles. Almost any area of education can be illuminated by synthesizing material from the extant autobiographical record of teachers, principals, school board members, and so on. A literary critic studying genre or voice, a clinician looking for signs of stress, a historian searching for evidence of a transition from teaching as a calling to teaching as a job, will all find grist for their respective mills. While local archives can be searched for unpublished material, the inter-library loan system will prove invaluable for tracking down published works that are no longer in print. Of course, a researcher can also collect life-history material from the living. One of the most direct sources is from our own students (Schoen 1991). Recent changes in the nature of the public school curriculum have provided impetus for student autobiography. In turn, and with proper safeguards, teachers can analyze these materials for themes so that we may gain a better understanding of how academic "careers" are constructed, for example.

The in-depth study of a single life in the conduct of biography also can be rewarding. Two issues need to be addressed by the aspiring biographer: Does this person's story illuminate issues that have contemporary significance? Is this someone that you can treat sympathetically but dispassionately? An area of biography that has an almost urgent appeal is that of the lives and stories of teachers who have had successful teaching careers in the inner city (e.g., Edwards 1989). Almost everyone has known or heard about these legendary figures, but we know almost nothing about what they have in common, what techniques they use in teaching, their philosophy, or their strategies for self-preservation and renewal.

With respect to the collection and analysis of multiple life histories, there are numerous topics waiting to be addressed. For example, innovation in education has been looked at from a number of perspectives, but no one, to my knowledge, has collected oral histories in which the subjects were asked to reflect on their encounters with new ideas. Where did these new ideas come from? How were they initially received? Was there a change in the classroom, school or school district? What does the wisdom of hindsight suggest to the subject?

As we have seen, the case study demands that the researcher acquire multiple sources of data on his/her subject—observation; collection of written material; and, perhaps, interviews with his/her colleagues, employers, and family members. The researcher now has the opportunity to construct a universal or etic characterization to set alongside the emic perspective provided in the interview and diary material. Here the field is truly wide open, so to speak. I have earlier mentioned the need for a case study or studies of women principals. But imagine how our personnel preparation courses would be enhanced if we had vivid and thorough case studies of gym teachers, guidance counselors, speech pathologists, secretaries, and assistant principals to draw on? Would we need to revise the text material used in training these individuals for their roles as real-world accounts became available?

Multiple case studies shorten the perspective—that is, we invest less in any single individual, we learn less about them, in order to obtain comparative data on several individuals. "Unpackaging" the teacher's or administrator's tool kit is amenable to study using several case studies. When a teacher says, ". . . the 'Quality Circle' is particularly important for me now. It's an opportunity for me to grow" (Marinera, in Raphael 1985:77), what does that mean?

In order to realize this promise, some limitations in the present personal accounts literature must be addressed. There is a tendency to locate at one or another end of the idiographic-nomothetic continuum, rather than attempting to strike a balance as Spencer (1986) does. I think we are rapidly reaching the saturation point with respect to single-subject narratives or collections of teachers' stories that do not address a problem. On the other hand, some problem-focused studies use such large samples that all sense of individual identity is lost.

The selection of subjects has been treated in a rather offhand fashion in too much of the personal account literature. Considering the enormous investment one makes over the course of the project, it is not sensible to select a subject who is unrepresentative of the class to which one wants to refer (e.g., a 45-year-old "beginning teacher") or someone who does not possess the qualities or attributes one is interested in studying (e.g., selecting an administrator who turns out to be widely regarded as incompetent for a study of leadership style). It is clearly unwise to study one's friends, whether or not they are treated as "collaborators."

We need a truth-in-advertising policy. Far too often when I expected to read a report of research, I was treated to a lecture in which the life-history material was not analyzed but instead selectively drawn on to illustrate the lecture. Fortunately, in some of these works sufficient material is presented so that one could use it to compare with other similar cases in the literature—this was particularly true of the works on beginning teachers. I am, obviously, an advocate of using life-history material for instructional purposes, and I see its usefulness in illustrating a novel thesis about the larger social forces that have an impact on teaching. However, one should be very careful to avoid claiming that one is reporting qualitative research findings (e.g., "I am not sure that I want to call what I do research" [Grumet 1991:71]).

Too many reports leave out what would seem to be essential pieces of the puzzle. Many scholars fail to gather and/or fail to report life-history details that might have a bearing on one's character in school. Critical contextual detail should include: the subject's family life, including the subject's role as parent; personal school history, especially details of the professional training; significant others, parents and favorite teachers; some sense of the individual's daily routines and lifestyle; the nature of the school and classroom environments; students' characteristics and background, especially regarding class and ethnicity; some sense of school climate and the prevailing teaching ethos; and classroom routines, including the use of prepared curricula, grouping arrangements, management strategies, predominant instructional mode, and so on. Again, I would cite Spencer (1986) as representing the ideal, although I missed any discussion of the teacher's pedagogical philosophy—another critical detail.

Let me now turn to two of the newer paradigms in the personal accounts tradition. The jointly constructed research project between a practitioner in the field and a researcher needs careful exploration. It certainly makes sense to suggest that, in pursuing a study where an individual's life history is a primary data source, the individual should have considerable say in the conduct, outcome and reporting of the research. However, in the published literature to date, the teachers seem not to have claimed ownership of the project. Largely, this seems to be due to *selecting* collaborators who are accessible rather than to *seeking out* teachers with a genuine interest in and understanding of research. When I contemplate this type of study, I think of a teacher of my acquaintance who did a superb job on her master's thesis; is widely recognized for her innovative teaching; and is called upon frequently to provide leadership in her school as well as in the district and state. She *knows* she is at the peak of her profession and would, I'm sure, be quite comfortable working with a researcher to pick apart some aspect of her pedagogical model (e.g., Gudmundsdottir 1990) or her practice.

ENDNOTES

[1] *Narrative* is an alternative label for this tradition (Polkinghorne 1995), but I find that work included under this heading is rather limited. Personal accounts is a broader, more inclusive and, I would argue, more useful category.

[2] The contradiction is intended.

[3] The personal accounts that are reviewed in this chapter are predominantly those of teachers—that's the nature of the literature. However, I have strived to find accounts of other actors on the education stage to provide some variety.

[4] The fact that Fordham herself is African American is also significant in this context.

[5] Two excellent sources on methods for psychologically oriented studies of personal accounts are Giele and Elder (1998) and Lieblich et al. (1998).

[6] Schoen's (1991) collection of autobiographies also grew out of a class with somewhat similar aims.

[7] But see Errante (2000), who crosschecked her teachers' recollections against archival records and found them to be quite accurate.

[8] In the course mentioned above, I used his (1984) *Growing Minds: On Becoming a Teacher* as the text.

[9] Another famous autobiography (*Teacher*), Sylvia Ashton-Warner's ([1963] 1986) encounter with Maori children, also resonates with the wisdom of hindsight.

[10] With McClaren, Kozol, Kohl, and Conroy, I have certainly not exhausted the store of autobiographical material focused on teaching impoverished elementary school children. Further, there is a parallel library of works on the challenges facing secondary school teachers (e.g., Best 1983; Channon 1970; Cherry 1978; James 1969; Kaufman 1964; Natkins 1986; Welsh 1986; Williams 1970) that I can't even touch on here.

[11] By contrast, Indian (Gibson 1988) and Chinese (Goto 1997) students do *not* feel they must sacrifice their ethnic identity and "become white" in order to be successful academically.

[12] I lasted only one quarter as a supervisor of student teachers because I ran into two intractable cases (out of six supervisees!). In one, I had to conclude that the individual would need far more than one quarter of student teaching before she would be considered competent, and yet she had earned all As and Bs in her teacher education classes and her "failure" in student teaching was unacceptable to my department head. In the second, the practicing teacher used an approach out of the Dark Ages, yet she was only aping her supervising teacher and following her directions.

[13] Wolcott (1983) himself describes a dramatically contrasting example that illustrates the difference between life history and case study. Here he discovers 19-year-old "Brad" squatting in a shack he has made for himself on a corner of Wolcott's wooded property. For two years, Wolcott gathers Brad's life history. A "stonie" and eventual dropout, Brad has gotten little from his schooling. Wolcott uses Brad's story to make the point that while school can teach you things it can't give you a reason for wanting to become educated; only your parents can do this. And Brad's parents have failed him. But what is interesting is that Wolcott treats Brad's case quite differently than Ed's; as he says, "There should be a high ratio of information to explanation in a life-story . . ." (p. 8). That's exactly what he does—his analysis is minor; instead he helps Brad tell his story.

[14] Districts vary a great deal in how concerned they are about "managing" research contact with schools. The best approach is a modified grass-roots approach where you search for the teacher/school/students that are right for your study while keeping contact with a "guardian angel" in central administration—someone who is sympathetic towards your project and can go to bat for you if someone in authority is upset that you didn't follow correct protocol. Of course, after getting informal agreement from teachers, principal, and so on, you need to seek formal permission through the district office.

[15] In the retrospective evaluation of Kensington School reviewed in the previous chapter, the researchers track down the principal actors 15 years later to conduct life-history interviews (Smith, Klein, Dwyer, & Prunty 1985). They were not surprised to find that the crusading

innovators who established this "open" school all revealed a history of deep involvement with organized religion. The authors refer to educational innovation as "secular religion."

[16] One of these is Phil Bingham (Clandinin & Connelly 1991), the very effective principal of an inner-city school in Toronto—he sounds like McClaren's (1980) principal, actually. Phil related a story about his being teased when he was sent to school in short pants to explain his empathy for minority students.

[17] See also Bullough's (1989:137–139) discussion of his relationship with Kerrie.

[18] Studying a friend is not a good idea. Even in a project that attempts to be collaborative, it is extremely difficult to keep a hierarchical relationship at bay. In the analysis, more may be revealed than is comfortable for either researcher or subject.

[19] Sarah seemed muddled about pedagogy for teaching English and unaware of the exciting developments taking place at the time, such as the National Writing Project, reader-response theory, and the integrated language arts curriculum.

[20] Aileen and Stephanie make guest appearances in a recent textbook (Connelly & Clandinin 1988) for new teachers, their narratives used illustratively as in Bullough (1989) and Fuchs (1969).

[21] I was distressed that, given the pervasive emphasis on the cooperative nature of this work, the teachers who should have been given co-authorship of the book aren't even identified by their real names (see also Shulman 1990)!

[22] A cautionary note comes from this review of one recent multiple-case study that incorporated personal account material in the report: ". . . the voices of so many people make the book a lengthy and sometimes laborious read" (Welner & Mickelson 2000:23).

7 Decisions, Decisions

As Dobbert (1982) rather pithily notes, "Just as a set of metric wrenches will not make a Volkswagen mechanic, neither will a set of research techniques make an ethnographer" (p. 86). Hence, I have taken an inductive and reflective approach throughout this book in order to show that, ultimately, qualitative research methods cannot be extracted from the traditions that spawned them and must be viewed within the context of specific research questions and problems. Nevertheless, in this chapter I venture to offer pointed direction to the would-be qualitative researcher and at the same time present highlights of what has gone before.

One way to characterize the conduct of qualitative research is as a decision structure much like the flowchart that precedes the composition of a computer program. If we start with a published study and retrace the investigator's steps backward, we find her hesitating at a number of decision points and then deciding to move in one direction and not another. Each qualitative research project is, for this reason, unique. It is not possible, therefore, to write a prescription or recipe that everyone can then follow to *do* a qualitative study. On the other hand, sending the novice out to grope around in the dark isn't very sensible either. Using our flowchart analogy, however, what we *can* do is call attention to these decision points, so you will know when these are coming up and what your options are.

THE IMPORTANCE OF SELF-ANALYSIS

Inevitably during the first few weeks of class, as they get into the material and agonize over the design for the mini-research project, some of my students confess that qualitative research makes them very uncomfortable. Shades of gray, ambiguity, and uncertainty may be fine for some aspects of their lives—how they decorate their homes, perhaps—but when it comes to their classes, their careers, their dissertations, they want the certainty afforded by an algorithm or at least an iron-clad heuristic. They want to be assured that if they invest time and energy in a project, they won't get lost in the middle and will have a recognizable (acceptable to a graduate committee, publishable) product when they are finished. If you are like this, qualitative research is not for you. Indeed, if you are uncomfortable with any degree of uncertainty, clearly quantitative research is not for you either. Of course, it is not at all uncommon to find students and faculty whose primary raison d'être is the *promotion* of a particular "treatment" or teaching technique, and they somehow see research as the means to this end. We do research when we are uncertain about what the state of the world is and are curious or concerned to reduce that uncertainty. If we are certain about the state of the world and what changes are needed, our means of attack will be political and/or rhetorical (Sleeter 1998). We will be activists in trying to persuade others to adopt our cause.

Next I would ask whether this research will be a once-in-a-lifetime effort—for example, you are doing a dissertation but, once finished, you will go into the public sector rather than academia. If so, consider doing a quantitative study. Your chances of achieving quick closure and a publishable product are much greater than if you chose qualitative research. Many doctoral dissertations that are qualitative in nature stretch out indefinitely and are unpublishable. "Getting it right" as a qualitative researcher sometimes takes at least one major false start. Hence, it is best to see the qualitative thesis/dissertation project as a lengthy and difficult apprenticeship preparing for what will be a long and distinguished research career.

So you've decided that there are some things in the world that you want to find out about, your degree of certainty is fairly low, you can maintain a "neutral" stance vis-à-vis this phenomenon, and you can live with the fluid and *ad hoc* nature of the qualitative study. How well do you write? Every aspect of one's work as a qualitative researcher demands more writing than would be the case for a quantitative scholar. Writing is to qualitative research what mathematics is to quantitative research. One's database consists of *written* notes; one's report is in *narrative* form and is inevitably *longer* than comparable reports of quantitative research. Can you write well in *English*? Academics, virtually anywhere in the world, are expected to publish in English-language journals.

Qualitative research means hundreds of pages of text—field notes, interview transcripts and the (inevitably lengthy) write-up, whether dissertation, article, book, or final report. If you plan to code your materials and/or plan to make use of qualitative data analysis programs, all this material must be *typed*.

Then ask whether there is a qualitative research tradition (pp. 4–7) to which you can attach yourself. Do you have an undergraduate major in *history*? Are you a Native American and aware how much the literature on

Native Americans has been done by *anthropologists*? One must first steep one-self in a particular tradition. An undergraduate degree and/or graduate minor in *sociology* would seem to be a prerequisite to doing a *field study*, for example.

Or, perhaps, you have an opportunity to work on a funded intervention project. You are a graduate assistant on a state-funded program to introduce "master" math teachers to new methods and have them mentor and train "cross-over" teachers. Clearly a case study is suggested. But will your case study focus on the intervention project, or will you do multiple case studies of a sample of the teacher pairs? To finesse one of these traditions altogether is unwise. As I write this, the analogy that comes to mind (from *All Creatures Great and Small*) is the orphan lamb that, because it is not chemically recognizable to any of the ewes, will not be nursed by them, even those that have lost their offspring. Pursuing your research within one of the traditions makes it recognizable. You'll know what to call it and how to talk about it. You'll find faculty colleagues/supervisors who are familiar with the area, if not at your own institution then at conferences where members of particular traditions are wont to gather. Most importantly, when you write up your work you'll know to what journal/book series to submit it. (If you're mistaken, you will receive nasty reviews that chide you for selecting an *inappropriate* journal.)

Finding a Problem in the Setting

The study may begin with the desire to describe/analyze/explore a particularly interesting phenomenon/situation/classroom that is already known to the researcher (e.g., Lancy 1976a). One negotiates entry, and obtains tentative agreement from the parties involved to cooperate in the study. The nature of the phenomenon one has chosen to investigate should immediately suggest a broader topic or issue to guide the study. Peshkin's (1986) initial look at Bethany Baptist Academy led him to examine it as a "total institution" (cf. Goffman 1961). Smith (1978) refers to this process as ". . . locating the case as an instance of a more general class of events" (p. 356).

It is also at this point that some refinement takes place in the selection of your tradition. You may recognize, in your study of staff interaction in a school, that not only are gender and power relations implicated—you had earlier decided to undertake a study of stratification from a sociological perspective—but you will need to draw on the literature in *discourse analysis*, because *how* people talk to each other seems very important.

Starting with a setting first is characteristic of anthropologists. We look for interesting and unusual settings or groups (e.g., MacLeod 1987) or those that have not been described often in the literature. The present ethnographic literature is very sparse with respect to: magnet schools; dance academies; montessori pre-schools; yeshivas; prep schools; and education in corporate settings; in the military; and in universities (Wisniewski 2000), among others. We need to understand the way unique cultural groups—such as people in Appalachia; Hmong immigrants; Paradise Valley, Arizona residents (a

wealthy bedroom community); and migrant workers, to name but a few—
relate to public schooling. Anthropology provides a theoretical framework
and the research methodology to help us gain such understanding.

Finding a Setting for the Problem

Contrariwise, the researcher may be motivated to address a particular
question, and this issue guides the selection of the research site(s). In my
comparative study in Papua New Guinea (Lancy, 1983) I was interested in
discovering whether different cultural/ecological configurations influenced
children's intellectual/academic development. Therefore, research sites were
chosen specifically with this aim in view. Here one has somewhat greater lee-
way; if one fails to gain entry to a particular site, one can search for a similar
site as an alternative. Barring anthropology and the case study, where one
begins with a site and searches for a problem, in other traditions the problem
comes first. Defining a problem is no easy task, as Meloy (1989) makes clear.
One way to move toward a clearer definition is through the process of
describing your problem to others. In the case of the study just mentioned,
the problem was residual from previous research. A piece of research (one's
own or that of others as reported in the literature) usually leaves one's questions only partially answered or opens up new questions not previously
addressed. Just as often, the existing literature reveals two or more contradictory findings or at least some tension between different points of view; or
there is an area of relatively little controversy that has been investigated primarily by quantitative means, where a qualitative approach might yield fresh
insights, such as *student motivation*.

THE REVIEW OF LITERATURE

The Review of Literature in a qualitative study describes both a piece of
prose—a section of one's research proposal or chapter in the dissertation—
and an ongoing *process*. There will always be several relevant areas to consider
in doing the review of literature. There will be a body of literature on the
topic (e.g., student groups, parent-school relations, gender and communication) or the particular culture/setting in which one has chosen to work (e.g.,
hearing-impaired youth, Punjabi Sikhs, inner-city parochial schools). Finally,
one will need to review appropriate literature relating to one's research design
(content analysis, multiple case studies, ethnoscience). All too often I have
had students tell me that there is "no literature on my topic." My standard
reply: "Well, that could mean one of two things: generations of scholars have
avoided the topic either because they thought it wasn't worth investigating or
because they thought it was too *difficult* to study given the present level of
research technology. Which is it in the case of your topic?" The point here is
that failure to find a literature base to support one's study is usually a sign
that we need to do some re-conceptualizing. Unfortunately, there seems to be

a lamentable tendency in some of the recent qualitative literature to include in the review of literature only other qualitative studies or, worse, only those studies that share a particular tradition or narrow theoretical/ideological framework. Don't fall into this trap. Review all the available literature on your topic, carefully weighing its relevance to your study.

Save yourself many headaches later on by beginning an *annotated bibliography* as soon as you have the merest hint of an idea for your setting/topic. Record all relevant citation information; it may be very difficult to relocate a reference to extract volume or page numbers three years after you've read it and are now ready to cite it in a publication. Extract other critical details: sample size, date study was conducted, class and ethnicity information, and so on. Store your annotated bibliography in *Pro-Cite*, for example, or another similar program that automatically converts your references from APA to MLA style. You can also quickly build new reference lists from your annotated bibliography, which in effect has become a database. As you would with your field notes (see below), include reflective comments in your annotated bibliography touching on emerging themes, contradictions, and linkages between unrelated studies. It is not at all a bad idea to think of the literature review for a major qualitative research undertaking (such as a doctoral dissertation) as publishable in its own right. I have found that I generate about 100 typed pages of notes for every 20 pages of final text in doing a review article. Bear in mind that a lengthy and thoroughly annotated bibliography can be drawn on, again and again, as you write additional articles/chapters.

As I have said, the literature review is an ongoing process. At some point fairly early in this process you will need to begin to project yourself into the studies you are reading as the "principal investigator." Like trying on clothing, some will clearly not look good on you; others will fit fairly well. Once you've found a study with which you are comfortable, you may need to learn more about the project than was reported in the publication(s). Seek out unpublished technical reports on the project in the ERIC microfiche section of the library. These usually provide critical methodological details. Additionally, write to the authors for information you are unable to find in these printed sources. Virtually all national scholarly organizations publish annual membership rosters, including addresses you can use to track down peripatetic academics.

You may also decide, at this point, that you need further training in specific areas of methodology that is not available at your present institution. Most national organizations sponsor workshops in research methodology, usually accompanying their annual conventions. Some universities are exceptionally strong in faculty who use qualitative methods and, consequently, offer a range of advanced courses.

THE PRELIMINARY PROPOSAL

One develops a two- to three-page "preliminary proposal" (see Locke et al. 1987, chapter 4). This includes rationale (reason for doing the study) and problem statement; background (description of previous research, history or *known* aspects of research site/culture/group); and method and plan for data analysis/write-up/dissemination. This mini-proposal can be used to give clients/informants/authority figures an idea of your plans so that they can make an informed decision about whether to permit you to do the research. Many public agencies, including schools, require just such a proposal as part of the project approval process. It will be submitted with the "human subjects" paperwork to your Institutional Review Board.[1] It can be circulated to members of one's committee in the case of thesis/dissertation research.[2] A number of funding sources encourage the submission of such preliminary proposals as a way of saving themselves and the principal investigator time wasted writing/reviewing an inappropriate proposal. The point to be stressed here is that the *tentative* nature of this mini-proposal encourages constructive input that could have a significant impact on the direction and success of the project.

Many, many decisions will be made in the process of preparing and revising the preliminary proposal. A tentative problem, site and tradition will be identified. The scope of the project will be established. When will it start and end?[3] All other things being equal, if it is a study in a school, it should begin on the first day of school or earlier. What is the unit of analysis: is this a *district*-level study; a study of primary-grade *teachers* in a medium-size elementary school; or a study of *fourth graders* learning fractions? How many of these units will be studied, and how will they be selected?—for example, whether the teachers will be "typical" or "expert," "beginning" or "experienced." What will be the role of the investigator? What will be the principal sources of data: field notes, interviews, artifacts, videotape recordings? Where will you get equipment—video camera; still camera; computer?[4] How will these sources be used? For example, will you use participant observation to identify general themes and then videotape recordings to meticulously quantify the variables that your more informal analysis suggested should be there? How much data will you collect? How will you analyze them?

Can you cite a similar, already published study to provide at least a partial *rationale* for the answers you provide (e.g., "Smithers and Smathers (1986), in their widely cited study, videotaped *four half-hour* lessons taught by their sample of *six* algebra teachers.")? Of course the tradition in which one chooses to work will also dictate many methodological choices. I tend to believe that "ethnography" is so often the method of choice because there are so many works on the subject that provide good materials for the "methods" sections of the proposal. Other traditions have not been as well documented, methodologically speaking, although I hope this book will redress that imbalance. Of course the principal source of inspiration for making these decisions is the topic you have chosen to study. If you are interested in cognitive processes underlying the composition of poetry, the database will be very different than if you're interested in the process whereby schools manage their relationships with irate parents.

Doesn't all this discussion about specifying one's topic, data sources, and analytical procedures in advance contradict what I said about qualitative research being fluid and *ad hoc*? It does. Many of the decisions you make at this stage will be reversed once the study gets underway. But sooner or later, you will have to justify whatever decisions you have made. Simply making decisions "on the fly" based on what is most expedient or convenient won't do. By being very specific in your preliminary proposal, you demonstrate to those who will review it that you understand the interactive and reciprocal nature of these choices—that making some choices precludes others, and also that you can successfully justify your choices in terms of optimizing the credibility and usability of your research. At the same time, you must leave loopholes for yourself in the proposal, indicating the sorts of contingencies that may arise that could cause you to change your plans—for example, to increase or decrease your sample, to rely less on video- and more on audiotape, shift from second to third grade, and so forth.

For a thesis/dissertation, or if one is seeking outside funding for the project, a longer, more formal version of the proposal will be necessary. Typically, in a dissertation proposal the review of literature is quite long because it serves to provide a rationale for the study at hand *and* to demonstrate that the student has mastered this particular topic—that he or she not only has read all the important and current pertinent works but also can synthesize and weave them together into a coherent pattern. A very common and sometimes fatal flaw that is revealed in the reviewers' comments on proposals is the failure to cite some critical piece or pieces of literature.

ENTERING THE FIELD

By now the project has been approved in principle by committees, funding agencies, or school authorities. The evolving proposal has been instrumental in this process, but it has also been helped along by frequent visits/ phone calls by the principal investigator to chat informally with interested parties and authority figures about the study. Ironically, it is not usually critical that the principal investigator demonstrate that the project provide a direct benefit/payoff to children, teachers, or administrators. Trying to argue that your research will provide direct benefits may promote skepticism; it may provoke anxiety that you will call attention to problems in your zeal to be helpful; it may raise false expectations. A far more credible approach is to argue that you will be the primary beneficiary: you will earn a degree, gather material for a publication, fulfill the terms of your fellowship. All educators have had to jump through these "hoops" at some point in their careers and will empathize with your situation. Don't expect approval and support on that basis alone, however. Your proposal must provide a convincing rationale that your work will contribute in important ways to helping us understand and, eventually, solve a particular problem. In this context make sure your audience agrees that what you've chosen to call a problem is, in their view, a problem. For example, many people see youth *un*employment as a problem, whereas most secondary school teachers see youth *employment* as the problem. Don't waste people's time on a fishing expedition when you are not sure what you'll catch (if anything), or by angling for the Loch Ness monster.

The point here is that you'd better get your story straight. Whereas your university colleagues might be comfortable with qualitative research, parents or practitioners in the field will be much less so. They will want to know how and in what ways your research will disrupt their routines; they will want to know the extent to which your work will highlight their assets and liabilities; they will want to know who will read your report and whether that report will reflect positively or negatively on individuals and/or the institution as a whole. Clearly you must establish trust, and qualitative research design offers some rather paradoxical features in this endeavor. Its openness makes it impossible to specify probable outcomes in advance, and this makes people nervous. On the other hand, that same openness allows you to adjust the project more easily to people's needs and concerns. (Also bear in mind that any research you contemplate with students under the age of 18, even "just" observing, requires the informed consent of the parents.) In short, you simply have to specify what your research will entail.

You can get *permission* to be an observer, but you must be *invited* to become a participant. If this is your goal, you should move fairly quickly to try to find a niche for yourself. You must be enough of a participant so that you can avoid being labeled a "spy" but not so much of a participant that you lose your detachment as well as foreclose on opportunities for research. If you become too much of an insider, some people will stop being candid with you because of who else in the institution is intimate and candid with you. It is not wise to do ethnographic research, field study, or personal-accounts research in a setting in which you are already identified as an insider. You will need to do a major piece of plastic surgery on the image you present to colleagues, and many of these may be so skeptical about your "neutrality" that they fail to accord you the level of trust and confidentiality they would willingly afford an outsider. By the same token do not assume, for example, that as a Hispanic your entrée into the Hispanic community will be eased. People expect researchers to be outsiders, as they expect politicians to lie.

DATA COLLECTION

Look for ways to gather data unobtrusively (Webb et al. 1966). If you are interested in how students learn about government, offer to tutor them. Working one-on-one in a tutorial capacity is a well-established niche. Go bowling with the teachers after school and conduct informal interviews in the car to and from the bowling alley. Volunteer to chaperone the Saturday night dances. Go along on the team bus to away games. Sign up to supervise student teachers.

Depending on the degree of trust you expect to establish, as well as the nature of your problem ("cheating" versus "school spirit") you must choose between videotaping, audiotaping, openly taking notes, taking notes after the fact but within the setting, or writing up your notes away from the setting. Where your work falls on this continuum will depend, again, on your problem. If you will need to quantify variables eventually or to study subtle aspects of discourse, audio and/or video recording are essential. However, if your subject demands discretion, you may want to just listen carefully. Obviously there are trade-offs, but consider that almost anything added to our knowledge base (e.g., about those who vandalize schools) would be welcome. However, if you are studying student activity in third-grade reading groups, you should be gathering the kind of data that permits very fine-grained analyses or should have discovered a kind of reading group arrangement/instructional strategy not, as yet, described in the literature.

Returning regularly to your problem statement and literature you've read will provide more focused questions for your observations and interviews. However, if you want to prime your pump, review Bogden and Biklen's (1982) very helpful listing of "observational questions for educational settings" (pp. 223–233). Your observation should include, as your annotated bibliography, critical details of person, place, and activity as well as date and time, class period, and so on. Use abbreviations, nicknames, and other shorthand to get it down more efficiently. Break up your notes into more easily codable blocks. When done describing an activity, leave white space before describing the next; likewise with turn taking in conversation. Draw diagrams, maps, and sketches and/or take photos to provide a record of the physical setting, especially where this might change over time (e.g., bulletin boards, seating patterns).

You should have several different kinds of notes. One type of notation provides a general description, background. Another type is precise, detailed. Use a specifically designed form to more easily check off or note behaviors that are fleeting. This is tedious work, so you'll want to observe on a schedule—for 30 seconds every 5 minutes, for example. A form containing space for contextual notes as well as boxes to check off specific behaviors of interest can be helpful. A third type of notation provides an "explanation" for what you are observing or links the present scene to antecedents in your database. Your notes should contain a running commentary in which you reflect on what it all means—you search for themes; you identify questions or issues to follow up later, perhaps something you observed in class about which you will ask the teacher/student after class. Your observation can be conceived of as a kind of zoom lens (Everhart 1983). Even if your analysis demands a close focus most of the time, it is important to zoom out occasionally to make sure you haven't lost sight of the larger picture. Also, if your analysis is broader and you observe mostly at the "normal" setting, it is important to zoom in for authenticating detail, documenting critical incidents, and obtaining juicy quotations that build the credibility of your report. Move the lens from normal to wide angle occasionally to take in a broader context; this helps to enhance the applicability of your research.

When recorded, even casual conversations can serve as "interview" data for the participant observer. Playing other roles may require a more formally constructed interview arrangement. However, do make all of your informants aware that even casual conversations will provide grist for your mill. These interviews can range all the way from "Say, can I talk to you guys in the teachers' lounge at break?" to "I'd like to set up an appointment to interview you." Generally speaking, unless you are conducting a case study using a personal accounts approach, you will want to interview multiple informants—it is not good to rely too heavily on the views of only one or two informants in the setting. How long these interviews last and how often they are done will depend on the evolving problem focus. One general rule is that you start with longer, more open-ended *exploratory* interviews and, as your thesis firms up, you shift to shorter, more focused *confirmatory* interviews.

Virtually any qualitative study will involve the collection of artifacts, primarily printed material of various sorts. Some of this material will come to you as a matter of course if you are a participant. Open public material, such as newsletters, is there for the asking. Access to other material must be negotiated during the initial entry stage. Minutes of meetings, interoffice memos, letters and material from student and personnel records is an even more delicate area. Resist the temptation to access this material without specific consent to do so from all parties involved. The very trust that you are struggling to achieve can be your downfall, if administrators and helpful secretaries give you ready access to material they really should be guarding more carefully.

Even when test scores, performance appraisals, and psychologist's reports fall legitimately into your hands, remember that all of these "objective" indicators have been socially constructed and cannot be treated as any more "real" or valid than your observations and conversations with the individual. Of course, the focus of your study may well be on unraveling how these facts were obtained and decisions were made, so official records may be the starting point for your study.

A final decision about data is to decide when you've got enough. If you are working within the biological traditions, you will have created a fairly strict schedule for yourself in order to adequately capture variation in the phenomena of interest over its life span or cycle. Most projects in education suggest gathering data, at least intermittently, over the course of the year with heaviest observation at the beginning. Otherwise, you continue collecting data until no new patterns emerge—until what you are observing/hearing you have heard or seen before. Then you consider the possibility of triangulation: would interviews with parents provide material which complements and supports what you have learned from the teachers? Would archived records indicate that what you have observed is a long-standing phenomenon or suggest that this is an effect of a change in leadership?

REFOCUSING THE STUDY

You are now in the field, your role established, and you have begun to collect data. There are further decisions yet to be made. It is virtually inevitable that, as a qualitative researcher, you will reassess your focus, methods, and purposes based on "what turns up." At an extreme, the original site/topic is abandoned completely as being unworkable and the investigator must start over. For example, Meeks and I were hired to evaluate student attitudes towards the use of a new microcomputer lab incorporated into composition classes. Our initial interviews turned up almost uniformly positive attitudes towards the computer and word processing; however, attitudes towards the instructional approach (*writing as a process*) were quite mixed, and this became the focus for our case study (Meeks & Lancy n.d.).

As you adjust your focus, it is critically important that you return to the library for additional material. Your annotated bibliography should continue to grow throughout the duration of the study.

At another intermediate stop in your ". . . voyage of discovery" (Peshkin 1986:15), you begin to develop a "theory," a "model," a "story" that will encapsulate/explain/represent the bulk of your findings. It is important that this process begin early so that you can start to test the model by looking for disconfirming evidence. For example, in my study (Lancy 1976a) of student culture in an elementary school it seemed that the primary organizing framework for them was "activity" rather than "type of kids," as the literature on older students (Cusick 1973; Palonsky 1975) indicated. Accordingly, in ongoing interviews I probed for these types (e.g., "jocks," "brains," "goody-goodies") and didn't get any positive response, thereby helping to confirm my initial impression. Hammersley and Atkinson (1983) refer to "progressive focusing," which may ". . . involve a gradual shift from concern with describing social events and processes to developing and testing explanations" (p. 175).

This grounded theory will dictate the foci of your data collection during the remainder of the study. You will need to seek patterns in your data and to begin some preliminary analyses.

DATA ANALYSIS

Once the data collection is complete (or you have run out of time/funds), you must review notes/tape recordings/archival material and firm up a scheme to *analyze* and *reduce* what has often been described as a "mountain" of material. There is such a thing as too much data. Many researchers founder at this point; the task seems so formidable and one is haunted by the specter of seriously distorting the phenomenon one has studied in the process that follows. Analysis schemes can be as simple as the investigator identifying a major "theme" from the material and then elucidating this theme with anecdotes, discourse transcripts, and snippets of "memos" (Ball 1981). On the other hand, one can develop an extremely complex "coding form" with dozens of categories for use in minutely analyzing the hours of videotape one has made of the phenomenon (e.g., Bergin, Lancy & Draper 1994). And, of course, there are innumerable points between these two extremes. You must wrestle with the decision of how far to go in reducing the data. Again, your best guide is the published literature.

Just as you prepared a preliminary proposal, you should prepare a *preliminary* report. If this is a case study, write up or prepare an oral presentation for your clients or the subjects of your study. Offer to make a presentation at a colloquium or "brown bag," or wrangle yourself a slot on a local or regional conference. This presentation forces you to pull your material together and to try to make sense of it. Anticipating your public debut is a wonderful antidote to procrastination, collecting too much data, and failing to define the problem. You really desperately need to get feedback on your thesis: Does it hang together? Is it, perhaps, less novel than you assumed, e.g., have you missed a precedent in the literature? Is it contradicted by other extant research? Have you failed to consider an equally plausible alternative thesis that better explains your observations? Is your thesis perhaps more complex than it needs to be or more complex than your slender database (interviews with two teachers) will support? Your audience will help you see these pitfalls *before* you fold your tent and leave the field, or at least before you have invested a lot of time in what may be a fruitless analytical scheme.

Your colleagues in the field also deserve to be informed about your emerging thesis and findings. However, they can only tell you whether your arguments make sense from their (emic) perspective; they are not a good audience as far as feedback regarding the value of your work to scholars.

STRUCTURING THE REPORT

During data analysis (if not sooner) major themes/issues emerge, and these serve as natural divisions as the investigator wrestles with the problem of how to *structure* the report. Other natural divisions reflect different databases (e.g., sections reporting "interview results," "classroom observations," "achievement records"). Unlike in quantitative research, these divisions aren't always anticipated at the outset of qualitative research; thus the report (thesis/dissertation/article) may be structured quite differently from the original proposal. Return to the model study or studies that you felt best reflected the assumptions and methods you would use in your study. How are the reports structured? If this is a dissertation, look at other dissertations that employed similar methodology. If this is a report to an agency, ask to see earlier reports; if this is to be an article, study the format of articles that appear in your target journals and read the "advice to authors" section.

If quantitative analyses are to be undertaken on some part of your database, arrange to have this done. Use multiple coders (fellow students?) and take full advantage of state-of-the-art technology to simplify this process. This analysis stage can be a welcome breather between being in the field and "writing it up." You are moving forward but, for the time being, you don't have to face your notes. Don't let this stage become a dead end, however. Don't keep looking for "significance" or patterns that may not be there. Get on with it, although it is not necessarily the case that your report will be written from the beginning straight through to the end. One way to avoid "writer's block" is to start with a section or chapter that is relatively straightforward, such as *methods* or *review of literature.*

A draft of the final report is prepared. This draft is shared with one's colleagues, professors, and key informants for feedback on clarity, cohesion, accuracy, creditability, and so on. Given the dearth of qualitative researchers, one often has to go far afield to seek informed scholarly feedback. A good strategy is to seek assistance from published scholars one has cited or relied upon heavily. However, don't be surprised if they fail to respond to your query. Your key informants may be very disappointed, even upset by your report. If they claim that you have misrepresented them or their institution, this is a serious charge. You must either alter your text or, if you believe this is a genuine difference of opinion, provide them with some means of rebuttal (perhaps in an appendix or by yourself reporting the contradictory views). If your report is "accurate" but unflattering, you can go to greater lengths to protect the anonymity of your subjects. Remember they have come to trust you; they believe you have come to share their view of the world. If this is not the case, they shouldn't find out for the first time when they read your report. On the other hand, don't be at all surprised if your colleagues in the field are indifferent to your report or if they evince selective attention, reading and perhaps enjoying the descriptive material but bypassing the analysis.

Colleagues in the university will also range in their level of interest and on what aspects of your study they choose to focus. Again, the fluid nature of qualitative research can create problems for you at this juncture. There may be differences of opinion on what direction to take the thesis. One colleague wants you to focus on aspects of "gender relations" and foreground that issue, while another feels your best material relates to the issue of "stages in teaching." If you are doing this as a dissertation, you can find yourself in a "tug of war" where you're the rope. This suggests the importance of selecting a mentor or supervisor with very high interest (ownership) in your problem with whom you will work closely throughout this process. This person should then be ready and willing to referee any of these disagreements. A journal editor plays, or should play, a similar role when two or more outside reviewers of your work provide contradictory recommendations.

The final draft, while possibly acceptable for a thesis/dissertation committee or a funding agency or client (e.g., "Lincoln School District"), will not usually be suitable for publication. It will be too long, particularly the review of literature and methods sections. A truly unique work, one that has uncovered some previously unreported aspect of mainstream public education (Mehan, Hertweck, & Miehls 1986) or some exotic species of educational endeavor (Peshkin 1986) has a fair chance of being published as a book. It is useful to ask colleagues who read your work to comment on its "publishability."

On the other hand, many qualitative studies can be broken into pieces along the "natural divisions" mentioned above. This is, once again, the time to return to your annotated bibliography to find out where people whose work you've cited are publishing. Also, don't be bashful at conferences. A very high proportion of qualitative research is now being published in edited collections, and these publishing opportunities arise almost entirely through personal contacts. If you want to get your qualitative research published you must become a joiner, so yet another decision relates to which organizations you should patronize.

Well, I guess it's time for you to be getting started. Good luck!

ENDNOTES

[1] Murphy and Johannsen (1990) suggest that Institutional Review Board (IRB) guidelines do not work very well with ethnographic research, created as they were primarily to deal with experimental research with a biomedical slant.

[2] Or peer input for post-doctoral research, e.g., "When this study was no more than an idea, I wrote proposal drafts that benefited from the criticism of Steve Asher, Eric Bredo . . ." (Peshkin 1986:x).

[3] A nice range of examples from 2 hours to 2 years can be found in Dobbert (1982).

[4] Do use *professional* standard equipment that is new and/or recently refurbished in order to avoid potentially great tragedy. I have audiotapes made on outmoded equipment that are nearly indecipherable and videotapes with an audible hum—from florescent lighting—made with a "home" video camera.

References

Abramovitch, R. (1976). "The relation of attention and proximity to rank in the preschool children." In M. R. A. Chance & R. R. Larsen (Eds.), *The social structure of attention*, pp. 154–176. London: Academic Press.

Acker, S. (Ed.) (1989). *Teachers, gender and careers*. London: Falmer Press.

Agar, M. H. (1986). *Speaking of ethnography*. Newbury Park, CA: Sage.

Aldis, O. (1975). *Play fighting*. New York: Academic Press.

Alkin, M., R. Daillak, & P. White. (1979). *Using evaluations: Does evaluation make a difference?* Newbury Park, CA: Sage.

Altman, J. (1974). "Observational study of behavior: Sampling methods." *Behaviour, 49,* 227–265.

Anderson, G. L. (1989). "Critical ethnography in education: Origins, current status and new directions." *Review of Educational Research, 59*(3), 249–270.

Anderson, R. B. (1977, April). *The effectiveness of follow through: What have we learned?* Paper presented at the annual meeting of the American Educational Research Association, New York.

Anderson, L. W., & R. B. Burns. (1990). *Research in classrooms*. New York: Pergamon Press.

Anyon, J. (1980). "Social class and the hidden curriculum of work." *Journal of Education, 162,* 67–92.

Ashton-Warner, S. (1986). *Teacher*. New York: Simon & Schuster.

Ayers, W. (1989). *The good preschool teacher: Six teachers reflect on their lives*. New York: Teacher's College Press.

Baker, C. (1969). *Ernest Hemingway: A life story*. New York: Scribners.

Baker, D., & D. Stevenson. (1986). "Mothers' strategies for school achievement: Managing the transition to high school." *Sociology of Education, 59,* 156–167.

Baker, V. J. (2000). "Village school in Sri Lanka." *Anthropology and Education Quarterly, 31*(1), 109–116.

Ball, D. L. (1990). "Reflections and deflections of policy: The case of Carol Turner." *Educational Evaluation and Policy Analysis, 12*(3), 263–275.

Ball, S. J. (1981). *Beachside comprehensive: A case study of secondary schooling.* Cambridge, MA: Cambridge University Press.

Ball, S. J. (1984). "Beachside revisited." In R. G. Burgess (Ed.), *Field research: A sourcebook and field manual,* pp. 69–96. London: Allen and Unwin.

Ball, S. J., & I. F. Goodson. (1985). "Understanding teachers: Concepts and contexts." In S. J. Ball & I. F. Goodson (Eds.), *Teachers' lives and careers,* pp. 1–26. London: Falmer Press.

Barker, R. G. (1976). "Naturalistic methods in psychological research." *Human Development, 10,* 223–229.

Barker, R. G., & P. B. Gump. (1964). *Big school, small school: High school size and student behavior.* Stanford: Stanford University Press.

Barone, T. (1987). "On equality, visibility and the fine arts program in a black elementary school: An example of educational criticism." *Curriculum Inquiry, 17*(4), 421–446.

Barone, T. (1995). "Persuasive writings, vigilant readings, and reconstructed characters: The paradox of trust in educational storysharing." *International Journal of Qualitative Studies in Education, 8*(1), 63–74.

Barr, R., & R. Dreeben. (1983). *How schools work.* Chicago: University of Chicago Press.

Becker, H. S. (1951). *Role and career problems of the Chicago public school teacher.* Unpublished dissertation. University of Chicago.

Becker, H. S. (1970). *Sociological work: Method and substance.* Chicago: Aldine.

Becker, H. S., B. Geer, E. C. Hughes, & L. A. Strauss. (1961). *Boys in white: Student culture in medical school.* Chicago: University of Chicago Press.

Bem, S. (1987). "Gender schema theory and the romantic tradition." In P. Shaver & C. Hendrick (Eds.), *Review of personality and social psychology, 7,* 251–271. Newbury Park, CA: Sage.

Bempechat, J., & E. Drago-Severson. (1999). "Cross-national differences in academic achievement: Beyond etic conceptions of children's understanding." *Review of Educational Research, 69,* 287–314.

Bengston, J. K. (1988). "What makes a study qualitative? A critique of Gershman's surviving through time." *Qualitative Studies in Education, 1*(4), 343–346.

Bennett, K. P., & M. D. LeCompte. (1990). *How schools work: A sociological analysis of education.* White Plains, NY: Longman.

Bergin, C., D. F. Lancy, & K. D. Draper. (1994). "Parents' interactions with beginning readers." In D. F. Lancy (Ed.), *Children's emergent literacy: From research to practice,* pp. 53–78. Westport, CT: Praeger.

Berk, L. E., & M. P. Berson. (1975). "The school bus as a development experience for young children." *Illinois School Research, 11*(3), 1–14.

Best, R. (1983). *We've all got scars.* Bloomington: University of Indiana Press.

Beynon, J. (1985). "Institutional change and career histories in a comprehensive school." In S. J. Ball & I. F. Goodson (Eds.). *Teachers' lives and careers,* pp. 158–179. London: Falmer.

Bickman, L., A. Teger, T. Gabriele, C. McLaughlin, M. Berger, & E. Sunaday. (1973). "Dormitory density and helping behavior." *Environment and Behavior, 5*(4), 465–490.

Bloch, M. N., & A. D. Pellegrini. (1989). *The ecological context of children's play.* Norwood, NJ: Ablex.

Blurton-Jones, N. G. (1967). "An ethological study of some aspects of social behavior of children in nursery school." In D. Morris (Ed.), *Primate ethology,* pp. 347–367. London: Weidenfield and Nicolson.

Blurton-Jones, N. G. (1968). "Observations and experiment on the causation of threat displays of the great Tit *Parus Major.*" *Animal Behavior Monographs, 1,* 75–158.

Bogdan, R. (1980). "Interviewing people labeled retarded." In W. B. Shaffer, R. A. Stebbins, & A. Turowetz (Eds.), *Fieldwork experience: Qualitative approaches to social research,* pp. 235–243. New York: St. Martins.

Bogdan, R. C., & S. K. Biklen. (1982). *Qualitative research for education: An introduction to theory and methods.* Boston: Allyn & Bacon.

Bourdieu, P. (1977). "Cultural reproduction and social reproduction." In J. Karabel & A. H. Halsey (Eds.), *Power and ideology in education,* pp. 487–511. New York: Oxford.

Bourdieu, P., & J. C. Passeron. (1977). *Reproduction in education, society and culture.* Newbury Park, CA: Sage.

Britzman, D. P. (1991). *Practice makes practice: A critical study of learning to teach.* Albany: SUNY Press.

Bronfenbrenner, U. (1979). *The ecology of human development.* Cambridge, MA: Harvard University Press.

Brown, L. D. (1985). "People-centered development and participatory research." *Harvard Education Review, 55*(1), 69–75.

Bruner, J. (1986). *Actual lives: Possible worlds.* Cambridge, MA: Harvard University Press.

Bullough, Jr., R. V. (1989). *First-year teacher: A case study.* New York: Teachers College Press.

Burnaford, G., J. Fisher, & P. Hobson. (Eds.) (1996). *Teachers doing research: Practical possibilities.* Mahwah, NJ: LEA.

Burton, L. M., D. A. Obeidallah, & K. Allison. (1996). "Ethnographic insights on social context and adolescent development among inner-city African-American teens." In R. Jessor, A. Colby, & R. A. Shweder (Eds.), *Ethnography and human development,* pp. 395–418. Chicago: University of Chicago Press.

Calhoun, J. B. (1962). "Population density and social pathology." *Scientific American, 206*(2), 138–148.

Carrier, J. (1979). "School and community on Ponam." In D. F. Lancy (Ed.), *The community school,* special issue of the *Papua New Guinea Journal of Education, 15,* 66–77.

Cazden, C. B. (1979). "Forward to Hugh Mehan's *Learning Lessons.*" Cambridge, MA: Harvard University Press, pp. vii–xi.

Cazden, C. B. (1988). *Classroom discourse: The language of teaching and learning.* Portsmouth, NH: Heinemann.

Champaign, A. B., & L. E. Klopfer. (1974). "An individualized elementary school science program." *Theory into Practice, 13,* 136–148.

Chance, M. R. A., & C. J. Jolly. (1970). *Social groups of monkeys, apes, and men.* New York: Dutton.

Channon, G. (1970). *Homework.* New York: Quaterbridge and Dienstfrey.

Charlesworth, W. R., & C. Dzur. (1987). "Gender comparisons of preschoolers' behavior and resource utilization in group problem solving." *Child Development, 58,* 191–200.

Cherry, M. (1978). *Train whistle blues.* Garden City, NY: Doubleday.

Chesterfield, R. A. (1986). "Qualitative methodology in the evaluation of early childhood bilingual curriculum models." In D. M. Fetterman & M. A. Pitman. (Eds.), *Educational evaluation: Ethnography in theory, practice and politics,* pp. 145–168. Newbury Park, CA: Sage.

Chilcott, J. H. (1962). "Enculturation in a Mexican rancheria." *Journal of Educational Sociology, 36*(1), 42–47.

Christman, J., J. Hirschman, A. Holtz, H. Perry, I. Spelkoman, & M. Williams. (1995). "Doing Eve's work: Women principals write about their practice." *Anthropology and Education Quarterly, 26*(2), 213–227.

Churchill, L. (1978). *Questioning strategies in sociolinguistics.* Rowley, MA: Newbury House.

Cicourel, A. V. (1968). *The social organization of juvenile justice.* New York: Wiley.

Cicourel, A. V. (1974). *Cognitive Sociology.* New York: Free Press.

Cicourel, A. V., K. H. Jennings, S. H. M. Jennings, K. C. W. Leiter, R. W. MacKay, H. Mehan, & D. R. Roth. (1974). *Language use and school performance.* New York: Academic.

Cicourel, A. V., & J. A. Kitsuse. (1963). *The educational decision makers.* Indianapolis, IN: Bobbs-Merrill.

Cicourel, A. V., & H. Mehan. (1983). "Universal development , stratifying practices, and status attainment." *Research in Social Stratification and Mobility, 4,* 3–27.

Clandinin, D. J. (1986). *Classroom practice: Teacher images in action.* London: Falmer Press.

Clandinin, D. J., & F. M. Connelly. (1991). "Narrative and story in practice and research." In D. A. Schön (Ed.), *The reflective eye: Case studies in and on educational practice,* pp. 258–281. New York: Teachers College.

Clifford, G. J. (1989). "Introduction." In G. J. Clifford (Ed.), *Lone voyagers: Academic women in coeducational universities 1870–1937,* pp. 1–46. New York: Feminist Press of CUNY.

Cohen, D. K. (1989). "Teaching practice: Plus a change . . ." In P. W. Jackson (Ed.), *Contributing to educational change: Perspectives on research and practice,* pp. 27–84. Berkeley, CA: McCutchan.

Cole, M., J. A. Gay, J. Glick, D. W. Sharp, T. Ciborowski, F. Frankel, J. Kellemu, & D. F. Lancy. (1971). *The cultural context of learning & thinking.* New York: Basic Books.

Cole, M., & S. Cole. (1989). *The development of children.* New York: Scientific American.

Collier, J. (1967). *Visual anthropology: Photography as a research method.* New York: Holt, Rinehart & Winston.

Collins, J. (1988). "Language and class in minority education." *Anthropology and Education Quarterly, 17,* 299–323.

Collins, T., & G. Noblit. (1978). *Stratification and desegregation: The case of Crossover High School.* Final Report of NIE Contract #400-76-009.

Connelly, F. M., & D. J. Clandinin. (1988). *Teachers as curriculum planners: Narratives of experience.* New York: Teachers College Press.

Connelly, F. M., & D. J. Clandinin. (1990). "Stories of experience and narrative inquiry." *Educational Researcher, 19*(5), 2–14.

Conroy, P. (1972/1987). *The water is wide.* New York: Bantam.

Convery, A. (1999). "Listening to teachers' stories: Are we siting too comfortably?" *International Journal of Qualitative Studies in Education, 12*(2), 131–146.

Cooper, J. E., & R. H. Heck. (1995). "Using narrative in the study of school administration." *International Journal of Qualitative Studies in Education, 8*(2), 195–210.

Corsario, W. A. (1985). *Friendship and peer culture in the early years.* Norwood, NJ: Ablex.

Corsario, W. A. (1988a). "Routines in the peer culture of American and Italian nursery school children." *Sociology of Education, 61,* 114.

Corsario, W. A. (1988b). "Peer culture in the preschool." *Theory into Practice, 27*(1), 19–24.

Corsario, W. A., & T. A. Rizzo. (1988). "Discussions and friendship: socialization processes in the peer culture of Italian nursery school children." *American Sociological Review, 53,* 879–894.

Cox, J. M. (1971). "Autobiography and America." In J. H. Miller (Ed.), *Aspects of narrative*, pp. 252–277. New York: Columbia University Press.

Cronbach, L., & Associates. (1980). *Toward reform of program evaluation*. San Francisco: Jossey Bass.

Csikszentmihalyi, M., & R. Larson. (1984). *Being adolescent: Conflict and growth in the teenage years*. New York: Basic Books.

Cusick, P. A. (1973). *Inside high school: The students world*. New York: Holt, Rinehart & Winston.

Datnow, A. (1977). "Using gender to preserve tracking's status hierarchy: The defensive strategy of entrenched teachers." *Anthropology and Education Quarterly, 28*(2), 204–228.

Davies, L. (1985). "Ethnography and status: Focusing on gender in educational research." In R. G. Burgess (Ed.), *Field methods in the study of education*, pp. 79–96. London: Falmer Press.

Davis, A. (1996, April). *Successful urban classrooms as communities of practice: Writing and identity*. Paper presented at annual meeting, American Educational Research Association, New York.

Davis, J. (1972). Teachers, kids and conflict: Ethnography of a junior high school. In J. P. Spradley & D. W. McCurdy (Eds.), *The cultural experience: Ethnography in complex society*, pp. 103–119. Chicago: SRA.

Delamont, S. (1984). "The old girl network: Reflections on fieldwork at St. Luke's." In R. G. Burgess (Ed.), *The research process in educational settings: Ten case studies*, pp. 15–38. London: Methuen.

Delgado-Gaitan, C. (1994). "Russian refugee families: Accommodating aspiration through education." *Anthropology and Education Quarterly, 25*(2), 137–155.

Dennis, W. (1943). "The Hopi child." In R. G. Barnes, J. S. Kounin, & H. F. Wright (Eds.), *Child behavior and development*, pp. 621–636. New York: McGraw Hill.

Denzin, N. K. (1970). *The research act: A theoretical introduction to sociological methods*. Chicago: Aldine.

Denzin, N. K. (1989). *Interpretive biography*. Newbury Park, CA: Sage.

Denzin, N. K. (1994). "Evaluating qualitative research in the post-structuralist moment: The lessons James Joyce teaches us." *International Journal for Qualitative Studies in Education, 7*(4), 295–308.

Derrida, J. (1981). *Positions*. Chicago: University of Chicago Press.

Devine, J. (1996). *Maximum security: The culture of violence in inner-city schools*. Chicago: University of Chicago Press.

DeWalt, M. K., & B. K. Troxell. (1989). "Old order Mennonite one room school." *Anthropology and Education Quarterly, 20*(4), 308–325.

Deyhle, D. (1986). "Break dancing and breaking out: Anglos, Utes and Navajos in a border reservation high school." *Anthropology and Education Quarterly, 17*(2), 111–127.

Deyhle, D. (1998). "The role of the applied anthropologist: Between schools and the Navajo Nation." In K. B. deMarrais (Ed.), *Qualitative research reflections*. Mahwah, NJ: Lawrence Erlbaum Associates.

Diesing, P. (1971). *Patterns of discovery in the social sciences*. Chicago: Aldine.

Dobbert, M. L. (1975). "Another route to a general theory of cultural transmission: A systems model." *Anthropology and Education Quarterly, 6*(2).

Dobbert, M. L. (1982). *Ethnographic research: Theory and application for modern societies and schools*. New York: Praeger.

Douglas, J. D. (1976). *Investigative social research*. Newbury Park, CA: Sage.

Douglas, J. D. (1985). *Creative interviewing.* Newbury Park, CA: Sage.

Dubois, C. (1944). *The people of Alor.* Minneapolis: University of Minnesota Press.

Eckert, P. (1989). *Jocks and burnouts: Social categories and identity in the high school.* New York: Teachers College Press.

Edelsky, C. (1990). "Whose agenda is this anyway?: A response to McKenna, Robinson & Miller." *Educational Researcher, 20*(8), 7–11.

Edelsky, C., B. Altwerger, & B. Flores. (1991). *Whole language: What's the difference?* Portsmouth, NH: Heinemann.

Edelsky, C., & K. Draper. (1989). "Reading/reading, writing/writing, text/text." *Reading-Canada-Lecture, 7,* 201–216.

Edelsky, C., K. Draper, & K. Smith. (1983). "Hookin' 'em in at the start of school in a 'whole language' classroom." *Anthropology and Education Quarterly, 14*(4), 257–281.

Eder, D. (1982). "Differences in communicative styles across ability groups." In L. C. Wilkinson (Ed.), *Communicating in classrooms,* pp. 245–264. New York: Academic Press.

Edwards, N. (1989). *Stand and deliver.* New York: Scholastic.

Eibl-Eibesfeldt, I. (1983). "Patterns of parent-child interaction in a cross-cultural perspective." In A. Oliverio & M. Cappella (Eds.), *The behavior of human infants,* pp. 177–217. New York: Plenum.

Eisner, E. W., & A. Peshkin. (Eds.) (1990). *Qualitative inquiry in education: The continuing debate.* New York: Columbia Teachers College Press.

Elbaz, F. (1983). *Teacher thinking: A study of practical knowledge.* London: Croom Helm.

Ellis, J. J., & R. Moore. (1974). *School for soldiers: West Point and the profession of arms.* New York: Oxford University Press.

Erickson, F. (1973/1984). "What makes school ethnography ethnographic? Revised version." *Anthropology and Education Quarterly, 15*(1), 51–66.

Erickson, F. (1982). "Classroom discourse as improvisation; relationships between academic task structure and social participation structure in lessons." In L. C. Wilkinson (Ed.), *Communicating in the classroom,* pp. 153–182. New York: Academic Press.

Erickson, F., & G. Mohatt. (1982). "Cultural organization of participation structures in two classrooms of Indian students." In G. Spindler (Ed.), *Doing the ethnography of schooling: Educational anthropology in action,* pp. 132–175. New York: Holt, Rinehart & Winston.

Erickson, F., & J. Schultz. (1982). *The counselor as gatekeeper: Social interaction in interviews.* New York: Academic Press.

Ericsson, K. A., & H. A. Simon. (1984). *Protocol analysis.* Cambridge, MA: MIT Press.

Errante, A. (2000). "But sometimes you're not part of the story: Oral histories and ways of remembering and telling." *Educational Researcher, 29*(2), pp. 16–27.

Everhart, R. B. (1975, December). *Cognitive mapping in the study of the social and formal organization of the school.* Paper presented to the meeting of the American Anthropological Association. San Francisco.

Everhart, R. B. (1983). *Reading, writing and resistance: Adolescence and labor in a junior high school.* Boston: Routledge, & Kegan Paul.

Ferrell, B. G., & D. W. Compton. (1986). "Use of ethnographic techniques for evaluation in a large school district: The Vanguard case." In D. M. Fetterman & M. A. Pitman (Eds.), *Educational evaluation: Ethnography in theory, practice and politics,* pp. 171–191. Newbury Park, CA: Sage.

Fetterman, D. M. (1989). *Ethnography: Step by step.* Newbury Park, CA: Sage.

Finders, M. J. (1997). *Just girls: Hidden literacies and life in junior high*. New York: Teacher's College Press.

Fine, G. A. (1983). *Shared fantasy*. Chicago: University of Chicago Press.

Fitzpatrick, E. (1989). "For the women of the university: Marion Talbot 1858-1948." In G. J. Clifford (Ed.), *Lone voyagers: Academic women in coeducational universities 1870–1937*, pp. 87–124. New York: Feminist Press of CUNY.

Fordham, S. (1996). *Blacked out: Dilemmas of race, identity and success at Capital High*. Chicago: University of Chicago Press.

Fordham, S. (1999). "Dissin' 'the standard': Ebonics as guerilla warfare at Capital High." *Anthropology and Education Quarterly, 30*(3), 272–293.

Fordham, S., & J. U. Obgu. (1986). "Black students' school success: Coping with the burden of 'acting white.'" *The Urban Review, 18*(3), 176–206.

Forsyth, A. S., & D. F. Lancy. (1987). "Simulated travel and place location learning in a computer adventure game." *Journal of Educational Computing Research, 3*, 377–394.

Forsyth, A. S., & D. F. Lancy. (1989). "Girls and micro computers: A hopeful finding regarding software." *Computers in the Schools, 6*(3/4), 51–59.

Frake, C. O. (1964). "The ethnographic study of cognitive systems." In S. A. Tyler (Ed.), *Cognitive anthropology*, pp. 28–41. New York: Holt, Rinehart & Winston.

Frazer, J. G. (1922). *The golden bough*. New York: Macmillan (abridged edition, originally published 1900).

Freedman, D. G. (1977). "The development of social hierarchies." In E. M. Hetherington & R. C. Parke (Eds.), *Contemporary readings in child psychology*, pp. 372–379. New York: McGraw-Hill.

Freedman, S. G. (1990). *Small victories: The real world of a teacher, her students and their high school*. New York: Harper & Row.

Freeman, D. (1983). *Margaret Mead and Samoa: The making and unmaking of an anthropological myth*. Cambridge, MA: Harvard University Press.

Fuchs, E. (1969). *Teacher's talk: Views from inside city schools*. Garden City, NY: Doubleday.

Gage, N. L. (1989). "The paradigm wars and their aftermath." *Educational Researcher, 18*(7), 4–10.

Gallimore, R. J., J. W. Boggs, & C. Jordan. (1974). *Culture, behavior and education: A study of Hawaiian Americans*. Beverly Hills: Sage.

Gamoran, A., & M. Berends. (1987). "The effects of stratification in secondary schools: Synthesis of survey and ethnographic research." *Review of Educational Research, 57*(4), 415–435.

Gardner, M. R. (1994). *On trying to teach*. Hillsdale, NJ: Analytic Press.

Garfinkel, H. (1967). *Studies in ethnomethodology*. Englewood Cliffs, NJ: Prentice Hall.

Gearing, F. O., & P. Epstein. (1982). "Learning to wait: An ethnographic probe into the operations of an item of hidden curriculum." In G. Spindler (Ed.), *Doing the ethnography of schooling: Educational anthropology in action*, pp. 240–267. New York: Holt, Rinehart & Winston.

Geertz, C. (1973). *The interpretation of cultures*. New York: Basic Books.

Gerlach, J. M., & V. R. Monseau. (1991). *Missing chapters: Ten pioneering women in NCTE and English education*. Urbana, IL: NCTE.

Gershman, K. (1988). "Surviving through time: A life history of a high school drama production." *International Journal of Qualitative Studies in Education, 1*(3), 239–262.

Gibson, M. A. (1982). "Reputation and respectability: How competing cultural systems affect students' performance in school." *Anthropology and Education Quarterly, 13*(1), 3–27.

Gibson, M. A. (1983). *Home-school-community linkages: A study of education opportunity for Punjabi youth.* Washington, DC: Final report to the National Institute of Education.

Gibson, M. A. (1985). "Collaborative educational ethnography: Problems and profits." *Anthropology and Education Quarterly, 16,* 124–148.

Gibson, M. A. (1987). "Punjabi immigrants in an American high school." In G. Spindler & L. Spindler (Eds.), *Interpretive ethnography of education,* pp. 281–310. Hillsdale, NJ: Erlbaum.

Gibson, M. A. (1988). *Accommodation without assimilation: Sikh immigrants in an American high school.* Ithaca, NY: Cornell University Press.

Giele, J. Z., & G. H. Elder, Jr. (1998). *Methods of life course research: Qualitative and quantitative approaches.* Thousand Oaks, CA: Sage.

Glaser, B. G., & A. L. Strauss. (1967). *The discovery of grounded theory: Strategies for qualitative research.* Chicago: Aldine.

Glaser, R. (1976). *Adaptive education: Individual diversity and learning.* New York: Holt, Rinehart &Winston.

Gleason, J. J. (1989). *Special education in context.* New York: Cambridge University Press.

Goetz. J. P., & M. D. LeCompte. (1984). *Ethnography and qualitative design in educational research.* New York: Academic Press.

Goffman, E. (1959). *The presentation of self in everyday life.* Garden City, NY: Doubleday, Anchor.

Goffman, E. (1961). *Asylums.* Garden City, NY: Anchor.

Goffman, E. (1963). *Behavior in public places.* Glencoe, IL: Free Press.

Goldstein, G., & D. F. Lancy. (1985). "Cognitive development in autistic children." In F. J. Morrison & L. S. Siegel (Eds.), *Cognitive development in atypical children,* pp. 83–112. New York: Springer.

Göncü, A. (Ed.) (1999). *Children's engagement in the world: Sociocultural perspectives.* New York: Cambridge University Press

Goodenough, W. M. (1971). *Culture, language and society.* Reading, MA: Addison-Wesley.

Goodlad, J. I. (1984). *A place called school .* New York: McGraw-Hill

Goodnow, J. J., J. Cashmore, S. Cotton, & R. Knight. (1984). "Mothers' developmental timetables in two cultural groups." *International Journal of Psychology, 19,* 193–205.

Goodson, I. F. (1989). "Teachers' lives." In J. B. Allen & J. P. Goetz (Eds.), *Qualitative research in education: Teaching and learning qualitative traditions,* pp. 150–159. Athens: University of Georgia.

Gorden, R. L. (1980). *Interviewing: Strategy, techniques & tactics* (rev. ed.). Homewood, IL: Dorsey.

Goto, S. T. (1997). "Nerds, normal people and homeboys: Accommodation and resistance among Chinese-American students." *Anthropology and Education Quarterly, 28*(1), 70–84.

Gould, S. J. (1981). *The mismeasure of man.* New York: Norton.

Graue, M. E., & D. J. Walsh. (1998). *Studying children in context: Theories, methods and ethics.* Thousand Oaks, CA: Sage.

Green, J. L., J. O. Harker, & J. M. Golden. (1987). In G. W. Noblit & W. T. Pink (Eds.), *Schooling in social context,* pp. 46–77. Norwood, NJ: Ablex.

Grindal, B. (1972). *Growing up in two worlds: Education and transition among the Sisala of Northern Ghana.* New York: Holt, Rinehart & Winston.

Gross, N., J. B. Giacquinta, & A. Bernstein. (1971). *Implementing organization innovations: A sociological analysis of planned educational change.* New York: Basic Books.

Grossman, P. L. (1991). "What are we talking about anyway?: Subject-matter knowledge of secondary English teachers." *Advances in Research on Teaching, 2,* 245–262.

Grumet, M. R. (1988). *Bitter milk: Women and teaching.* Amherst: University of Massachusetts Press.

Grumet, M. R. (1991). "The politics of personal knowledge." In C. Witherel & N. Noddings (Eds.), *Stories lives tell: Narrative and dialogue in education,* pp. 67–77. New York: Teachers College Press.

Gudmundsdottir, S. (1990). "Values in pedagogical content knowledge." *Journal of Teacher Education, 41*(3), 44–52.

Gump, P. V. (1974). "Operating environments in schools of open and traditional design." *School Review, 84*(4), 575–593.

Gump, P. V. (1978). "School environment." In I. Altman & J. F. Wohlwill (Eds.), *Children and the environment,* pp. 33–51. New York: Plenum.

Hallpike, C. R. (1977). *Bloodshed and vengeance in the Papuan Mountains.* Oxford: Oxford University Press.

Hammersley, M. (1984). "Staffroom news." In A. Hargreaves & P. Woods (Eds.), *Classrooms and staffrooms,* pp. 203–214. London: Open University Press.

Hammersley, M., & P. Atkinson. (1983). *Ethnography: Principles in practice.* London: Tavistock.

Hanks, L. M. (1973). "Indifference to modern education in a Thai farming community." In F. A. J. Ianni & E. Storey (Eds.), *Cultural relevance and educational issues,* pp. 357–371. Boston: Little, Brown.

Hanna, J. L. (1988). *Disruptive school behavior: Class, race, and culture.* New York: Holmes & Meier.

Hargreaves, A. (1984). "Experience counts, theory doesn't: Teachers talk about their work." *Sociology of Education, 57,* 244–254.

Hargreaves, D. H. (1982). *The challenge for the comprehensive school.* London: Routledge.

Harklau, L. (1994). "Jumping tracks: How language minority students negotiate evaluations of ability." *Anthropology and Education Quarterly, 25*(3), 347–363.

Harkness, S., & C. M. Super. (Eds.). (1996). *Parents' cultural belief systems.* New York: Guilford .

Harris, M. (1968). *The rise of anthropological theory.* New York: Crowell.

Hart-Landsberg, S. (1982). *Toward a clear picture of Thinkabout: An account of classroom use.* Bloomington, IN: Agency for Instructional Television.

Hartwig, F., & B. E. Dearing. (1979). *Exploratory data analysis.* Newberry Park, CA: Sage.

Hatch, J. A. (1987). "Status and power in a kindergarten peer group." *The Elementary School Journal, 88*(1), 79–92.

Heath, S. B. (1982). "What no bedtime story means." *Language in Society, 11*(1), 49–76.

Heath, S. B. (1983). *Ways with words.* New York: Cambridge University Press.

Hemwall, M. K. (1984). "Hearing impaired students in the mainstream." In D. M. Fetterman (Ed.), *Ethnography in educational evaluation,* pp. 133–152. Newbury Park, CA: Sage.

Herndon, J. (1968). *The way it spozed to be.* New York: Simon & Schuster.

Hirsch, E. D. (1987). *Cultural literacy.* Boston: Houghton-Mifflin.

Hitchcock, G., & D. Hughes. (1989). *Research and the teacher.* London: Routledge.

Hoffman, N. (1981). *Woman's "true" profession: Voices from the history of teaching.* Old Westbury, NY: Feminist Press.

Hold, B. C. L. (1976). "Attention structure and rank specific behavior in preschool children." In M. R. A. Chance & R. R. Larsen (Eds.), *The social structure of attention*. London: Academic Press.

Hollingshead, A. B. (1949/1975). *Elmtown's youth and Elmtown revisited*. New York: Wiley.

Hoover, J. H. (1985). "A comparison of traditional pre-school and companion play from a social/cognitive perspective." Unpublished Master's Theses. Utah State University.

Horowitz, R. (1983). *Honor and the American dream*. Brunswick, NJ: Rutgers University Press.

Hostetler, J. A. (1974). "Education in communitarian societies—The old order Amish and Hutterite brethren." In G. D. Spindler (Ed.), *Education and cultural process* (3rd ed., pp. 119–138). New York: Holt, Rinehart & Winston.

Hostetler, J. A., & G. E. Huntington. (1971). *Children in Amish society* . New York: Holt, Rinehart & Winston.

Howard, A. (1970). *Learning to be Rotuman*. New York: Teachers College Press.

Howe, K. R., & M. Eisenhart. (1990). "Standards for qualitative (and quantitative) research: A prolegomenon." *Educational Researcher, 19*(4), 2–9.

Huberman, A. M., & M. B. Miles. (1984). *Innovation up close: How school improvement works*. New York: Plenum.

Hull, G. (1993). "Critical literacy and beyond: Issues learned from students and workers in a vocational program." *Anthropology and Education Quarterly, 24*(4), 373–396.

Humphreys, A. P., & P. K. Smith. (1987). "Rough and tumble, friendship and dominance in school children: Evidence for continuity and change with age." *Child Development, 58*, 201–212.

Husserl, E. (1962). *Ideas: General introduction to pure phenomenology.* New York: Macmillan.

Hutt, S., & C. Hutt. (1970). *Direct observation and measurement of behavior.* Springfield, IL: Thomas.

Hutt, S. J., C. Hutt, D. Lee, & C. Ounsted. (1965). "A behavioral & encephalogical study of autistic children." *Journal of Psychiatric Research, 3*, 181–197.

Hymes, D. H. (1977). *What is ethnography?* (Unpublished manuscript) Philadelphia: University of Pennsylvania, ED 159–234.

Jacob, E. (1987). "Qualitative research traditions: A review." *Review of Educational Research, 57*, 1–50.

James, D. (1969). *The taming: A teacher speaks*. New York: McGraw Hill.

Jelinek, E. C. (1980). *Women's autobiography: Essays in criticism*. Bloomington, IN: University Press.

Jenkins, R. (1983). *Lads, citizens and ordinary kids: Working class life styles in Belfast*. London: Routledge.

Jocano, F. L. (1969). *Growing up in a Philippine barrio*. New York: Holt, Rinehart & Winston.

Johnson, N. B. (1980). "The material culture of public school classrooms: The symbolic integration of local schools and national culture." *Anthropology and Education Quarterly, 9*(3), 173–190.

Kaufman, B. (1964). *Up the down staircase*. Englewood Cliffs, NJ: Prentice Hall.

Kennedy, M. M. (1979). "Generalizing from single case studies." *Evaluation Quarterly, 3*(4), 661–679.

Kidder, T. (1989). *Among schoolchildren*. Boston: Houghton Mifflin.

King, A. R. (1967). *The School at Mopass*. New York: Holt, Rinehart & Winston.

Kinkead, J. A. (1997). *A schoolmarm all my life: Personal narratives from frontier Utah*. Salt Lake City: Signature Press

Kirk, J., & M. L. Miller. (1986). *Reliability and validity in qualitative research.* Beverly Hills: Sage.

Knowles, J. G. (1990). "A beginning teacher's experience: Reflections on becoming a teacher." *Language Arts, 65*(7), 702–712.

Knowles, J. G., & V. B. Hoefler. (1989). "The student teacher who couldn't go away: Learning from failure." *Journal of Experiential Education, 12*(2), 14–21.

Knupfer, A. M. (1996). "Ethnographic studies of children: The difficulties of entry, rapport and presentation of their world." *International Journal of Qualitative Studies in Education, 9*(2), 135–149.

Kohl, H. (1967). *36 children.* New York: New American Library.

Kotlowitz, A. (1991). *There are no children here.* New York: Doubleday.

Kozol, J. (1967/1985). *Death at an early age: The destruction of the hearts and minds of Negro children in the Boston public schools.* New York: New American Library.

Kroeber, T. (1961). *Ishi in two worlds: A biography of the last wild Indian in North America.* Berkeley: University of California Press.

Kuhn, T. (1970). *The structure of scientific revolutions.* Chicago: University of Chicago Press.

Kvale, S. (1995). "What is anthropological research? An interview with Jean Lave." *International Journal of Qualitative Studies in Education, 8*(3), 219–228.

LaFreniere, P. J., & W. R. Charlesworth. (1987). "Effects of friendship and dominance status on pupils' resource utilization in cooperative/competitive situation." *International Journal of Behavior Development, 10*(3), 345–358.

Lancy, D. F. (1975). "The social organization of learning: Initiation rituals and public schools." *Human Organization, 34,* 371–380.

Lancy, D. F. (1976a). "The beliefs and behaviors of pupils in an experimental school: Introduction and overview." *Learning Research and Development Center Publication Series,* 3 ED127301.

Lancy, D. F. (1976b). "The beliefs and behaviors of pupils in an experimental school: The science lab." *Learning Research and Development Center Publication Series,* 6, ED127300.

Lancy, D. F. (1976c). "The beliefs and behaviors of pupils in an experimental school: School settings." *Learning Research and Development Center Publication Series,* 21, ED134573.

Lancy, D. F. (1977). "The impact of the modern world on village life: Gbarngasuak-welle." *Papua New Guinea Journal of Education, 13*(1), 36–44.

Lancy, D. F. (1978). "The classroom as phenomenon." In D. Bar-Tal & L. Saxe. (Eds.), *The contribution of social psychology to education,* pp. 111–132. New York: Wiley.

Lancy, D. F. (Ed.) (1979). "The community school." *Papua New Guinea Journal of Education* (special issue), *15.*

Lancy, D. F. (1980a). "Becoming a blacksmith in Gbarngasuakwelle." *Anthropology and Education Quarterly, 11,* 266–274.

Lancy, D. F. (1980b). "Play in species adaptation." *Annual Review of Anthropology 9,* 471–495.

Lancy, D. F. (1983). *Cross-cultural studies in cognition and mathematics.* New York: Academic Press.

Lancy, D. F. (1984). "Play in anthropological perspective." In P. K. Smith (Ed.), *Play in animals and humans,* pp. 295–303. Oxford: Basil Blackwell.

Lancy, D. F. (1987). "Will video games alter the relationship between play and development?" In G. A. Fine (Ed.), *Meaningful play, playful meanings,* pp. 219–230. Champaign, IL: Human Kinetics.

Lancy, D. F. (1989). "An information processing framework for the study of culture and thought." In D. Topping, V. Kobayashi, & D. Crowell (Eds.), *Thinking across cultures*, pp. 13–26. Hillsdale, NJ: Erlbaum.

Lancy, D. F. (1990). "The microcomputer and social studies." *OCCS Review, 26*(1), 30–38.

Lancy, D. F. (1991). "The autotelic learning environment revisited: An exploratory study." *Play and Culture, 4*, 24–128.

Lancy, D. F. (1993). *Qualitative research in education* . White Plains, NY: Longman.

Lancy, D. F. (1994). "The conditions that support emergent literacy." In D. F. Lancy (Ed.), *Children's emergent literacy: From research to practice*, pp. 1–20. Westport, CT: Praeger.

Lancy, D. F. (1996). *Playing on the motherground: Cultural routines for childrens' development*. New York: Guilford.

Lancy, D. F., K. Draper, & G. Boyce. (1989). "Parental influence on children's acquisition of reading." *Contemporary Issues in Reading, 4*(1), 83–93.

Lancy, D. F., A. S. Forsyth, Jr., & L. L. Meeks. (1987). "An after-school program utilizing computers." *National Association of Laboratory Schools Journal, 11*(2), 1–9.

Lancy, D. F., & G. Goldstein. (1982). "Using nonverbal Piagetian tasks to assess the cognitive development of autistic children." *Child Development, 53*, 1233–1244.

Lancy, D. F., & B. L. Hayes. (1988). "Interactive fiction and the reluctant reader." *English Journal, 77*(6), 42–46.

Lancy, D. F., & M. C. Madsen. (1981). "Cultural patterns and the social behavior of children: Two studies from Papua New Guinea." *Ethos, 9*, 201–216.

Lancy, D. F., & A. Nattiv. (1992) "Parents as volunteers: Storybook readers/listeners." *Childhood Education, 68*(4), 208–212.

Lancy, D. F., R. J. Souviney, & V. Kada. (1981). "Intracultural variation in cognitive development: Conservation of length among the Imbonggu." *International Journal of Behavioral Development, 4*, 455–468.

Lancy, D. F., & A. J. Strathern. (1981). "Making-twos: Pairing as an alternative to the taxonomic mode of representation." *American Anthropologist, 81*, 777–795.

Lancy, D. F., & A. B. Zupsic. (1994) "Too little, too late: A case study of Running Start" In D. F. Lancy (Ed.), *Children's emergent literacy: From research to practice*, pp. 157–168. Westport, CT: Praeger.

Langness, L. L., & G. Frank. (1981). *Lives: An anthropological approach to biography.* Novato, CA: Chandler and Sharp.

Lareau, A. (1989a). "Family-school relationships: A view from the classroom." *Educational Policy, 3*(3), 245–259.

Lareau, A. (1989b). *Home advantage: Social class and parental intervention in elementary education*. New York: Falmer Press.

Lather, P. (1986). "Research as praxis." *Harvard Educational Review, 56*(3), 257–277.

Lauer, J. M., & J. W. Asher. (1988). *Composition research: Empirical designs*. New York: Oxford University Press.

Leacock, E. B. (1969). *Teaching and learning in city schools*. New York: Basic.

Leis, P. E. (1972). *Enculturation and socialization in Ijaw village*. New York: Holt, Rinehart & Winston.

Leinhardt, G. (1989). "Math lessons: A contrast of novice and expert competence." *Journal of Research and Mathematics Education, 20*(1), 52–75.

Leiter, K. C. W. (1976). "Teachers' use of background knowledge to interpret test scores." *Sociology of Education, 49*, 59–65.

Leiter, K. C. W. (1980). *A primer on ethnomethodology.* New York: Oxford University Press.

Lewis, C. C. (1996). "Fostering social and intellectual development: The roots of Japan's educational success." In T. P. Rohlen & G. K. LeTendre (Eds.), *Thinking and learning in Japan,* pp. 79–97. Cambridge: Cambridge University Press.

Lewis, O. (1966). *La vida: A Puerto Rican family in the culture of poverty—San Juan and New York.* New York: Random House.

Lieblich, A. Tuval-Mashiac, & T. Zilber. (1998). *Narrative research: Reading, analysis & interpretation.* Applied Social Research Method Series, Vol. 47. Thousand Oaks, CA: Sage.

Lightfoot, S. L. (1978). *Worlds apart: Relationships between families and schools.* New York: Basic Books.

Lincoln, Y. S., & E. G. Guba. (1985). *Naturalistic inquiry.* Newbury Park: Sage.

Little, J. W. (1990). "The persistence of privacy: Autonomy and initiative in teachers' professional relations." *Teachers College Record, 91*(4), 509–536.

Locke, L. F., W. W. Spirduso, & S. J. Silverman. (1987). *Proposals that work,.* Newbury Park, CA: Sage.

Logsdon, D. M., N. Taylor, & I. H. Bloom. (1988). "It was a good learning experience: The problems and trials of implementing and evaluating a parent participation program." In D. Fetterman (Ed.), *Qualitative approaches to evaluation in education,* pp. 23–41. New York: Praeger.

Lomask, M. (1986). *The biographer's craft.* New York: Harper & Row.

London, H. B. (1978). *The culture of a community college.* New York: Praeger.

Lubeck, S. (1984). "Kinship and classrooms: An ethnographic perspective on education as cultural transmission." *Sociology of Education, 57,* 219–232.

MacLeod, J. (1987). *Ain't no makin' it.* Boulder, CO: Westview.

Macrorie, K. (1974). *A vulnerable teacher.* Rochelle Park, NJ: Hayden.

Macrorie, K. (1984). *20 teachers.* New York: Oxford University Press.

Makler, A. (1991). "Imagining history: A good story and a well-formed argument." In C. Witherell & N. Noddings (Eds.), *Stories lives tell: Narrative and dialogue in education,* pp. 29–47. New York: Teachers College Press.

Malinowski, B. (1922). *Argonauts of the western Pacific.* London: Routledge; Dutton.

Malinowski, B. (1967). *A diary in the strict sense of the term.* (N. Guterman, trans.). New York: Harcourt, Brace, & Jovanovich.

Manning, D. (1990). *Hill country teacher: Oral histories from the one-room school and beyond.* Boston: Twayne.

McClaren, P. (1980). *Cries from the corridor.* Toronto: Methuen.

McClaren, P. (1989). *Life in schools: An introduction to critical pedagogy in the foundations of education.* White Plains, NY: Longman.

McClaren, P. L., & J. M. Giarelli (Eds.) (1995). *Critical theory and educational research.* Albany, NY: SUNY Press.

McCracken, G. (1988). *The long interview.* Newbury Park, CA: Sage.

McDermott, R. (1976). *Kids make sense.* Unpublished dissertation. Stanford University.

McDermott, R., & L. Hood. (1982). "Institutionalized psychology and the ethnography of schooling." In P. Gilmore & A. A. Glatthorn (Eds.), *Children in and out of school.* Washington, DC: Center for Applied Linguistics.

McGrew, W. C. (1972a). *An ethological study of children's behavior.* New York: Academic Press.

McGrew, W. C. (1972b). "Aspects of social development in nursery school children with emphasis on introduction to the group." In N. Blurton-Jones (Ed.), *Ethnological studies of child behavior,* pp. 129–156. Cambridge: Cambridge University Press.

McGrew, W. C. (1992). *Chimpanzee material culture: Implications for human evolution.* New York: Cambridge University Press.

McNeil, L. M. (1986). *Contradictions of control: School structure and school knowledge.* New York: Routledge, Kegan Paul.

McNeil, L. M. (1988). "Contradictions of control: Part III: Contradictions of reform." *Phi Delta Kappan, 69*(7), 478–785.

McPherson, G. H. (1972). *Small town teacher.* Cambridge: Harvard University Press.

Mead, M. (1928). *Coming of age in Samoa.* New York: Morrow.

Mead, M. (1972). *Blackberry winter: My earlier years.* New York: Morrow.

Measor, L. (1985). "Critical incidents in the classroom: Identities, choices and careers." In S. J. Ball & I. F. Goodson (Eds.), *Teachers' lives and careers*, pp. 61–77. London: Falmer Press.

Meeks, L. L., & D. F. Lancy. (nd). *Varying student conceptions of writing: Implications for teaching composition with the aid of computers.* Unpublished Master Theses, Utah State University.

Mehan, H. (1978). "Structuring school structure." *Harvard Education Review, 48*(1), 32–64.

Mehan, H. (1979). *Learning lessons: Social organization in the classroom.* Cambridge, MA: Harvard University Press.

Mehan, H., A. Hertweck, S. E. Coombs, & P. J. Flynn. (1982). "Teachers' interpretations of students' behavior." In L. C. Wilkinson (Ed.), *Communicating in the classroom*, pp. 297–321. New York: Academic Press.

Mehan, H., A. Hertweck, & J. L. Meihls. (1986). *Handicapping the handicapped.* Stanford: Stanford University Press.

Mehan, H., I. Vilaneuva, L. Hubbard, & A. Lintz. (1996). *Constructing school success: The consequences of un-tracking low achieving students.* Cambridge: Cambridge University Press.

Mehan, H., & H. Wood. (1975). *The reality of ethnomethodology.* New York: Wiley.

Meier, D. R. (1997). *Learning in small moments: Life in an Urban classroom.* New York City: Teachers College Press.

Meloy, J. (1989). "Got a problem?" In J. Allen & J. P. Goetz (Eds.), *Qualitative research in education: Teaching and learning qualitative traditions*, pp. 29–35. Athens, GA: University of Georgia College of Education.

Melson, G. F., & D. Dyar. (1987). "Dominance and visual attention rank orders in preschool groups." *Perceptual and Motor Skills, 65*, 570.

Merriam, S. B. (1988). *Case study research in education.* San Francisco: Jossey Bass.

Metz, M. (1978). *Classrooms and corridors.* Los Angeles: University of California Press.

Mickelson, R. A. (1989). "Why does Jane read and write so well? The anomaly of women's achievement." *Sociology of Education, 62*, 47–63.

Middleton, J. (1970). *From child to adult.* Garden City, NY: Natural History Press.

Miles, M. B., & A. M. Huberman. (1984a). "Drawing valid meaning from qualitative data: Toward a shared craft." *Educational Researcher, 13*, 12–20.

Miles, M. B., & A. M. Huberman. (1984b). *Qualitative data analysis: A source book of new methods.* Newbury Park, CA: Sage.

Miles, M. B., & A. M. Huberman. (1988). "Drawing valid meaning from qualitative data: Toward a shared craft." In D. Getterman (Ed.), *Qualitative approaches to evaluation in education*, pp. 222–244. New York: Praeger.

Miller, S. E., G. Leinhardt, & N. Zigmond. (1988). "Influencing engagement through accommodation: An ethnographic study of at-risk students." *American Educational Research Journal, 25*(4), 465–487.

Mischler, E. G. (1979). "Meaning in context: Is there any other kind?" *Harvard Educational Review, 49*(1), 1–19.

Modiano, N. (1973). *Indian education in the Chiapas highlands.* New York: Holt, Rinehart & Winston.

Moffatt, M. (1989). *Coming of age in New Jersey: College and American culture.* New Brunswick: Rutgers University Press.

Moore, D. T. (1986). "Learning at work: Case studies in non-school education." *Anthropology and Education Quarterly, 17*(3), 166–184.

Moore, R. C. (1989). "Before and after asphalt: Diversity as an ecological measure of quality in children's outdoor environments." In M. N. Bloch & A. D. Pellegrini (Eds.), *The ecological context of children's play,* pp. 191–213. Norwood, NJ: Ablex.

Morine-Dershimer, G. (1983). "Instructional strategy and the 'creation' of classroom status." *American Educational Research Journal, 20*(4), 645–661.

Morine-Dershimer, G. (1985). *Talking, listening and learning in elementary classrooms.* White Plains, NY: Longman.

Munro, P. (1991, April). *Multiple 'Is': Dilemmas of life history research.* Page presented at the annual meeting of the American Educational Research Association, Chicago.

Murdock, G. P. (1967). *Ethnographic atlas.* Pittsburgh: University of Pittsburgh Press.

Murphy, M. D., & A. Johannsen. (1990). "Ethical obligations and federal regulations in ethnographic research and anthropological education." *Human Organization, 49*(2), 127–154.

Natkins, L. G. (1986). *Our last term: A teacher's diary.* Lanham, MD: University Press of America.

New, D. A. (1985). *History of the Deseret alphabet and other attempts to reform English orthography.* Unpublished doctoral dissertation, Utah State University.

Newman, K. K. (1980). "Stages in an unstaged occupation." *Educational Leadership, 37,* 514–516.

Ngana-Mundeke, A. (2000). Language barriers to learning. *Anthropology News 41*(4), 25.

Nias, J. (1985). "Reference groups in primary teaching: Talking, listening and identity." In S. J. Ball & I. F. Goodson (Eds.), *Teachers' lives and careers,* pp. 105–119. London: Falmer Press.

Ninio, A. (1979). "The naive theory of the infant and other maternal attitudes in two subgroups in Israel." *Child Development, 50,* 976–980.

Noblit, G. W., & R. D. Hare. (1988). *Meta-ethnography: Synthesizing qualitative studies.* Newbury Park, CA: Sage.

Noblit, G. W., & W. T. Pink. (1987). *Schooling in social context.* Norwood, NJ: Ablex.

Oakes, J. (1986). "Tracking, inequality, and the rhetoric of reform: Why schools don't change." *Journal of Education, 168*(1), 60–80.

Ogbu, J. (1974). *The next generation: An ethnography of education in an urban community.* New York: Academic Press.

Ogbu, J. U. (1978) *Minority education and caste: The American system in cross-cultural perspective.* New York: Academic.

Ogbu, J. U. (1982). "Cultural discontinuities and schooling." *Anthropology and Education Quarterly, 13*(4), 290–307.

Ogbu, J. U. (1987). "Variability in minority school performance: A problem in search of an explanation." *Anthropology and Education Quarterly, 18*(4), 312–334.

Ohanian, S. (1989, September 6). "Searching for the 'soul' of a classroom review of *Among Schoolchildren.*" *Education Week,* 35–36.

Omark, D. R., & M. S. Edelman. (1976). "The development of attention structures in young children." In M. R. A. Chance & R. R. Larsen (Eds.), *The social structure of attention,* pp. 120–151. London: Academic Press.

Osborne, J. M. (1961). *The autobiography of Thomas Whythorne.* Oxford: The Clarendon Press.

Paley, V. G. (1992) *You can't say you can't play.* Cambridge, MA: Harvard University Press.

Palincsar, A. M. (1986). "Review of Hugh Mehan, Alma Hertweck, J. Lee Meihls, *Handicapping the handicapped*" (Stanford: Stanford University Press). *Anthropology and Education Quarterly, 17*(3), 190–192.

Palonsky, S. B. (1975). Hempies and squeaks, truckers and cruisers: A participant observer study in a city high school. *Educational Administration Quarterly, 11*(2), 86–103.

Papert, S. (1980). *Mindstorms.* New York: Basic Books.

Pascal, R. (1960). *Design and truth in autobiography.* Cambridge, MA: Harvard University Press.

Patthey-Chavez, G. G. (1993). "High school as an arena for cultural conflict and acculturation for Latino Angelinos." *Anthropology and Education Quarterly, 24*(1), 33–60.

Patton, M. Q. (1990). *Qualitative evaluation and research methods* (2nd ed.). Newbury Park, CA: Sage.

Payne, G. C. F. (1982). "Dealing with the late-comer." In G. C. F. Payne & E. C. Cuff (Eds.), *Doing teaching,* pp. 90–103. London: Batsford.

Pellegrini, A. D. (1988). "Elementary school children's rough and tumble play and social competence." *Developmental Psychology, 24*(6), 802–806.

Pellegrini, A. D. (1989). "Elementary school children's rough and tumble play." *Early Childhood Research Quarterly, 4,* 245–260.

Pellegrini, A. D. (1991). *Applied child study* (2nd ed.). Hillsdale, NJ: Erlbaum.

Pellegrini, A. D. (1996) *Observing children in their natural worlds: A methodological primer.* Mahwah, NJ: LEA.

Pelto, P. J., & G. H. Pelto. (1978). *Anthropological research* (2nd ed.). Cambridge: Cambridge University Press.

Peshkin, A. (1972). *Kanuri schoolchildren.* New York: Holt, Rinehart & Winston.

Peshkin, A. (1986). *God's choice: The total world of a fundamentalist Christian school.* Chicago: University of Chicago Press.

Pfaffenberger, B. (1988). *Microcomputer applications in qualitative research.* Newbury Park, CA: Sage.

Phillips, D.C. (1983). "After the wake: Post positivist educational thought." *Educational Researcher, 12*(5), 4–12.

Phillips, S. U. (1972) "Participant structures and communicative competence: Warm Springs children in community and classroom." In C. B. Cazden, V. P. John, & D. Hymes (Eds.), *Functions of language in the classroom,* pp. 370–394. New York: Teachers College Press.

Phillips, S. (1983). *Invisible culture: Communication in classroom and community on the Warm Springs Indian Reservation.* New York: Longman.

Piestrup, A. (1973). *Black dialect interference and accommodation in first grade* [Monograph No. 4]. Berkeley, CA: Language Behavior Research Laboratory.

Pike, K. (1954). *Language in relation to a unified theory of the structure of human behavior.* Orange, CA: Summer Institute of Linguistics.

Pinar, W. F. (1980). "Life history and educational experience." *Journal of Curriculum Theorizing, 2*(2), 159–212.

Poirer, F. E. (1972). *Primate socialization*. New York: Random House.

Polkinghorne, D. E. (1988). *Narrative psychology.* Albany, NY: SUNY Press.

Polkinghorne, D. E. (1995). "Narrative configuration in qualitative analysis." *International Journal of Qualitative Studies in Education, 8*(1), 5–23.

Pomponio, A., & D. F. Lancy. (1986). "A pen or a bush knife: School, work and personal investment in Papua New Guinea." *Anthropology and Education Quarterly, 17,* 40–61.

Proshansky, H. M, W. H. Ittelson, & L. G. Rivlin. (Eds.) (1970). *Environmental psychology.* New York: Holt, Rinehart & Winston.

Raitt, M., & D. F. Lancy. (1988). "Rhinestone cowgirl: The education of a rodeo queen." *Play and Culture, 1*(4), 267–281.

Raphael, R., (1985). *The teacher's voice: A sense of who we are.* Portsmouth, NH: Heinemann.

Ray, L. C. (1987). "Reflections on classroom research." In D. Goswami & P. R. Stillman (Eds.), *Reclaiming the classroom: Research as an agency for change*, pp. 219–242. Portsmouth, NH: Heinemann.

Raymond, C. (1991). "Videotaped data pose legal and ethical problems for social scientists." *Chronicle for Higher Education, 37*(28), A9.

Read, M. H. [1960] (1968). *Children of their fathers: Growing up among the Ngoni of Nyasaland.* New York: Holt, Rinehart & Winston.

Reilly, W. E. (Ed.) (1990). *Sarah Jane Foster: Teacher of the Freedman, a diary and letters.* Charlottesville: University of Virginia Press.

Rist, R. C. (1978). *The invisible children: School integration in American society.* Cambridge, MA: Harvard University Press.

Rist, R. C. (Ed.) (1979). *Desegregated schools: Appraisals of an American experiment.* New York: Academic Press.

Rist, R. C. (1980). "Blizkrieg ethnography: On the transformation of a method into a movement." *Educational Researcher, 9*(2), 8–10.

Rist, R. C. (1987). "Research in the shadows: A critique." *Curriculum Inquiry, 17*(4), 447–451.

Robbins, P. (1986). "The Napa Vacaville follow-through project: Qualitative outcomes, related procedures and implications for practice." *Elementary School Journal, 87*(2), 139–157.

Roberts, J. M. (1951). *Three Navajo households: A comparative study in small group culture.* Peabody Museum of Harvard University papers, 40, No. 3.

Roberts, J. M., M. J. Arth, & R. R. Bush. (1959). "Games in culture." *American Anthropologist, 61,* 597–605.

Robinson, D. R. (1978) *The bell rings at four: A black teacher's chronicle of change.* Austin: Madrona.

Rodriguez, R. (1982). *Hunger of memory: The education of Richard Rodriguez.* New York: David R. Godine.

Rogoff, B. (1990). *Apprenticeship in thinking: Cognitive development in social context.* New York: Oxford University Press.

Rogoff, B., & W. Gardner. (1984). "Adult guidance of cognitive development." In B. Rogoff & J. Lave (Eds.), *Everyday cognition: Its development in social context*, pp. 95–116. Cambridge, MA: Harvard University Press.

Romo, H. D., & T. Falbo. (1996). *Latino high school graduation: Defying the odds.* Austin: University of Texas Press.

Rosenfeld, G. (1971). *"Shut those thick lips!": A study of slum school failure.* Prospect Heights, IL: Waveland Press.

Roth, D. R. (1973). "Intelligence testing as a social activity." In Cicourel et al. (Eds.), *Language use and school performance*, pp. 143–217. New York: Academic Press.

Rury, J. L. (1991). *Education and women's work: Female schooling and the division of labor in urban America 1870–1930*. Albany, NY: SUNY Press

Rury, J., and G. Harper. (1986). "The trouble with coeducation: Mann and women at Antioch, 1953–1959." *History of Education Quarterly, 26*(4), 481–502.

Ryan, J., & C. Sackrey. (1984). *Strangers in paradise: Academics from the working class.* Boston: South End.

Ryan, K. (1986). *The induction of new teachers.* Bloomington, IN: Phi Delta Kappa Education Foundation.

Sachar, E. (1991). *Shut up and let the lady teach.* New York: Poseidon Press.

Sage, G. H. (1989). "Becoming a high school coach: From playing sports to coaching." *Research Quarterly of Exercise and Sports, 60*(1), 81–92.

Sanders, J. R., & S. R. Sonnad. (1982). *Research on the introduction, use and impact of the Thinkabout instructional series.* Bloomington, IN: Agency for Instructional Television.

Savin-Williams, R. C. (1979). "Dominance hierarchies in groups of early adolescents." *Child Development, 50*, 923–935.

Savin-Williams, R. C. (1982). "A field study of adolescent social interactions: Developmental and contextual influences." *The Journal of Social Psychology, 117*, 203–209.

Savin-Williams, R. C. (1987). *Adolescence: An ethological perspective.* New York: Springer-Verlag.

Schjeldesup-Ebbe, T. (1922). "Beitrage Zur Sozial Psycholgie des Haushuhns." *Zeitschrift fur Tierpsycholgie, 88*, 225–252.

Schneider, B., & Y. Lee. (1990). "A model for academic success: The school and home environment of East Asian students." *Anthropology and Education Quarterly, 21*(4), 358–377.

Schoen, D. (1991). *Inside separate worlds: Life stories of young blacks, Jews and Latinos.* Ann Arbor: University of Michigan Press.

Schofield, J. W. (1989). *Black and white in school.* New York: Teacher College Press.

Schofield, J. W. (1990). "Increasing the generalizability of qualitative research." In E. W. Eisner & A. Peshkin (Eds.), *Qualitative inquiry in education: The continuing debate*, pp. 201–232. New York: Columbia Teachers College Press.

Schubert, W. H. (1991). "Teacher lore: A basis for understanding praxis." In C. Witherell & N. Noddings (Eds.), *Stories lives tell: Narrative and dialogue in education*, pp. 207–233. New York: Teachers College Press.

Schwartz, F. (1981). "Supporting or subverting learning: Peer group patterns in four tracked schools." *Anthropology and Education Quarterly, 12*, 99–121.

Scott, S. (1985). "Working through the contradictions of researching post-graduate education." In R. G. Burgess (Ed.), *Field methods in the study of education*, pp. 115–130. London: Falmer Press.

Scriven, M. (1967). "The methodology of evaluation." In R. E. Stake (Ed.), *Perspectives of curriculum evaluation*, pp. 39–89. Chicago: Rand McNally.

Shavelson, R., & P. Stern, P. (1981). "Research on teachers' pedagogical thoughts, judgements, decisions, and behavior." In *Review of Educational Research, 51*(4), 455–498.

Shaw, C. (1930/1966). *The jack-roller.* Chicago: University of Chicago Press.

Shulman, J. M. (1990). "Now you see them, now you don't: Anonymity versus visibility in case studies of teachers." *Educational Researcher, 19*(5), 11–15.

Sikes, P. J. (1985). "The life cycle of the teacher." In S. J. Ball & I. F. Goodson (Eds.), *Teachers' lives and careers*, pp. 27–60. London: Falmer Press.

Silverman, D. (1985). *Qualitative methodology and sociology.* Aldershot, UK: Gower.

Singleton, J. (1967). *Nichu: A Japanese school.* New York: Holt, Rinehart & Winston.

Singleton, J. (1984). "Origins of the AEQ: Methods, myths, and cultural transmission."*Anthropology and Education Quarterly, 15*(1), 11–16.

Sleeter, C. (1998). "Activist or ethnographer? Researchers, teachers, and voice in ethnographies that critique." In K. B. deMarrais (Ed.), *Inside stories: Qualitative research reflections*, pp. 49–58. Mahwah, NJ: LEA.

Sleeter, C. S. M., & C. A. Grant. (1985). "Race, class, and gender in an urban school: A case study." *Urban Education, 10*(1), 31–60.

Smith, L. M. (1978). "An evolving logic of participant observation, educational ethnography and other case studies." In L. S. Shulman (Ed.), *Review of Research in Education*, pp. 316–377. Itasca, IL: Peacock.

Smith, L. M., & W. Geoffrey. (1968). *The complexities of an urban classroom.* New York: Holt, Rinehart & Winston.

Smith, L. M., & P. M. Keith. (1971). *Anatomy of educational innovation: An organizational analysis of an elementary school.* New York: Wiley.

Smith, L. M., P. F. Klein, D. C. Dwyer, & J. J. Prunty. (1985). "Pupils, teachers' careers and schooling: An empirical study." In S. J. Ball & I. F. Goodson (Eds.), *Teachers' lives and careers*, pp. 27–60. London: Falmer Press.

Smith, L. M., J. P. Prunty, D. C. Dwyer, & P. F. Kleine. (1987). *The fate of an innovative school.* Philadelphia: Falmer Press.

Smith, M. L. (1982). *How educators decide who is learning disabled.* Springfield, IL: Thomas.

Smith, M. L. (1986). "The whole is greater: Combining qualitative and quantitative approaches in evaluation studies." In D. D. Williams (Ed.), *Naturalistic evaluation*, pp. 37–54. San Francisco: Jossey Bass.

Smith, M. L., & G. V. Glass. (1987). *Research and evaluation in education and the social sciences.* Englewood Cliffs, NJ: Prentice-Hall.

Smith, P. K. (1974). "Ethological methods." In B. Foss (Ed.), *New perspective in child development*, pp. 85–137. Hammondsworth, U.K.: Penguin.

Smith, P. K. (1982). "Does play matter? Functional and evolutionary aspects of animal and human play." *The Behavioral and Brain Sciences, 5*, 139–184.

Smith, P. K. (1990). "Ethology, sociobiology, and developmental psychology: In memory of Niki Tenbergen and Konrad Lorenz." *British Journal of Developmental Psychology, 8*, 187–200.

Smith, P. K., & K. J. Connolly. (1980). *The ecology of preschool behaviour.* Cambridge: Cambridge University Press.

Smith, P. K., & K. Lewis. (1985). "Rough & tumble play, fighting and chasing in nursery school children." *Ethology and Sociobiology, 6*, 175–181.

Smith, P. L. (1980). "On the distinction between quantitative and qualitative research." *CEDR Quarterly, 13*(3), 3–6.

Speier, M. (1973). *How to observe face-to-face communication: A sociological introduction.* Pacific Palisades, CA: Goodyear.

Spencer, D. A. (1986). *Contemporary women teachers: Balancing school and home.* New York: Longman.

Spindler, G. D. (1983). "Review of R. T. Sieber and A. J. Gordon (Eds.), *Children and their organizations.*" *Anthropology and Education Quarterly, 14*(1), 70–72.

Spindler, G. D. (Ed.) (1955). *Education and anthropology.* Palo Alto: Stanford University Press.

Spradley, J. P. (1979). *The ethnographic interview.* New York: Holt, Rinehart & Winston.

Spradley, J. P. (1980). *Participant observation*. New York: Holt, Rinehart & Winston.

Spradley, J. P., & D. W. McCurdy. (1972). *The cultural experience: Ethnography in complex society*. Chicago: SRA.

Stake, R. E. (1978). "The case study method in social inquiry." *Educational Researcher, 7*, 5–8.

Stake, R. E. (1983). "Program evaluation, particularly responsive evaluation." In G. F. Madaus, M. S. Scriven, & D. K. Stufflebeam (Eds.), *Evaluation models*, pp. 287–310. Boston, MA: Kluwer-Nijhoff.

Stenhouse, L. (1975). *An introduction to curriculum research and development*. London: Heinemann.

Stenhouse, L. (1985). "A note on case study and educational practice." In R. G. Burgess (Ed.), *Field methods in the study of education*, pp. 263–271. London: Falmer Press.

Stodolsky, S. S. (1988). *The subject matters: Classroom activity in math and social studies*. Chicago: University of Chicago Press.

Strane, S. (1990). *A whole-souled woman: Prudence Crandall and the education of black women*. New York: W. W. Norton.

Strayer, F. F., & J. Strayer. (1976). "An ethological analysis of social agonism and dominance relations among preschool children." *Child Development, 47*, 980–989.

Stuart, J. (1970). *To teach, to love*. New York: World.

Sturtevant, W. G. (1964). "Studies in ethnoscience." *American Anthropologist, 66*(1), 99–131.

Suransky, V. P. (1982). *The erosion of childhood*. Chicago: University of Chicago Press.

Tabulawa, R. (1998) "Teachers' perspectives on classroom practice in Botswana: Implications for pedagogical change." *International Journal of Qualitative Studies in Education, 11*(2), 249–268.

Tammivaara, J., & D. S. Enright. (1986). "On eliciting information: Dialogues with child informants." *Anthropology and Education Quarterly, 17*(4), 218–238.

Tesch, R. (1990). *Qualitative research*. Philadelphia: Falmer Press.

Theroux, P. (1989). "One woman against the odds, review of *Among Schoolchildren*." *New York Times Review of Books, 94*(1), 1, 46.

Thrasher, F. (1927). *The gang*. Chicago: University of Chicago Press.

Tinbergen, E. A., & N. Tinbergen. (1972). "Early childhood autism: An ethological approach." *Zeitschrift Fur Tierpsychologie*, Supplement 10, 1–53.

Tinbergen, N. (1951). *The study of instinct*. Oxford: Clarendon Press.

Treisman, P. U. (1983). *Improving the performance of minority students in college-level mathematics*. Unpublished MS, ED 234874.

Trueba, H. T. (1988). "Culturally based explanations of minority students' academic achievement." *Anthropology and Education Quarterly, 19*(3), 270–287.

Turkle, S. (1984). *The second self: The computer and the human spirit*. New York: Simon & Schuster.

Tyack, D. B., & E. Hansot. (1982). *Managers of virtue: Public school leadership in America 1820–1980*. New York: Basic Books.

Valentine, C. A. (1968). *Culture and poverty*. Chicago: University of Chicago Press.

Van Galen, J. (1987) "Maintaining control: The structuring of parent involvement." In G. Noblitt & W. T. Pink (Eds.), *Schooling in social context: Qualitative studies*, pp. 78–90. Norwood, NJ: Ablex.

Van Maanen, J. (1988). *Tales of the field: On writing ethnography*. Chicago: University of Chicago Press.

Varenne, H. (1976). "American culture in the school: A case study." In C. J. Calhoun & F. A. J. Ianni (Eds.), *The anthropological study of education*, pp. 227–239. The Hague: Mouton.

Varenne, H. (1982). "Jocks and freaks." In G. D. Spindler (Ed.), *Doing the ethnography of schooling*. New York: Holt, Rinehart & Winston.

von Frisch, K. (1954). *The dancing bees: An account of the life and senses of the honeybee.* (D. L. Ilse, trans.). London: Methuen.

Walker, D. F. (1975). "Curriculum development in an art project." In W. A. Reid & D. F. Walker (Eds.), *Case studies in curriculum change: Great Britain and the United States*, pp. 91–135. London: Routledge, Kegan Paul.

Waller, W. [1932] (1961). *Sociology of teaching.* New York: J. Wiley.

Walter, G. (1981). *So where's my apple: The diary of a first-year teacher.* Prospect Heights, IL: Waveland Press.

Ward, M. C. (1971). *Them children: A study in language learning.* Prospect Heights, IL: Waveland Press.

Watson, L. C., & M. B. Watson-Franke. (1985). *Interpreting life histories: An anthropological inquiry.* New Brunswick, NJ: Rutgers.

Wax, R. (1971). *Doing fieldwork: Warning and advice.* Chicago: University of Chicago Press.

Wax, M., R. H. Wax, & R. V. Dumont, Jr. (1964). "Formal education in an American Indian community with assistance from Roselyn Holyrock & Gerald Onefeather." *Supplement to Social Problems, 11*(4), (126 pp., app).

Webb, E. J., D. T. Campbell, R. D. Schwartz, & L. Sechrest. (1966). *Unobtrusive measures.* Chicago: Rand McNally.

Weiner, A. (1976). *Women of value, men of renown.* Austin: University of Texas Press.

Weis, L. (1985). *Between two worlds: Black students in an urban community college.* Boston: Routledge, Kegan Paul.

Weisfeld, G. E., & C. C. Weisfeld. (1984). "An observational study of social evaluation: An application of the dominance hierarchy model." *Journal of Genetic Psychology, 145*, 89–99.

Welner, K. G., & R. A. Mickelson. (2000) "School reform, politics, and tracking: Should we pursue virtue?" *Educational Researcher, 29*(5), 22–26.

Welsh, P. (1986). *Tales out of school: A teacher's candid account from the front lines of the American high school today.* New York: Viking Penguin.

Wertsch, J. (1985). *Vygotsky and the social formation of mind.* Cambridge, MA: Harvard University Press.

Whiting, B. B. (Ed.) (1963). *Six cultures: Studies of child rearing.* New York: John Wiley.

Whiting, B. B., & C. P. Edwards. (1988). *Children of different worlds.* Cambridge, MA: Harvard University Press.

Whiting, B. B., & J. W. M. Whiting. (1975). *Children of six cultures: A psycho-cultural analysis* Cambridge, MA: Harvard University Press.

Whiting, B. B. et al. (Eds.). (1963). *Children of six cultures.* New York: John Wiley.

Whiting, J. M. W., & I. L. Child. (Eds.). (1953). *Child training and personality: A cross-cultural study.* New York: Yale University Press.

Whyte, W. F. (1982). "Interviewing in field research." In R. G. Burgess (Ed.), *Field research: A sourcebook and field manual.* London: Allen & Unwin.

Whyte, W. F. (1984). *Learning from the field.* Newbury Park, CA: Sage.

Wilkinson, A. C. (1981). *Children's understanding of written and spoken discourse.* Washington, DC: National Institute of Education.

Williams, S. B. (1970). *Hassling: Two years in a suburban high school.* Boston: Little, Brown.

Williams, T. R. (1969). *A Borneo childhood: Enculturation in Dusun society.* New York: Holt, Rinehart & Winston.

Willis, P. E. (1977). *Learning to labour: How working class kids get working class jobs.* Westmead, UK: Saxon House.

Willis, G. (Ed.). (1978). *Qualitative evaluation: Concepts and cases in curriculum criticism.* Berkeley, CA: McCutchan.

Wilson, S. M. (1990). "A conflict of interest: The case of Mark Black." *Educational Evaluation and Policy Analysis, 12*(3), 309–326.

Wisniewski, R. (2000). "The averted gaze." *Anthropology and Education Quarterly, 31*(1), 5–23.

Witherell, C., & N. Noddings. (Eds.) (1991). *Stories lives tell: Narrative and dialogue in education.* New York: Teachers College Press.

Wohlberg, K. (1979). "The teacher as missionary: Teaching as moral imperative in Papua New Guinea schools." In D. F. Lancy (Ed.), *The community school*, special issue of the *Papua New Guinea Journal of Education, 15*, 120–136.

Wolcott, H. F. (1967). *Kwakiutl Village and school.* New York: Holt, Rinehart & Winston.

Wolcott, H. F. (1973). *The man in the principal's office: An ethnography.* New York: Holt, Rinehart & Winston.

Wolcott, H. F. (1974). "The elementary school principal: Notes from a field study." In G. D. Spindler (Ed.), *Education and cultural process in modern societies*, pp. 176–204. New York: Holt, Rinehart & Winston.

Wolcott, H. F. (1975). "Criteria for an ethnographic approach to research in schools." *Human Organization, 34*, 111–127.

Wolcott, H. F. (1977). *Teachers vs. technocrats.* Eugene, OR: Center for Educational Policy and Management.

Wolcott, H. F. (1983). "Adequate schools and an inadequate education: The life history of a sneaky kid." *Anthropology and Education Quarterly, 14*, 3–32.

Wolcott, H. F. (1987). "On ethnographic intent." In G. Spindler & L. Spindler (Eds.), *Interpretive ethnography of education*, pp. 37–57. Hillsdale, NJ: Erlbaum.

Wolcott, H. F. (1990). *Writing-up qualitative research.* Newbury Park, CA: Sage.

Wolcott, M. (1980). "How to look like an anthropologist without being one." *Practicing Anthropology, 3*(1), 6–7.

Wolfe, J. F. (1987, October). "Effects of development guidance curriculum on the interpersonal cognitive problem solving skills and social behavior of elementary pupils." Paper presented at the fifth annual meeting of Northern Rocky Educational Research Association. Park City, UT.

Woods, P. (1986). *Inside schools: Ethnography in education.* London: Routledge.

Woods, P., M. Boyle, B. Jeffrey, & G. Troman. (2000). "A research team in ethnography." *International Journal of Qualitative Studies in Education, 13*(1), 85–98.

Yin, R. K. (1984). *Case study research: Design and methods.* Newbury Park, CA: Sage.

Zerby, C. (1975). "John Dewey and the Polish question: A response to the revisionist historians." *History of Education Quarterly, 15*(1), 17–30.

Name Index

Subject Index